THE PICTORIAL HISTORY OF
BASEBALL

THE PICTORIAL HISTORY OF BASEBALL

JOHN S. BOWMAN
AND
JOEL ZOSS

GALLERY BOOKS
An imprint of W.H. Smith Publishers Inc.
112 Madison Avenue
New York, New York 10016

PART I
The Early Years

PART II
The Golden Years;
the Sunlight Years, 1920-1939

Published by Gallery Books
A Division of W H Smith Publishers Inc.
112 Madison Avenue
New York, New York 10016

Produced by
Brompton Books Corp.
15 Sherwood Place
Greenwich, CT 06830

Copyright © 1986 Brompton Books Corp.

All rights reserved. No part of this book
may be reproduced or transmitted in any form
or by any means without written permission
from the Publisher.

ISBN 0-8317-6872-X

Printed in Hong Kong

10 9 8 7 6

PART III
The War Years
and Baseball Comes of Age, 1940-1959

PART IV
The Games Goes On, Since 1960

INTRODUCTION

By now it is a universal truism that baseball is America's national pastime, but as much as this is intended as a tribute to baseball's unique role in Americans' lives, it actually does not begin to do justice to the sport – or that role. Baseball is far more than a 'pastime', as even a glance at the sports pages of the nation's newspapers will make clear. Far more than a game played on a field for recreation – although it is that, too – it is even more than a professional sport watched by millions of people in ballparks or before television sets.

Baseball is intrinsic to American society as both a common basis for discussion among people and as a group activity, and indeed the game of baseball itself, as an outdoor and timeless sport, reflects America's rural roots. Baseball is every Americans' shared youth, the Garden of Eden in a world beset by half-truths and compromise.

Baseball plays other functions in American life that are hardly suggested by the word 'pastime.' For example, it has long served as a hobby or almost cult for young boys who, if they could barely recall the date that Columbus discovered America, could recite reams of statistics about baseball. This underlines yet another function of baseball: these same statistics offer to all Americans a rock of certainty in a world of shifting relativities. It may not be absolutely clear who is on the right side of a boundary dispute or missile counts, there may be much to be said on all sides in the Middle East or in Central America, but there is only one thing to be said about the modern pitcher with the most career victories: it is Cy Young with his 511. To keep things interesting, this rock of certainty has many facets, and baseball fans can argue forever whether the records amassed in 162-game seasons should really be compared with those of 154-game seasons.

Baseball, then, is less a pastime among a people and more a microcosm of their history. Consider just one instance – the role of various ethnic and racial groups in organized baseball. The sport, which began as a leisure activity among mostly Waspish gentlemen, proceeded to absorb one ethnic group after the other in pretty much the same sequence these groups were absorbed into American society as a whole. Or consider that when most people hear 'baseball' they probably think of the major leagues: but what about the youth leagues that engage the energies and talents of literally millions of young Americans (not to mention their families, coaches, and fans)? Then there are the minor leagues – or college baseball teams – an increasingly more visible and significant force in American baseball.

All this, and much more, is the history of baseball. And this, and much more, awaits the reader of this volume, a history of a pastime – and a people.

PART I

The Early Years

Origins and the
Earliest Amateur Teams

While the origin of organized baseball as an American game can be traced to the mid-nineteenth century reforms of Alexander Cartwright, the origins of games with balls and bats will probably always remain impenetrably vague. The first recorded instance of 'batting contests' occurs more than 5000 years ago, with Egyptian priests engaged in mock combat with bats. Fertility of crops and people was undoubtedly the goal, and balls which sometimes represented such symbols of springtime potency as the sun or the mumified head of Osiris eventually found their way into the game. By 2000 BC, pictures of half-naked women playing ball were included in the carvings on the tomb of Beni Hasan. Various fertility rituals involving the cycles of the seasons gradually evolved into tremendously popular rites which climaxed in ball games, and these games which so enthralled the Egyptian populace were carried to Europe – and eventually to America – by the conquering Moors.

In Europe, ball games were rapidly incorporated into Christian ceremonies from Austria to France. During the Middle Ages, the Cathedral of Rheims wound up Easter services with a ball game in which contending teams either kicked or swatted a ball with a stick. When these post-mass games crossed the Channel into England, they evolved into a game called stoolball, in which a pitcher tried to hit an upturned stool with a ball before a batter could bat it away with a stick. Legend has it that when the game moved out of the churchyard into the countryside, milkmaids added more stools or 'bases,' which had to be circled after the ball was struck. The English children's game of 'rounders,' baseball's most likely modern precursor, was born when

the rule was added that a base runner could be put out by being struck with a thrown ball. Posts called 'goals' or 'bases' came to be driven into the ground, and the game was called 'goal ball' or 'base ball' as early as 1700. *A Pretty Little Pocket Book*, published in London in 1744, contains a rhymed description of the game and a picture captioned, 'Base-Ball.' The book was republished in America several times between 1762 and 1787.

While nineteenth-century America was changing from a rural society into a nation of large cities and giant factories, baseball developed from the children's game of rounders to a highly skilled game of professionals performing for the entertainment of paying spectators.

THE AMERICAN NATIONAL GAME OF BASE BALL.
GRAND MATCH FOR THE CHAMPIONSHIP AT THE ELYSIAN FIELDS, HOBOKEN, N.J.

OPPOSITE TOP: *A drawing from the tomb of Beni Hasan shows Egyptian women playing a ball game.*

OPPOSITE BOTTOM: *Alexander Joy Cartwright is in the center of the rear row of Old Knickerbockers.*

ABOVE: *Probably a game played on 3 August 1865 in Hoboken, New Jersey.*

BELOW: *'Club ball' was played in England around 1200.*

RIGHT: *The Book of Sports, published in 1834, included illustrations and directions on how to play 'base ball.'*

On its way to becoming commercialized entertainment, baseball became the province of the elite. Oliver Wendell Holmes played baseball on a diamond-shaped field at Harvard in 1829, and by the 1840s, the basic pattern of the game was being shaped in snobbish gentlemen's clubs centered in eastern cities. By then baseball had already evolved to a point which would have made the game recognizable to a visitor from the twentieth century.

Alexander J Cartwright, a bank clerk who played with New York friends, was selected by his mates to head a committee to form a baseball club. On 23 September 1845, the Knickerbocker Base Ball Club was formally organized, and on the same date the Knickerbockers adopted the 20 rules Cartwright proposed to standardize the game. Until then, the most popular ball game variant had been 'town ball' or the 'Massachusetts game,' in which runners were declared out when hit with a thrown ball.

While the most significant rule of the Knickerbockers' new game provided that a player could be tagged or forced out but not thrown at, his code also provided for such enduring regulations as three strikes to a batter, three outs in an inning, and equal and standardized distances between bases. An umpire was to mediate disputes. Pitchers were penalized for balking.

The first game under these rules was played on 19 June 1846 in Hoboken, New Jersey. The Knickerbockers were badly beaten by the New York Nine, 23-1, and player J W Davis was fined six cents for swearing at the man who umpired the game. The ball was still pitched underhand, and the dimensions of the diamond were still to face important changes, but Cartwright's game, which systematized the field as well as the playing rules, serves to mark the real beginning of organized baseball, and the 'New York Game' soon became the basis for intercity competition.

11

Baseball in American Culture

It is a truism that baseball, as America's national pastime, has become part of the warp and woof of the country's social fabric, but what is perhaps less widely appreciated is how quickly baseball began to spin off into the general culture. The first authenticated game between two organized teams had barely been played in Hoboken, New Jersey, on 19 June 1846, when Currier & Ives was selling colored lithographs depicting it. Even something as seemingly modern as commercial endorsements by ballplayers was beginning by the turn of the century.

Or consider popular music. Baseball had just begun to enter the awareness of Americans in the 1850s when music referring to baseball in the title began to appear – 'The Baseball Quadrille' being one such song. Eventually, another song took over top spot on baseball's hit parade: 'Take Me Out to the Ball-Game,' published in 1908, and the work of two men who had never seen a professional baseball game. Jack Norworth, a vaudeville entertainer of the day, was allegedly inspired to write the words when he happened to see a notice in a New York City subway announcing that day's ballgame at the Polo Grounds; his words were set to music by his friend Albert von Tilzer, also the manager of the York Music Publishing Company that first brought it out. The song caught on quite quickly, aided by 'song slides,' a series of hand-colored slides illustrating the action of the lyrics and shown in the nickelodeons, the early movie theaters, where patrons soon began to sing along. The song's great success inspired several outright imitations, but the original 'Take Me Out to the Ball-Game' outlasted them all and remains a perennial favorite. (It might also be mentioned that for many Americans, baseball games are inextricably associated

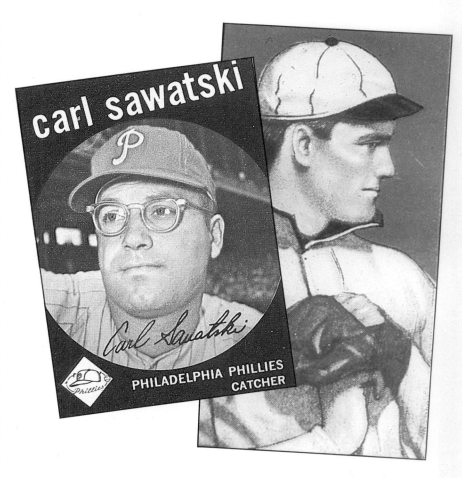

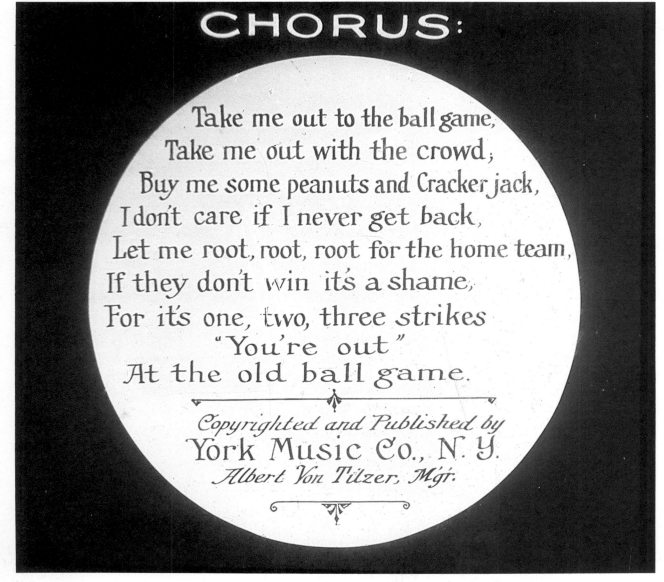

ABOVE: *Baseball cards depict the Phillies' catcher Carl Sawatski (1958-59) and the Senators' pitcher Walter Johnson (1907-27). First included in cigarette packages, then in packs of chewing gum, baseball cards have become an American collectible.*

LEFT: *A 'song slide' segment displays the words to the popular song, 'Take Me Out to the Ball-Game,' written in 1908.*

OPPOSITE: *Norman Rockwell's depiction of family baseball from issue of* The Saturday Evening Post, *illustrates the integral role of the sport in the American consciousness.*

THE SATURDAY EVENING POST

An Illustrated Weekly
Founded A. D. 1728 by Benj. Franklin

AUGUST 5, 1916

5c. THE COPY

Norman Rockwell

In This Number: Harry Leon Wilson—Samuel G. Blythe—George Lee Burton
Joseph Hergesheimer—Stewart Edward White—Charles E. Van Loan

with yet another piece of music – 'The Star Spangled Banner': never is the national anthem sung with more enthusiasm!)

Norman Rockwell had some fun with baseball pictures and various other artists have used baseball motifs as well. Baseball has also inspired some poetry – undoubtedly the most beloved being 'Casey at the Bat,' composed by Ernest Lawrence Thayer and first published in the San Francisco *Examiner* in 1888. It, too, enjoyed almost immediate success, due in part to a well-known vaudevillian, William deWolf Hopper, who recited it thousands of times over the years. (Thayer never took the poem seriously – and never bothered to collect a cent from its many reprintings and recitations. What is also little known is that Thayer wrote a sequel, 'Casey's Revenge,' in which Casey hits a homer off the same pitcher in a later game.) The other best-known verse inspired by baseball, of course, is the 'Tinker to Evers to Chance' ditty written by Franklin P Adams and published in 1910 in his column in the *New York Mail*.

There have been numerous works of fiction inspired by baseball, starting back with the 'pulp' or popular novels such as the Frank Merriwell stories by Gilbert Patten; Merriwell was only an amateur baseball player, but baseball was often a crucial element in his life. Eventually, more serious writers would turn to baseball as a subject for their artful work: Ring Lardner's *You Know Me Al*; James T Farrell's *My Baseball Diary*; Mark Harris' trilogy: *The Southpaw, A Ticket for Seamstitch*, and *Bang the Drum Slowly*; Robert Coover's *The Universal Baseball Association*; Irwin Shaw's *Voices of a Summer Day*; and Bernard Malamud's *The Natural*. Beyond such books that focus on baseball, many fictional works allude to baseball in a telling way: any American writer worth his grain of salty indigenousness knows how to deftly define a character or situation by a reference to baseball – Joe DiMaggio being a frequent symbol, cropping up, for instance, in Hemingway's *The Old Man and the Sea*.

There have been a number of movies about baseball (some based on books referred to above) but none have been especially memorable: perhaps no re-creation can compete with the real drama and human interest of baseball. The language and lore of baseball, however, permeate American conversation, whether it is a single word ('strike-out'), a phrase ('Wait till next year!') or yet another recounting of the

OPPOSITE: *Scenes of the 1908 Polo Grounds, from 'song slides' that were projected onto movie-house screens while the audience sang 'Take Me Out to the Ball-Game'.*

RIGHT: *A first day cover with postage stamps depicting Jackie Robinson, Babe Ruth, Roberto Clemente and other famous players are collectors' items.*

BELOW: *A Cubs souvenir vendor in Chicago's Wrigley Field sells everything from bats to hats.*

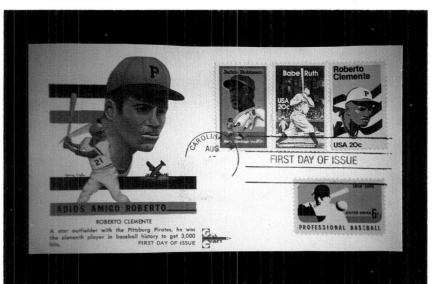

ABOVE: *A souvenir Temple Cup scorecard from the 1894 New York over Baltimore contest. The Temple Cup series, which pitted the National League's first and second place teams against each other, undercut the pennant series and was played for only four years (1894-97).*

time Babe Ruth pointed with his bat to where he would hit a home run and. . . . But of all the many holds on the American consciousness that baseball can claim, perhaps none is more tenacious than baseball cards. They began to appear before the end of the nineteenth century, although they were then aimed at adults, for they were included in cigarette packages. Eventually they were taken up by chewing gum (and since 1951 they have been associated with the Topps brand) and a whole subculture grew up around them: cards are collected, compared, traded (with subtle values assigned); and games involving flipping or skimming baseball cards have been developed. And now baseball cards are an expensive collectible – the first Mickey Mantle in the 1952 series selling for at least $3000.

But whether it is 'Casey at the Bat' or 'Take Me Out to the Ball-Game' or *The Natural* or Topps cards, baseball is secure in its niche in American popular culture.

Teams Become Professional

By the 1850s teams playing baseball under Cartwright's rules had created a spectator sport whose phenomenal popularity amazed the most seasoned observers of the contemporary scene. Cartwright's conception of the game, which included a code of conduct to ensure gentlemanly decorum, served as the foundation upon which organized amateur teams flourished for 23 years.

On 10 March 1858, representatives from 25 of the 60 to 100 clubs in the North which played the New York Game formed history's first baseball league, the staunchly amateur National Association of Base Ball Players. By 1860 fervent national attention surrounded the 60-odd clubs then in the Association as they battled for a mythical championship of the United States. Henry Chadwick, whose sports-writing career spanned fifty years and earned him the title 'Father of the Game,' fueled enthusiasm.

One of the Association's earliest acts was to choose a nine-inning game. Balls were not called on a batter until 1863. In what purported to be an attempt to preserve baseball's gentlemanly nature, in 1867 the Association passed a resolution which barred blacks and the clubs they played for from admission. At least in theory baseball was amateur and high-toned, but in the same year as the formation of the league, on 20 July 1858 the first admission ever charged in the history of the game – fifty cents to cover costs of preparing the grounds – was levied by Brooklyn and Manhattan teams playing an All-Star game.

Despite gentlemanly pretensions after the English model of sportsmanship, this was America, and winning was important. In 1858 Harry Wright, a cricket professional and jeweler's apprentice, was invited to join the Knickerbockers, largely to bolster the team against their arch-rivals, the Brooklyn Atlantics. Similar processes were at work throughout baseball. As early as 1860 James P Creighton, probably the first professional player, was paid under the table to pitch for the Excelsiors of Brooklyn. Two years later, players on the New York Mutuals were splitting the gate after expenses from their ten cent admission at the Union Grounds, and the Atlantics were doing the same at their Capitoline Grounds.

While the Civil War dampened enthusiasm and forced many of the gentlemen clubs from New York to Chicago to go under, it contributed greatly to the geographical spread of the game. A throng of over 40,000 Union soldiers – probably the largest crowd at any sporting event in the nineteenth century – watched a game between teams selected from the 165th New York Volunteer Infantry, Duryea's Zouaves, on Christmas Day, 1862. After the war, many businesses began hiring young men to work in their industries with a view toward using their baseball talent in the teams they sponsored. By the late 1860s, with teams touring and taking on all comers for the gate, the gentlemanly amateur code had entirely given way to the ethic of winning, and amateurism was a sham. The Excelsiors, the first team to go on tour, visited several cities in western and central New York in 1860. The Washington Nationals traveled as far as Rockport, Illinois, in 1867, where they suffered the only defeat of their tour at the hands of a 17-year-old pitcher named Albert G Spalding.

In 1869, largely in response to the trouncing the local favorites had experienced at the hands of the Nationals, Harry Wright was offered

ABOVE: *Off-duty army officers play a friendly baseball game at Fort Riley, Kansas, in 1870.*

LEFT: *The Excelsior Baseball Club of Brooklyn, New York, was the first team to go on tour.*

RIGHT: *Hall of Famer Albert Spalding was the premier pitcher of his day. His baseball career included roles as club president, manager, and founder of an international sporting goods manufacturer.*

LEFT: *English-born journalist Henry Chadwick pioneered modern baseball's scoring system in 1857.*

ABOVE: *Sometimes called the 'Father of Professional Baseball,' Harry Wright played or managed from 1858 to 1893. A jeweler and former cricket player, Wright played for the Knickerbockers and managed three National League teams.*

$1200 to head up a professional team from Cincinnati. Salaries to stars were already commonplace on many teams, but the Red Stockings were the first all-salaried professional team. Only one player, first baseman Charlie Gould, was a native of Cincinnati.

The Red Stockings traveled almost 12,000 miles by boat and rail from Massachusetts to California and took on all comers, playing before more than 200,000 people and achieving a record of 56 wins and one tie. Their outstanding success and the caliber of their play transformed baseball in America, uprooting the foundation of 'amateur' baseball and demonstrating beyond doubt that baseball could succeed as a professional venture.

On 17 March 1871, ten men met at Collier's Cafe on Broadway and 13th Street in New York and established the National Association of Professional Base-Ball Players, the first professional league. James N Kerns, representing the Philadelphia Athletics, was elected president. Charter members included the Athletics, the Boston Red Stockings, the Chicago White Stockings, Cleveland Forest Citys, New York Mutuals, Rockford Forest Citys, Washington Nationals, Washington

Olympics and the Fort Wayne Kekiogas, who folded in August and were replaced by the Brooklyn Eckfords, who had at first balked at the $10 fee required to join an organization they considered precarious.

Philadelphia took the 1871 championship with a season record of 22-7, Chicago placing second, and the Boston Red Stockings, staffed by Harry Wright and many of his former Cincinnati stars, took the next four consecutive pennants. Although baseball was as popular as ever, attendance declined for each of the league's five years of existence, partly because of the dominance of the Red Stockings, partly because of weak organization which permitted players to jump from team to team, and partly because of poor scheduling which in 1875 saw the Red Stockings play 79 games and Keokuk, Iowa, play 13.

Even more damaging was the degree to which gambling and bribery infiltrated the league. By 1875 National Association clubs were so riddled with heavy gambling, game-throwing, drunkenness, player desertion, contract jumping and plain rowdiness on both sides of the dugout that public confidence in the integrity of the game was reaching a point which did not bode well for baseball's future.

The National League Begins

William Ambrose Hulbert, Chicago businessman and president of the Chicago White Stockings, feared for professional baseball's future as much as he was excited by its potential, and decided to do something about it. During the 1875 season he convinced Boston's star pitcher Al Spalding (founder of the sporting goods concern that bears his name) and the rest of Boston's 'Big Four' (Cal McVey, Ross Barnes and Deacon Jim White), as well as Philadelphia star Adrian 'Cap' Anson to come to Chicago, where he hoped to set an example with a higher caliber of players than had previously played together on one team.

Joining forces with Spalding, Hulbert decided that the reforms necessary for baseball to survive and thrive could not be effected within the existing structure of the rickety National Association, and proposed to form a new league to be called the 'National League of Professional Base Ball Clubs.' Such a move would also protect him from actions by the National Association which might prevent the players he had signed from taking the field, since Hulbert had not followed Association regulations in obtaining them.

At a secret meeting in Louisville in January 1876, Hulbert convinced representatives of the St Louis, Cincinnati and Louisville clubs that his scheme for a new league was sound. On 2 February 1876 he met with representatives of Boston, Hartford, Philadelphia and New York at the Grand Central Hotel in New York. Hulbert reportedly locked the hotel room door while he read the proposed constitution and player contract he and Spalding had prepared. Equally worried about the effects of gambling and other evils, the Easterners unanimously agreed to the formation of a new league, and the National League, with eight clubs,

was born.

Hulbert and Spalding's constitution has provided the basis of the National League for more than a century. Its main objective was to make baseball-playing respectable and honorable. The constitution forbade gambling and the sale of alcohol on the grounds, obligated each team to play a complete schedule, and required each franchise to represent a city with a population of at least 75,000. Each club paid an entry fee and annual dues of $100, and was required to play 70 games, meeting each opponent ten times, five at home and five away. Admission was set at fifty cents (then considered rather high), and the team winning the most games would receive a pennant costing not less than $100.

Above all, Hulbert wanted a league that would be run in a disciplined, profitable and businesslike manner. For the first time control of the

ABOVE: *The dynamic businessman William A Hulbert, part-owner and official of the Chicago White Stockings, formed the National League in 1876 with the adoption of his new league constitution.*

LEFT: *Hall of Famer Adrian 'Cap' Anson played for the National Association's Athletics for five years, then in 1876 played the first of his 22 years with the Chicago White*

Stockings. The first player to achieve 3000 hits, Anson also led his team to five pennants in his 19 years as manager.

OPPOSITE TOP: *The Boston 1874 team.*

OPPOSITE BOTTOM: *Boston and Providence teams pose before a game in 1879.*

ABOVE: *The National League's 1882
Detroit Wolverines finished the season
in sixth place.*

LEFT: *Abraham G Mills was the
National League president in the early
1880s.*

game was placed firmly in the hands of the owners. Players were
bound to one club by an ingenious reserve clause, which guaranteed a
club a player's services for as long as it wished, and were no longer to
have any voice in the operation of the league.

Philadelphia and Boston thoroughly dominated the league during its
first decade, although Chicago took the first pennant. The first game of
the new league was played in Philadelphia on 22 April 1876, Boston
defeating Philadelphia 6-5.

Hulbert gained respect for his new organization by expelling New
York and Philadelphia at the end of the first season for refusing to
complete their schedules, and by banishing four players from Louisville for gambling. By the mid-1880s, the enterprise was successfully
launched, and National League clubs were making money. Teams
from 23 cities came and went until 1900, when the National League
settled into the same eight franchises it would maintain for 53 years.

In 1882 an opposing major league was founded around the nucleus of
the Cincinnati club that had been expelled from the National League for
permitting Sunday games and liquor on the grounds. The American
Assocation of Base Ball Clubs, featuring both of these practices, as
well as a twenty-five cent admission, soon gained the edge in attendance. Player raids and league war weakened both leagues until
National League president A G Mills wisely brought about a National
Agreement in 1883, which granted some mutual protection, especially
over player contracts, and eventuated in post-season playoffs (or
World Series) between league champions which greatly enhanced the
popularity of the game.

In 1884 both major leagues faced a challenge from St Louis million-aire Henry V Lucas, whose Union Assocation repudiated the reserve rule and lured many players from the other leagues. In return, the National League and the American Assocation raided so many of the Union Assocation's players that it was reduced to five of its twelve franchises by the end of the year, and folded after a single season.

A more serious threat was mounted in 1890 by the National Brotherhood of Professional Players, a players' benevolent associa-tion started in 1885, which responded to salary ceilings, the reserve clause, arbitrary fines and other abuses of the owners by forming the Players' League. Eighty percent of National League players, including the entire Washington team, left to join the new league.

With three leagues battling for attendance, the 1890 season was a financial disaster for all concerned. Over the winter the debt-ridden Players' League, represented by former New York Giant John Mont-gomery Ward, was out-maneuvered and dissolved by the National League. The crippled American Association barely made it through the next season. When it folded the National League acquired its Baltimore, St Louis, Washington and Louisville clubs, bringing its roster to twelve teams. Beginning in 1892 peace and the twelve-club National League monopoly would reign in baseball until the turn of the century.

LEFT: *Hall of Famer John Montgomery Ward pitched for Providence for five years, beginning in 1878; he won a league-leading 47 games the following year. In 1883 he moved to the Giants, and seven years later he helped form the Brotherhood of Professional Base Ball Players.*

BELOW: *The pennant-winning Giants of 1889.*

The Stars of the Nineties

With all quiet on the league war front in 1892, the National League, hoping to replace the post-season World Series with a play-off of champions from among its own 12 clubs, instituted its first and only split season. Despite this tactic and across-the-board slashes of players' salaries from 30 to 40 percent, only Cleveland and Pittsburgh broke even, and the league as a whole experienced the most disappointing season in its history.

The Boston Beaneaters took the pennant again in 1892, their second of three consecutive flags, and one of five they would take in the 1890s. Pitching this superb club to 11 wins out of its first 13 contests was Charles 'Kid' Nichols, whom Boston manager Frank Selee had brought to Boston from the Western League in 1890. With a fastball and good control as his primary weapons, Hall of Famer Nichols pitched a decade of games unequalled since pitchers began throwing overhand in 1883. From 1890 to 1899 Nichols' win totals were 27, 30, 35, 33, 32, 30, 30, 30, 29 and 21. For the first 7 years he averaged over 30 wins a season. He never fell below 20 wins for all ten years, during which he pitched as many as 50 complete games a season, and failed to finish only 22 games. His lifetime total of 360 wins is still respectable by any standards.

Supporting Nichols on those Boston teams were sluggers Bobby Lowe and Hugh Duffy, pitchers Jack Stivetts, Harry Staley and Vic Willis, and master catcher Charlie Ganzel. Tommy Tucker joined Lowe, Herman Long and Billy Nash in an exceptional infield, which was later bolstered by Fred Tenny and Jimmy Collins; and heavy hitters Tommy McCarthy and Cliff Carroll joined Duffy in the outfield.

1880s superstars Mike 'King' Kelly, who had been purchased from Chicago with John Clarkson for the astounding figure of $10,000 each, and the great Harry Stovey were nearing the ends of their careers, but also made solid contributions. Bobby Lowe set the as yet unsurpassed record of hitting four home runs in a single nine-inning game. Hugh Duffy also established an all-time season record, hitting .438 – the highest ever under modern rules – in 1894. The diminutive Duffy hit over .300 in each of his first ten full seasons in the majors. His 236 hits in 1894 included 18 home runs, 13 triples and 50 doubles for a .679 slugging average.

Boston's repeat championship in 1893 apparently restored the interest of the fans, who made the 1893 season the best-attended in professional baseball history. A factor not to be overlooked in increased public interest was the 1893 rule change which increased the pitching distance from 55 feet to 60 feet 6 inches. This move was made in an effort to encourage hitting, and succeeded to a remarkable degree. While pitchers went through a period of remastery and readjustment, the number of players hitting over .300 jumped from 12 in 1892 to 94 in 1894.

Denton True Young, nicknamed 'Cy' for 'Cyclone,' after his fastball, was like Nichols one of the great pitchers of all times. A farm boy from Ohio who joined Cleveland in 1890, Young won more than 20 games during each of the nine years from 1891 to 1899, including totals of 36, 32 and 35. He was the only major star to perform with equal brilliance in both centuries, winning seven more 20-game seasons from 1900 to 1908, including 33- and 32-win seasons in 1901 and 1902, on his way to

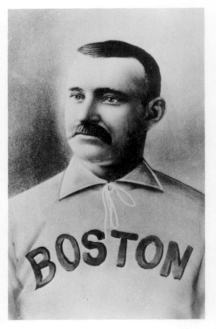

ABOVE: *Hall of Famer Charles Gardner 'Old Hoss' Radbourn in a Boston Beaneaters uniform. When he played for Providence in 1884 Radbourn hurled his way to an unbelievable 60 victories.*

LEFT: *A silk badge awarded to Sam Jackson of the Boston Red Stockings in 1871.*

TOP FAR LEFT: *Amos Wilson Rusie, 'The Hoosier Thunderbolt,' pitched for New York from 1890 to 1898, leading the league in strikeouts five times.*

TOP LEFT: *Hall of Famer Michael Joseph Kelly played outfield, catcher, first base, second base, third base, shortstop and pitcher for Chicago from 1880 to 1889. The premier hitter ended his 16-year career with the New York Giants in 1893.*

BELOW LEFT: *Hall of Famer Denton True 'Cy' Young pitched from 1890 to 1909. His legendary career featured three no-hitters – one of them a perfect game. The great pitcher holds lifetime records for wins, complete games and innings pitched.*

RIGHT: *Kid Nichols led his Boston team to greatness in the 1890s, where his unhittable change-ups brought him seven consecutive 30-win seasons. He was elected to the Hall of Fame in 1949.*

the incredible lifetime record of 511 wins. Young completed a mind-boggling 758 games in 816 starts.

The legendary Baltimore Orioles, managed by Ned Hanlon, took three consecutive pennants starting in 1894 (placing second the next two years) to share domination of the 1890s with the Boston Bean-eaters. Baltimore won its games through an exciting and rowdy style which featured intimidating the umpire, intentional spiking, insulting profanity, and such tricks as holding on to a baserunner's belt to break his stride and hiding extra balls in the outfield grass. Excitement on the field, whether caused by the new baseball idols, who had emerged as objects of hero-worship during the 1880s, or by the Orioles' vicious tactics, which transformed umpires into evil villains, paid off at the gate. In the face of profits, league policy was lenient, and the Orioles were soon imitated by all the other teams.

But the Baltimore club was also one of the greatest collections of ball players ever assembled. Hanlon's lineup included six future Hall of Famers: John J McGraw, Hughey Jennings, Wilbert Robinson, Joe Kelley (all of whom became great managers), Dan Brouthers and Wee Willie Keeler, whose famous prescription for batting success was, 'Keep your eyes clear and hit 'em where they ain't.' Moving from last place in 1892 to the top of the league in two years, in 1894 the team batted .343, led the league in fielding, and stole 343 bases. Brouthers hit .347, McGraw .340, and the star outfield of Steve Brodie, Keeler

and Kelley hit .366, .371 and .393! When Hanlon took his methods and a few key players to Brooklyn in 1899, that club took pennants in 1899 and 1900.

Under Hanlon, the Orioles can be credited for evolving much of the 'scientific' style that was to predominate in baseball until the introduction of the lively ball altered the game's basic offensive concepts. In 1894 Hanlon took his players south for spring training, then an unusual move. He taught his players to back up bases and each other and to change position for cutoff throws at a time when the game consisted almost entirely of individual effort. The same teams that imitated the Orioles' rowdy style also imitated and advanced their brand of 'inside' baseball, and it was in the twelve-club circuit of the 1890s that intricate team strategy was developed.

The hit-and-run play, perfected by Boston and Baltimore in the 1890s, had been pioneered by Cap Anson and King Kelly in the 1880s. Anson, who lured thousands to games with his genius for showmanship and batted over .300 for twenty years, was as popular as any player until Babe Ruth, and is universally acknowledged to be the outstanding player of organized baseball's first quarter century. After he became Chicago's playing manager in 1879 he greatly influenced the direction of baseball strategy.

On the negative side, Anson took a leading role in excluding the black man from major-league baseball. While at least 20 blacks played ball with major-league white clubs during the 1880s, for reasons known best to himself Anson used all his tremendous influence and prestige in baseball circles to enforce the unwritten rule, a holdover from old National Association days, which kept blacks out of baseball, and succeeded, at a time when it looked like blacks would permanently enter white organized baseball's structure, in setting a precedent that kept blacks out of major league baseball until 1947.

ABOVE: *Hall of Famer Willie Henry 'Wee Willie' Keeler played for the New York Giants at the close of his career. The outfielder also played for Brooklyn and Baltimore National League teams, and for New York in the American League. In his 19-year career (1892-1910), Keeler struck out only 36 times, and ended up with a lifetime batting average of .345.*

RIGHT: *A standing-room-only crowd fills the stands in Boston's Grand Pavilion in the early 1890s.*

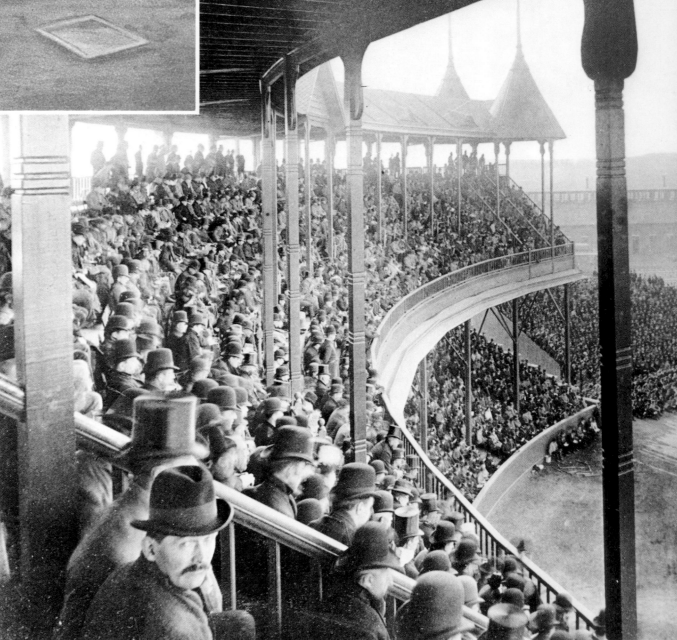

ABOVE: *Enthusiastic baseball fans of Boston accompanied their 1897 National League Champions to Baltimore for the Temple Cup Series with the second-place Orioles. Here they pose for a photograph in front of Boston's hotel headquarters. Baltimore won this last Temple Cup Series, four games to one.*

RIGHT: *Outfielder Jessie Caie Burkett, known as 'The Crab' for his rather dour disposition, played for the Cleveland Spiders through most of the 1890s. Adept at bunting, Burkett hit .400 three times in his 16-year career. He moved to the American League's St Louis Browns in 1902, and ended his career in 1905 playing for the Boston Somersets. Burkett was elected to the Hall of Fame in 1946.*

The American League Organizes

The National League, having outlasted or destroyed all attempts to create another major league, was the dominant force in professional baseball at the turn of the century. But as the new century began, the efforts of two men, Charles Albert Comiskey and Byron Bancroft Johnson, bore fruit in the permanent establishment of the American League. By the end of the first decade of the twentieth century, the American League outdrew the Senior Circuit, and had established a pattern of dominance which would continue until the end of the Second World War.

Ban Johnson and Charlie Comiskey, both of whom played baseball in college (Comiskey also played professionally), met in 1892 in Cincinnati, where Johnson was a sportswriter for the *Commercial-Gazette* and Comiskey was managing the Cincinnati Reds. They soon became drinking and cardplaying buddies, and found that they were united, with much of the country, in their dislike of the magnate-ridden 12-club National League, and in their desire to see an end to the rowdyism that characterized the baseball of the day.

With Comiskey's help, Johnson became president of the newly reorganized Western League, the strongest of the minors, in 1893.

OPPOSITE: *In an early game at New York's Polo Grounds, Philadelphia's Nap Lajoie bats while New York's Jack Warner catches. Second baseman Lajoie jumped to the American League in 1901, playing 12 of his 21 years with Cleveland.*

BELOW: *Charles 'The Old Roman' Comiskey both played and managed baseball before joining with Ban Johnson to work toward the formation of the new American League.*
BELOW RIGHT: *The founder of the American League, Ban Johnson.*

The following year Comiskey took over the Western League's Sioux City franchise and moved it to St Paul. Cornelius McGillicuddy, a former major-league catcher known to the world as Connie Mack, purchased the Milwaukee franchise, which he eventually moved to Philadelphia.

Johnson and Comiskey then set about upgrading the Western League to major-league status. The autocratic Johnson ran his league with dignity, strictly upholding the authority of umpires, discouraging profanity and the sale of liquor, and encouraging women to attend. Soon most of the clubs in the league were thriving. Unlike the organizers of previous attempts to fight the National League, Johnson and Comiskey had real executive ability, and attracted men with brains and energy.

After securing the financial backing of coal magnate Charles Somers, in October 1899, Johnson renamed his circuit the American League in order to create a more national image. It was still a minor in 1900 (the year the National League pared its roster to eight clubs, enabling Johnson to pick up the Cleveland franchise); but after the National League refused even to discuss Johnson's honorable intentions to launch a stable second circuit, Johnson announced that the American League would begin the 1901 season as a major league, and withdrew from the minor-league National Agreement. He placed franchises in three National League cities, Chicago, Philadelphia, and down east in Boston, to compete with American League franchises already located in Detroit, Baltimore, Washington, Cleveland and Milwaukee. In 1902 St Louis replaced Milwaukee, and in 1903 New

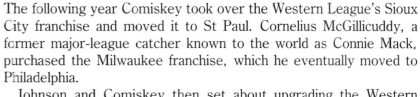

York replaced Baltimore, creating the American League lineup that was to remain unchanged until 1954. The American and the National League were direct competitors in five of their eight cities by 1903.

Since the National League owners had established a players' salary ceiling of $2400, creating great discontent, and the American League withdrawal from the National Agreement meant that the new league did not have to respect the National League's reserve clause, Johnson had no trouble buying the stars he needed to make his new league a success. In 1901, 111 out of 182 American League players were former National Leaguers. Napoleon Lajoie, perhaps the greatest star of the age, jumped from the Phillies to the Athletics for an offer of almost $6000, more than twice what he was earning with the Phillies, and that first season took the American League's Triple Crown with a .422 average still unequalled in the league, 14 home runs and 125 RBI's. Cy Young, the game's greatest pitcher, also jumped, as did such luminaries as Joe McGinnity, John J McGraw, Jimmy Collins, Bobby Wallace, Jesse Burkett, Ed Delahanty, Jack Chesbro, Wild Bill Donovan, Sam Crawford and Wee Willie Keeler.

The end of the 1902 season showed attendance totals of 2,228,000 for the American League and 1,684,000 for the National League, and the National League decided to negotiate. Ban Johnson passed on the offer of a merger from the Senior Circuit, and received recognition for the American as a major league. Both leagues then agreed to respect contracts and reserve clauses, and a three-man National Commission composed of both league presidents and secretary August Herrmann, owner of the Cincinnati Reds, was formed to govern organized ball. Ten years after the game had achieved technical maturity with the establishment of the modern pitching distance in 1893, baseball achieved organizational maturity with the two-league structure we know today.

The Chicago White Sox took the American League pennant in 1901, spurred by the pitching of manager Clark Griffith, who was 24-7 for the season. Despite a 33-10 record from Cy Young, who also led the league in ERA, strikeouts and shutouts, his Boston Somersets finished four games out, with Detroit placing third, four and a half games behind Boston.

OPPOSITE LEFT: Hall of Famer Eddie Plank pitched for the Philadelphia A's for 14 years, finishing up in 1914 with a career ERA of 2.34 and a .630 winning percentage.

OPPOSITE BOTTOM: Connie Mack described Rube Waddell as 'the pitcher with the best combination of speed and curve.' This big lefthander moved to the American League's Philadelphia team in 1902 and finished his career in 1910 with St Louis. He was elected to the Hall of Fame in 1946.

OPPOSITE TOP: Connie Mack in a Pittsburgh Ivoryettes uniform in 1894, the first year he managed in

addition to playing catcher. 'The Tall Tactician' spent 49 of his 53 managing years in the American League, leading his Athletics to a first-place finish nine times.

BELOW: Hall of Famer Clark Griffith pitched and managed his Chicago White Sox to a pennant in 1901, with a league-leading .774 winning percentage.

RIGHT: Hall of Famer Jimmy Collins, who revolutionized the playing style of third base, came to the American League in 1901 as player manager for Boston, and directed the team to pennants in 1903 and 1904.

Connie Mack's Athletics gave him the first of his nine pennants in 1902, the St Louis Browns placing second, five games behind. One half of Mack's 83 wins came from George Edward 'Rube' Waddell (24-7), who led the American League in strikeouts for six straight seasons, and from Eddie Plank, a poker-faced lefty who recorded seven 20-game seasons and became the twentieth century's first 300-game winner.

Both hurlers took 20-game seasons again in 1903, but the Boston Somersets, managed by third base great Jimmy Collins and propelled by 28 wins from Cy Young, ran away with the pennant, finishing 14 and a half games ahead of the Athletics. An equally lopsided race in the National League moved Pittsburgh owner Barney Dreyfuss and Boston owner Henry Killilea to work out details for a post-season competition, and the modern World Series was born. Boston took the first Series from a strong Pittsburgh team 5-3, thereby ending any doubts that may have remained about the quality of play in the American League. Since 1903 America's most universally followed sporting event has continued without interruption, with one notable exception.

Horner
Photo

The Modern Era Begins

Following the 1903 settlement between the two major leagues, baseball entered a period of peace and returning prosperity, an era inspired by the scientific style of play, and by such legendary players as Christy Mathewson and the incomparable Ty Cobb. Above all it was an era when pitching decided the games, and hurlers such as Jack Chesbro, Joe McGinnity, Eddie Plank, Ed Walsh, Addie Joss, Mathewson, Mordecai Brown and Rube Waddell, who struck out 343 in 1904, ruled the diamond. Until 1909, when cork was first added to the rubber center of the baseball, foreshadowing the end of what is often called the dead-ball era, hitting became almost a lost art.

The war with the American League had caused a shift in the balance of power in the National League. Beginning in 1901 Pittsburgh, New York and Chicago were to share domination of the National League for the next two decades. In 1904 the Giants took the first of two back-to-back pennants behind the pitching of 'Iron Man' Joe McGinnity, who won 35, and Mathewson, who won 33, their twin total of 68 still an unequalled record for a single season. Teammate George Wiltse, in his first year in the majors, won his first 12 decisions.

In the American League, spitballing Jack Chesbro of the New York Highlanders won the all-time record of 41 games in 1904, completing 48 of 51 starts. But Boston became the league's first repeater, beating New York in a tight race that ended on the final day when Chesbro threw history's most famous wild pitch. Cy Young, now 37, topped the Somersets' pitching staff with 26 wins and a perfect game on his way to compiling an unassailable 511 lifetime victories: Young pitched 11 years and recorded 289 victories in the National League, and pitched 11 years for 222 wins in the American.

In honor of a long-standing feud with Ban Johnson, Giant manager John J McGraw refused to field his team against the Somersets, and there was no World Series in 1904. Before the next year the post-season play-offs were made mandatory, and America's most famous sporting event has continued without interruption ever since.

LEFT: *John Dwight 'Happy Jack' Chesbro pitched for 11 years, reaching his zenith in 1904 with 41 wins for the New York Highlanders. On 10 October a wild pitch which allowed Boston to clinch the pennant diminished the glory of his achievement.*

ABOVE: *During his 10-year career, Hall of Famer Joseph McGinnity pitched eight consecutive 20-win seasons, twice topping the 30-win mark. McGinnity helped the New York Giants to two pennants.*

LEFT: *In the 17 years that Hall of Fame shortstop Honus Wagner, 'The Flying Dutchman,' played for Pittsburg, he won the batting title eight times. In 1903 his .355 batting average helped his team take the pennant.*

BELOW LEFT: *Hall of Famer Elmer Flick poses with his bat and glove. Flick, who switched to the A's and then Cleveland in the American League in 1902, played his first four years with the Phillies. Flick retired in 1910 with a .315 lifetime batting average.*

BELOW: *New York Giants' manager John McGraw and pitcher Christy Mathewson wait in the dugout. Both future Hall of Famers, McGraw and Mathewson championed their team to the Series in 1905. Mathewson, who had won 31 games that season and led the league in winning percentage (.795), ERA (1.27), strikeouts (206) and shutouts (8), hurled three shutouts in the Series.*

Although offensive play bottomed out in 1908 with the American League batting .239 overall and the National League batting .238 (Brooklyn set a modern low with .213), hitting was so anemic in 1905 that Cleveland's Elmer Flick led his league with .306, one of the lowest averages ever to take the title, and was seconded by New York's Wee Willie Keeler, with .302. The Athletics' Harry Davis led the American League with eight home runs, and Cincinnati's Fred Odwell led the National with nine. The American League's Nap Lajoie, who led the league with .381 in 1904, was limited by injury to 65 games that season. Despite the brutal pitching, Pittsburgh's Honus Wagner took his fourth National League batting championship with .339 in 1906.

The man who, with Wagner, brought the place-hitting, base-stealing, dead-ball style to its greatest heights, the demonic Tyrus Raymond Cobb, made his debut with the Tigers in 1905. After his

ABOVE: *Considered possibly the best shortstop of all time, slugger Honus Wagner slaps an infield hit.*

ABOVE RIGHT: *Ty Cobb at bat. The legendary ballplayer achieved a lifetime record of 2245 runs with a .367 batting average. In 24 years Cobb won the batting title 12 times.*

He was elected to the Hall of Fame in 1936.

RIGHT: *Hall of Famer Mordecai 'Three Finger' Brown pitched six consecutive 20-win seasons for the Cubs, helping his team take four pennants.*

rookie year, he never batted under .300 for 23 years, 16 times batted over .350, and three times hit over .400, leading the American League in batting 12 times, including nine years in a row beginning in 1907. His record of 4191 lifetime hits stood until 11 September 1985, and his lifetime average of .367 has still not been touched. As a player, his fanatic, near-psychotic zeal to excel made him all but unique. Cobb was the most hated, the most feared and perhaps the greatest ball player of all times.

In 1906 the National League's Chicago Cubs, led by Three Finger Brown's 26 wins, won 116 games, still the major-league record, and took the first of three consecutive pennants. The Chicago White Sox, protected by Ed Walsh's awesome spitball, became known to the world as 'The Hitless Wonders,' taking the American League pennant with the lowest team batting average (.228) and the lowest home run total (six) in the league. Third-place Cleveland had a team average 49 points higher than the Sox', as well as three 20-game winners, but a 19-game winning streak late in the season landed the Sox three games ahead of New York and five in front of Cleveland.

The Cubs' tight pitching gave them the flag again in 1907 with a team ERA of 1.73 that is still the lowest in National League history. Fired by Ty Cobb, who led the league in hits, average and RBI's three years running, the Tigers took the first of three consecutive American League pennants in 1907. The battle for the flag was hard-fought, but the real news in the American League that season was the debut of three players who with Cobb helped keep the new league on top for decades to come. Eddie Collins, with the Athletics, batted .333 for his 25-year career and set the standard for second base; Tristam

RIGHT: *Addie Joss pitched for Cleveland for nine years (1902-10), achieving a 1.88 career ERA. In 1908, when Cleveland and the White Sox were embroiled in a pennant race, he pitched a perfect game, turning in a league-leading 1.16 ERA that year.*

ABOVE: *Fred Merkle slides home in a close play. Merkle joined the Giants in 1907, and subsequently played for Brooklyn and the Cubs, ending his career in 1926 with the Yankees.*

Speaker, with the Red Sox, wrote the book on playing center field while compiling one of the highest lifetime batting averages (.344) in the twentieth century; and Walter Perry Johnson, called by Cobb and others the fastest pitcher ever, began his legendary 21-year career with the Washington Senators.

The Cubs' last of three consecutive pennants in 1908 saw a tight race that will always be remembered for the controversial play by the New York Giants' Fred Merkel, in which he was called out after failing to touch second base after the apparent winning run had scored in a tie game against the Cubs. A high point of the equally close race in the American League was the 2 October game between Chicago's 40-game winner Ed Walsh, one of the great spitballers of the era, and Cleveland's Addie Joss. Walsh struck out 15, allowing one run on four hits, but Joss, whose fine career was cut short by tubercular meningitis, pitched the new league's second perfect game, retiring 27 men in order.

Honus Wagner, taking another batting title with a .354 average, spurred the Pittsburgh Pirates to 110 wins and the pennant in 1909. In a hard-fought Series battle against the Tigers and their new infield, Wagner hit .333 and stole six bases (to Cobb's .231 and two), spiriting his team to victory in the first championship to go a full seven games. The two greatest exponents of the dead-ball era style of play were never to face each other again.

The American League had now won only one Series in nine years, causing some to wonder just how major a league it was; but with aging heroes such as Nap Lajoie and Cy Young being replaced by a precocious crop of youngsters, the situation was soon to change.

Two Baseball Dynasties and Another War

The opening of the second decade of the twentieth century saw Connie Mack's Athletics take four pennants (and three world championships) to become the American League's first dynasty team. In the National League, after the Chicago Cubs returned to the winner's circle in 1910, John McGraw's Giants started a dynasty of their own, taking pennants in 1911, 1912 and 1913.

National League batting averages rose by 12 points in 1910 over the preceding season, and the hit-and-run play began to replace the sacrifice bunt as the somewhat livelier cork-center ball patented by A J Reach became available for major-league play. The emphasis was still on place-hitting, bunting and base-stealing, but the dead-ball era was on the way out. Not to be forgotten was the suicide of National League president Harry Pulliam, caused at least in part by the badgering he received from McGraw for supporting the umpires' ruling in the Merkle affair. Also in 1910, President Taft tossed out the first ball at the Washington season opener, beginning a practice that developed into the tradition of American presidents tossing out the first ball at significant games.

The championship Cubs of 1910, essentially the same team that had been successful in 1906, featured the fabled double-play combination of Joe Tinker, Johnny Evers and Frank Chance, immortalized in verse by sportswriter Franklin P Adams on 10 July ('Tinker to Evers to Chance'). While part of an excellent infield, they were probably not the era's best, and the way the game was played in those days made double plays a relatively rare occurrence anyway. More than anything else, the enduring fame of this trio testifies to the power of the pen in an era when newsprint was the only medium, and sportswriters could make or break reputations. More to the point, Cub pitchers, sparked by Leonard Cole's 20-4 rookie year, again led the league, but with an ERA of 2.51, reflecting the arrival of Reach's ball. Pitching for the Senators, Walter Johnson had his first great year with 25 wins, starting a streak of ten consecutive seasons in which he averaged over 26 wins a season.

ABOVE: *President William Howard Taft was the first President of the United States to toss out the first ball of the season, in 1910.*

RIGHT: *As part of Connie Mack's $100,000 infield, John Phalen 'Stuffy' McInnis played first base for nine years (1909-17). McInnis ended his career in 1927 with a .308 lifetime batting average.*

Second baseman Johnny Evers and shortstop Joe Tinker (left), together with first baseman manager Frank Chance (above) formed the Cubs' lethal double-play combination, immortalized in verse during the 1908 World Series:

These are the saddest of possible
  words –
Tinker to Evers to Chance.
Trio of Bear Cubs and fleeter than
  birds –
Tinker to Evers to Chance.

Thoughtlessly pricking our
  gonfalon bubble,
Making a Giant hit into a double,
Words that are weighty with
  nothing but trouble,
Tinker to Evers to Chance.

RIGHT: Hall of Famer Rube Marquard pitched for the New York Giants from 1908 to 1915, moving in midseason to Brooklyn, and finishing his 18-year career with the Boston Braves in 1925. In 1911 Marquard led the league in winning percentage (.774) and strikeouts (237).

The Athletics, led by Jack Coombs' 31 wins and Chief Bender's 23, finished 14 and a half games ahead of second-place New York – their 102 victories marking the first time an American League club had won over 100 games – and went on to take the Series from the Cubs in five games, setting a team Series batting mark of .316 that stood for fifty years. Mack's winning teams featured .300-hitters Danny Murphy and Rube Oldring in the outfield, Eddie Collins at second, Jack Barry at short, and Frank 'Home Run' Baker at third. Veteran Harry Davis at first was replaced by John 'Stuffy' McInnis in 1911, completing what Mack called his 'hundred-thousand-dollar infield.'

Cobb took his fourth straight batting title with a .385 average in 1910, beating out Lajoie's .384 by sitting out the last game of the season to preserve his lead. Manager Jack O'Connor and coach Harry Howell of the Browns, against whom Lajoie played his last double-header, were banished from baseball forever for trying to make it easy for Lajoie to break the unpopular Cobb's record. (Both the third baseman, to whom Lajoie repeatedly bunted, and the score-keeper, appeared to be involved in the scheme.)

The McGraw Giants who took the pennant in 1911, 1912 and 1913 were powered by the pitching of the great Christy Mathewson, whose wins totaled 26, 23 and 25 in those years (in 1913 Mathewson pitched 68 consecutive innings without walking a man); and by Rube Marquard, who took 24, 26 and 23, including 19 straight in 1912. The Giants stole 347 bases in 1911, still the major-league record. Staffing

Frank 'Home Run' Baker at bat. This third baseman for the Philadelphia Athletics earned his nickname in the 1911 World Series, smashing a two-run homer in game two, and a ninth-inning homer in game three. The A's took the Series against the Giants, four games to two.

those winning teams were Fred Merkle, Larry Doyle, Art Fletcher and Charles 'Buck' Herzog in the infield; Chief Meyers behind the plate; and Red Murray, Fred Snodgrass, Josh Devore and George Burns in the outfield. The team was drilled to perfection in McGraw's system, receptive to his signalled commands.

Ty Cobb hit .420 in 1911, followed by .410 in 1912, to set an as yet unequalled two-year record. Teammate Sam Crawford hit .378 that

first year, the two combining for a total of 465 Tiger hits. 'Shoeless' Joe Jackson, in his rookie year with Cleveland, hit .408. Soon to gain a reputation as one of the game's greatest natural hitters, Jackson would be studied for batting style secrets by both Ty Cobb and Babe Ruth.

In his first year with the Phillies, pitcher Grover Cleveland Alexander set a still-standing rookie record of 28 wins, seven shutouts and 227 strikeouts. In 1911 the Athletics' Frank Baker became 'Home Run Baker,' leading the league with nine homers, including two in the Series as the A's took the championship from the Giants. Reflecting more effects of the cork-center ball, the Cubs' Frank 'Wildfire' Schulte hit an astounding 21 homers to break the previous major-league record of 16.

In 1912 Joseph 'Smokey Joe' Wood, a young righthander who threw 23-17 for the Red Sox the year before, spirited his team to victory with a 34-5 season (he also batted .290). Walter Johnson, picking up speed, was 32-12, with 303 strikeouts and a 1.39 ERA. Both Johnson and Wood pitched 16 consecutive wins, surpassing Jack Chesbro's 1904 record of 14 to tie for the new mark. Tris Speaker's .383 average combined with Wood's performance to give the Red Sox 105 wins, a new league record. In the National League, Cub first baseman Heinie

RIGHT: *Red Sox righthander Joe Wood warms up before a game. Wood had his finest year in 1912, winning 34 games and losing only five for a .872 winning percentage. His three Series victories spirited the Sox to a World championship that year.*

BELOW RIGHT: *Walter Johnson poses with Captain Edith Ivings of the Salvation Army. 'The Big Train' pitched his magic for the Washington Senators from 1907 to 1927, his stamina and talent bringing him 416 career victories with 3508 strikeouts. He was elected to the Hall of Fame in 1936.*

Zimmerman led his league with 207 hits, including 14 home runs and 42 doubles, for a batting average of .372. The Sox took the Series from the Giants in a close contest that went into eight games.

Joe Wood hurt his arm in spring training in 1913 and vanished from pitching greatness as quickly as a shooting star, but Walter Johnson, now known as 'The Big Train,' his era's epitome of great speed, had his greatest season ever, and by definition the greatest year any pitcher has ever enjoyed. Johnson was 36-7 in 1913, pitched 55 and two-thirds consecutive scoreless innings, led his league in every pitching category, and walked only 38 men in 346 innings. But despite his performance, the Senators finished six and a half games behind the A's, who went on to an easy victory over the Giants in the Series. Cobb took his seventh straight batting title with .390, seconded for the third year in a row by Joe Jackson – who had batted .395 the year before – with .373.

No pennant or World Series race since 1914 ever passes without some reference to the 'Miracle Braves' of 1914. In last place on 19 July, they won 60 of their last 76 games to take the pennant 10 and a half games ahead of the Giants, the first time a club other than the Giants, Cubs or Pirates had taken a National League pennant since 1900. Mack's Athletics were universally expected to put the upstart Braves in their place in the World Series, but instead became the first team to be counted out in four games. The Braves' Hank Gowdy set a long-standing batting mark of .545 for the Series, second baseman Johnny Evers hit .438, and pitchers Dick Rudolph and Bill James, who had won 27 and 26 games each for manager George Stallings during the regular season, each took two games.

In the spring of 1914, with the beginning of war in Europe, the exceptionally well-funded Federal League announced plans to move from minor- to major-league status for the coming season. When Ban Johnson, who from his powerful seat on the National Commission virtually ruled organized baseball, refused to countenance a third league, the Federals began raiding players from both leagues. Despite an edict which blacklisted players who deserted the two established major leagues, the Federal League managed to buy such players as Eddie Plank and Three Finger Brown, although it failed to land such major draws as Walter Johnson and Ty Cobb.

ABOVE: *The 1914 Boston Braves pose for a team picture. With a 94-59 record, the Braves won the pennant by an 11 and a half game margin, then went all the way in the Series.*

BELOW: *American League founder and member of the National Commission, Ban Johnson dealt harshly with the Federal League.*

BELOW RIGHT: *Judge Kenesaw Mountain Landis (named for a Civil War battle) became baseball's first commissioner in 1920.*

Unable to obtain big-name stars when the two major leagues upped their players' salaries, the new league never really got anywhere. The Federals took the battle to the courts, suing to invalidate the structure of organized baseball. All parties concerned suffered financially, but Judge Kenesaw Mountain Landis' skillful handling of the case led to a negotiated settlement which preserved organized baseball's status quo, and the Federal League folded completely before the 1916 season.

Baseball in the Great War

Stung by his team's defeat at the hands of the Miracle Braves and convinced that the times demanded retrenchment (the A's had lost money in 1914 despite a championship year, and the Federal League wolves were at the door with fat checkbooks), after the 1914 season Connie Mack released the high-salaried Jack Coombs, sold Eddie Collins to the White Sox, Jack Barry and Herb Pennock to the Red Sox, and Bob Shawkey to New York (Frank Baker retired and re-appeared with New York a year later; Eddie Plank and Chief Bender had already jumped to the Federals). True to Mack's gloomiest vision, 1915 was the blackest year in baseball since the 1890s. Only seven major-league clubs made minimal profits; nine others, as well as six Federal clubs and most of the minors, lost money. But in the midst of this carnage, owners Joe Lanin of the Red Sox and Comiskey of the White Sox bought superstars at bargain basement prices. Boston and Chicago took the next five pennants, while Philadelphia finished at the bottom of the American League for the next seven years.

The Red Sox team that won three out of four pennants beginning in 1915 featured the legendary outfield of Tris Speaker, Duffy Lewis, and Harry Hooper (Speaker was dealt to Cleveland in April of 1916 after he asked for a salary increase; he hit .386 that year and ended Cobb's nine-year string of batting championships). Boston sported a strong infield as well, but it was the Red Sox pitching staff, among the strongest of all times, that carried the day. The war-era hurlers included Carl Mays, George 'Rube' Foster, Hubert 'Dutch' Leonard, Ernie Shore, and George Herman 'Babe' Ruth, the last two purchased after Mack declined to buy them both for $10,000. In 1915, his first full

season in the majors, Babe Ruth was 18-6 with a 2.44 ERA, batted .315 and hit four home runs. In 1916 he was 23-12 and led the league in ERA and shutouts; and in 1917 he was 24-13, with a 2.02 ERA, and batted .325.

Grover Cleveland Alexander established himself as the National League's leading pitcher in 1915, throwing 31-10 with 12 shutouts for an ERA of 1.22 that remained a league record for 53 years. Teammate Gavvy Cravath, anticipating the coming of the long-ball style of play, set a new major-league record of 24 homers to help the Phillies take their first pennant. But National League hitting on the whole was weak that year, with Larry Doyle of the Giants taking the title with a record-low .320 average. That year McGraw's Giants finished in the cellar for the first and only time, and the Phillies dropped the Series to the Red Sox, 4-1.

LEFT: *The Philadelphia Athletics won three of the four World Series they played with Jack Barry at shortstop. Here he warms up with infield practice.*

ABOVE: *Hall of Famer outfielder Tris Speaker played for Cleveland from 1916 to 1926, after nine years with the Boston Red Sox. Speaker's record of 793 doubles still stands today.*

The Brooklyn Dodgers, then known as the Robins after clownish manager Wilbert Robinson, who had played on the Orioles teams of the 1890s with McGraw, took the pennant in 1916, becoming the third National League team in a row to earn its first pennant. Pitcher Ed Pfeffer won 25 games to lead a pitching staff that included Marquard and Jack Coombs. Slugging power was supplied by Zack Wheat, Jake Daubert and Casey Stengel; and ex-Giants Merkle and Meyers were also aboard, adding fuel to rumors that the Giants helped the Robins to

ABOVE LEFT: *Cubs pitcher from 1913 to 1921, James Leslie 'Hippo' Vaughn was almost unstoppable, turning in five 20-win seasons during that time. Vaughn's 1.74 ERA with 148 strikeouts and eight shutouts helped the Cubs win the pennant in 1918.*

ABOVE: *Grover Cleveland Alexander pitched for Philadelphia from 1911 to 1917, helping his team take the pennant in 1915 with a league-leading 31-10 record and a 1.22 ERA. Alexander ended his 20-year career in 1930, and was elected to the Hall of Fame in 1938.*

LEFT: *Larry Doyle played for the Cubs in 1916 and 1917, but played the rest of his 14-year career for the New York Giants. In 1915 Doyle's .320 batting average and 40 doubles led the league.*

BROWN vs. MATHEWSON
GREATEST TREAT of THE YEAR for BASEBALL FANS

CINCINNATI, OHIO, SEPT. 1, 1916.

"YOU CAN POSITIVELY COUNT ON MY PITCHING AGAINST BROWN ON SEPT. 4th."

CHRISTY MATHEWSON,
MANAGER CINCINNATI REDS.

CHRISTY MATHEWSON

BROWN'S TWIRLING HAND

—1916.—

"THREE FINGERED" BROWN

CHICAGO, ILL.
"MORDECAI BROWN WILL BE READY TO BATTLE AGAINST MATHEWSON LABOR DAY."

JOE TINKER,
MANAGER CUBS.

| First Game at 1:30 P.M. | **DOUBLE HEADER LABOR DAY** | First Game at 1:30 P.M. |

WEEGHMAN PARK

STARS OF MANY YEARS TO PITCH FOR CHICAGO CUBS AND CINCINNATI REDS

NORTH CLARK AND ADDISON STREETS.
RESERVED SEATS AT A. G. SPALDING & BROS. 28 S WABASH AVE. TEL. CEN. 448.

THE DAILY NEWS BOYS BAND WILL RENDER MUSIC

ABOVE: *A poster advertises a match between two of the greatest pitchers of the day – the Cubs' Three Finger Brown and the Reds' Christy Mathewson.*

RIGHT: *A pick-up baseball game at Camp Gordon in Georgia during World War I.*

win by lying down for a crucial series.

Despite a 26-game winning streak in September, the Giants finished fourth. Alexander won 33 games, setting the all-time record of 16 shutouts, and young Rogers Hornsby of the Cardinals batted .313 in his first full season. With Chick Shorten and Clarence 'Tilly' Walker replacing Tris Speaker, the Red Sox repeated in the American League in 1916, and repeated in the Series, dropping the Robins by 4-1, the same margin they had set over the Phillies the year before.

On 2 May 1917 Fred Toney of the Reds and Jim 'Hippo' Vaughan of the Cubs pitched the only double no-hitter in major-league history, each pitcher issuing only two bases on balls during the first nine innings. Vaughan gave up two hits and the Reds scored one run in the top of the tenth inning, but Toney maintained his no-hitter through the tenth inning, retiring the Cubs in order.

Featuring strong pitching, a fine infield, and Shoeless Joe Jackson in the outfield, the White Sox stopped the Red Sox roll in 1917. In the

RIGHT: *Detroit Tigers Ty Cobb (left) and Sam Crawford (right) talk with Chicago's Shoeless Joe Jackson.*

BELOW: *Babe Ruth at bat in a Boston Red Sox uniform. Ruth batted .309 during his six years as a Red Sox pitcher, while winning 89 games and losing only 46.*

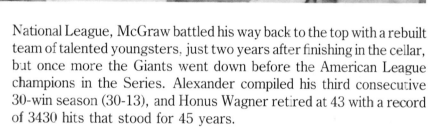

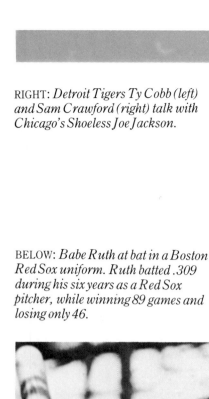

National League, McGraw battled his way back to the top with a rebuilt team of talented youngsters, just two years after finishing in the cellar, but once more the Giants went down before the American League champions in the Series. Alexander compiled his third consecutive 30-win season (30-13), and Honus Wagner retired at 43 with a record of 3430 hits that stood for 45 years.

A few days after the 1917 season began, Congress declared war on the Central Powers of Europe, but it was not until the next season that baseball, classified as a non-essential industry, its players subject to General Crowder's 'Work-or-Fight' order, began to feel the heat. As attendance declined some owners panicked. Correctly fearing Alexander's conscription, the Phillies sold him to the Cubs in November of 1917; in 1918, Giant owner Harry Hempstead sold out to Charles Stoneham. In all, 103 National League players entered the service by the November 1918 Armistice, including such greats as Casey Stengel, Christy Mathewson and Grover Alexander. The 1918 season was shortened to end on Labor Day, although eventually a dispensation was allowed to permit the repeating Red Sox and the Chicago Cubs, led by Hippo Vaughan's 22 wins, to play the Series. The Red Sox, who lost such stars as Duffy Lewis, Jack Barry and Dutch Leonard to the war effort, took the Series 4-2, marking the fourth straight American League victory and the eighth American League World Series win in nine years.

Babe Ruth started twice in the Series with the Cubs, and by winning both his games, compiled a record of 29 and two-thirds consecutive scoreless Series innings that stood for 45 years. By now acknowledged as the American League's leading lefty, Babe Ruth had started in only 19 games in 1918, manager Ed Barrow preferring to play him in the outfield or at first base to make fuller use of his batting. Ruth obligingly hit .300 in 95 games and tied Tilly Walker for league home run honors with 11 that season. The next year he pitched even fewer games, but set the first of the home run records which were to revolutionize the way the game was played.

The Turning Point:
1919 and the Black Sox Scandal

Disrupted by the war and plagued by flagging attendance, baseball reached a low point in 1918. No major-league team played more than 130 games in that year's shortened season, and in 1919, owners uncertain over the future of the economy scheduled only 140 of the usual 154 games. But postwar enthusiasm for baseball took everyone by surprise. Attendance tripled in Cincinnati, quadrupled in Brooklyn, and increased by almost half a million for the New York Giants. The 1919 World Series broke all attendance records and earned nearly fifty percent more than the half-million Series of 1912, the previous all-time high.

In 1919 Babe Ruth played 111 games in the outfield and started in only 15 games on the mound. He led the American League in RBI's (114), set a new record for slugging average with .657, and set a new major-league record for home runs with 29 – the second of 12 home run titles he took or tied (he shared the 1918 American League record of 11 with Tilly Walker). But in spite of his performance, the Red Sox finished fifth, and the American League pennant went to Comiskey's Chicago White Sox, one of baseball's all-time great teams.

In the National League the Cincinnati Reds, led by slugger Edd Roush, took their first pennant ever in 1919, finishing nine games ahead of the Giants. A good-to-average team that experienced one brief summer of success, the Reds went on to defeat the unquestionably superior White Sox 5-3 in that season's best-out-of-nine Series. Just as surprisingly, at the time the Series took place, the gamblers established Cincinnati as favorite. While almost every major sports event generates rumors of conspiracy, to many observers the White

Sox performance was suspiciously substandard. The following year it was established that some members of the White Sox, known forever after as the 'Black Sox,' had conspired with gamblers to throw the 1919 Series.

It now seems probable that the Black Sox Series scandal was the tip of an iceberg rather than an isolated incident. In an era when miserly owners paid players astonishingly low salaries, Charlie Comiskey paid his White Sox the lowest salaries in both major leagues. Furthermore, the White Sox were a notoriously clique-ridden team, one faction led by sophisticated captain Eddie Collins, whose 1919 salary was $15,000; and another, less polished crew, none of whom made over $6000, led by Arnold 'Chick' Gandil. Player resentment was high, and gamblers' offers, which could amount to several times an annual salary, must have been hard to refuse.

Nor were the White Sox the only team whose players threw games or were suspected of throwing games. In 1919 two of McGraw's most brilliant stars, first baseman Hal Chase and third baseman Heinie Zimmerman, were barred from organized baseball forever for trying to induce players to throw games. Chicago's Lee Magee was barred a year later, for the same reasons, and similar fixing, encouraged by the climate of the times, had evidently been going on for some time. Even such greats as Ty Cobb and Tris Speaker did not escape the breath of scandal. The Black Sox conspiracy capped a sordid era that had been taxing public faith in the national game for some time.

In September 1920, the story broke when boxer Abe Attell confessed to being involved in the deal to throw the 1919 Series and

OPPOSITE: *The 1919 Chicago White Sox team, eight players of which threw the World Series in a gambling scandal that was discovered the following year. The players were barred from the major leagues for life.*

ABOVE: *Called the 'finest infielder of all time' by Connie Mack, second baseman Eddie Collins moved from the A's to the White Sox in 1915, where he would stay until 1926. A lifetime .333 hitter, Collins had speed as well: twice he stole six bases in a game. 'Cocky' Collins was elected to the Hall of Fame in 1939.*

RIGHT: *Outfielder Edd Roush places a bunt. Roush played for the Cincinnati Reds from 1917 to 1926, winning the batting title in 1919 to help his team to the Series.*

ABOVE: *The Black Sox scandal ended shortstop Charles 'Swede' Risberg's career after only four years in the majors.*

ABOVE: *Judge Kenesaw Mountain Landis throws out the first ball of the season. The Black Sox scandal hastened the formation of the commissioner role that Landis was appointed to fill in 1920. To restore baseball's image, Landis dealt harshly with the offenders.*

LEFT: *White Sox pitchers Claude 'Lefty' Williams and Eddie Cicotte were involved in the 1919 scandal.*

Williams lost all three Series games he pitched, while Cicotte lost two of the three Series games he pitched, his 2.91 Series ERA a dismal contrast to his regular-season ERA of 1.82.

OPPOSITE: *Babe Ruth tips his hat to acknowledge applause after belting a home run. One of the game's most talented and popular players, Ruth rose to glory in the roaring twenties, the era of the lively ball.*

named eight White Sox – seven of them regular starters – as co-conspirators. 'Shoeless' Joe Jackson, Eddie Cicotte, Charles 'Swede' Risberg, Claude 'Lefty' Williams, Chick Gandil, George 'Buck' Weaver, Oscar 'Happy' Felsch and Fred McMullin were in due course summoned before a Chicago grand jury. Cicotte, Jackson and Williams confessed in detail how the games were rigged, and a conspiracy trial began in Chicago in June 1921. This proceeding soon turned into a farce. Witnesses fled the country, and the confessions of Cicotte, Jackson and Williams mysteriously disappeared, as did all the grand jury records, enabling the accused to repudiate their confessions. In the face of this lack of hard evidence, no conviction was possible, and a not guilty verdict was rendered on 2 August.

But the trial of the Black Sox was not yet over. While the events of the sport's most notorious scandal were unfolding, baseball completed the last step in the evolution of its government, and the three-man National Commission, in trouble as a governing body since the Federal League war, was replaced by a single commissioner, Judge Kenesaw Mountain Landis. Landis had risen to favor and prominence in baseball circles for his handling of the Federal League suit, and was now charged with cleaning up the game, for which purpose he was given sweeping, dictatorial powers, and a seven-year contract at $50,000 annually. Famous for theatrical posturing and fully conscious of the symbolic value of his role, according to Heywood Broun, the career of Commissioner Landis 'typifies the heights to which dramatic talent may carry a man in America if only he has the foresight not to go on the stage.' Landis served as baseball's first commissioner until 1944.

The new commissioner's first major ruling was to bar the eight Chicago Black Sox from professional baseball for life, regardless of their acquittal. Some felt some of the players deserved a pardon – Buck Weaver played .324 ball in the Series and Joe Jackson led both leagues with a Series average of .375 – but such was the crisis in public confidence in the national pastime that the commissioner's firm handling of the situation was generally acknowledged as necessary to put the game back on solid ground, and he did much to make the game a respected and admired sport.

With trust in the integrity of the game restored by his presence and the postwar economy booming, the beginning of the Roaring Twenties marked a turning point for baseball. But Commissioner Landis alone was not enough to account for the great outpouring of baseball enthusiasm. The final element in this successful equation was a young slugger named Babe Ruth. It took his bat to wipe the slate clean, to turn the glare of media attention away from the greatest baseball scandal of all time and to usher in an era of unprecedented prosperity for baseball.

PART II

The Golden Years; The Sunlight Years

1920-1939

Black Players, Black Leagues

In 1867 history's first baseball league, the National Association of Base Ball Players, then nine years old, passed a resolution which barred blacks and the clubs they played for from membership. Theoretically, the resolution was designed to protect the amateur, high-tone, gentlemanly nature of the game, as it was then conceived; but more than anything else, the resolution reflected the racism that grew increasingly virulent in the North after the Civil War. Blacks might be legally free, but segregation was rapidly becoming a fact of American life. As early as 1867, black teams in their own league had played a 'colored championship' in Brooklyn. The Excelsiors of Philadelphia took the crown that year, besting the Brooklyn Uniques and the Brooklyn Monitors.

While no other association or league ever adopted a *written* resolution barring blacks, the 1867 National Association resolution set a precedent and served as the basis for what became known as the 'gentleman's agreement,' in effect an unwritten rule which rigorously excluded blacks from organized ball. Many white men believed there was a law against blacks playing major league baseball.

Such may have been the case for the legendary Cap Anson, a major force in baseball after he became Chicago's playing manager in 1879. Yet support for the color line was by no means universal, and in the 1880s, Moses Fleetwood Walker and his brother William Welday Walker, for instance, both of whom played for the American Association's Toledo club, were among the at least 20 blacks who played ball with white major-league clubs. Over 30 blacks played major-league ball before 1900.

In 1884, Anson's Chicago White Stockings played an exhibition game with Toledo. When Anson saw Fleetwood Walker take the diamond, he bellowed with characteristic tact, 'Get that nigger off the field!' On that occasion Anson was forced to play or see his team forfeit its share of the gate, but five years later he refused to play against a Newark team which featured George Stovey, considered by many the greatest black pitcher of all time. Stovey walked off the field and refused to play the White Stockings.

Still, by 1887 it looked like blacks would enter organized baseball's structure. John Montgomery Ward tried to bring Stovey up to pitch for the Giants that year, but Anson, mustering all of his tremendous prestige and popularity in baseball circles – he was the single most popular figure in baseball until Babe Ruth – was able to prevent it. Declaring, 'There's a law against that,' Anson succeeded in setting a precedent that excluded blacks from major-league baseball for over half a century.

Not that others didn't try to bring blacks to the majors. In 1901, for instance, manager John J McGraw attempted to sneak black second baseman Charlie Grant onto the Orioles team by passing him off as a full-blooded Cherokee. White Sox president Charlie Comiskey recognized Grant as a former member of the Chicago Columbia Eagles and made sure it didn't happen. Similar attempts met similar fates.

With the door to organized baseball closed, black Americans continued to establish amateur and professional teams and leagues. In the early part of this century, black baseball was a semi-professional affair, but the quality of black play was never in doubt. Black talent, cultivated

ABOVE: *Moses Fleetwood Walker played 42 games for Toledo of the American Association in 1884 – 41 of them as a catcher and the other in the outfield – all at the ripe old age of 26.*

LEFT: *Leon Walter 'Buck' Leonard played first base for the Homestead Grays of the Negro National League from 1933 to 1950, and batted in the high .300s. At his peak he was earning $100 per month, which was pretty small potatoes for the best first baseman in the league – a player who eventually made it to the Hall of Fame. Leonard often led the Negro National League in home runs.*

ABOVE: *Joshua 'Josh' Gibson caught for the Homestead Grays from 1930 to 1946, and was considered one of the all-time great ball players of any color.*
ABOVE RIGHT: *Charlie Grant was discovered by John J McGraw, who signed him and tried to pass him off as Charlie Tokohama, a Cherokee Indian, but the owners rebelled.*

BELOW: *The Kansas City Monarchs of 1936. The Monarchs were probably the all-time great Negro National League team, and won the first Negro World Series in 1924. Like many black teams, they had to barnstorm around the country, and carried with them a portable lighting system to get in an extra game at night.*

on such teams as the Kansas City Monarchs, the Chicago Leland Giants, the New York Lincoln Giants, and the St Louis Stars, was everywhere acknowledged to be equal to anything the white majors had to offer.

One of the early giants of black baseball, shortstop John Henry 'Pop' Lloyd, was often called the black Honus Wagner. Honus himself commented, 'It's a privilege to have been compared with him.' Wagner considered Andrew 'Rube' Foster, who pitched for the Chicago Lelands and later founded the National Negro Baseball League, 'the smartest pitcher I have ever seen in all my years in baseball.' Dizzy Dean was to remark in the 1930s, 'I have played against a Negro All-Star team that was so good, we didn't think we had an even chance against them.' Indeed, while not all teams in the black leagues, according to the great Judy Johnson – who Connie Mack said could have named his price if he'd been white – were major-league quality, black teams regularly beat white major-league all-stars.

Rube Foster, with the cooperation of Ban Johnson, formed the first black professional league in 1920. His National Negro Baseball League was eventually joined by the Negro Eastern League and the Negro American League, and there was a Negro World Series. It was during this period that players with the reputation of Satchel Paige and Josh Gibson, doing for black baseball what Babe Ruth did for white, began to emerge.

Backing for black clubs came from various sources. During the thirties, for instance, Louis Armstrong sponsored a team called the 'Secret Nine,' and the Cab Calloway band had a team of its own. While black leagues never enjoyed the stability and prosperity of their white counterparts, and had to put up with intolerable traveling and playing conditions, organized Negro baseball survived the Depression and thrived until black players began to enter the majors after the Second World War.

Just as they never had the benefit of organized baseball's salaries, black players never had the benefit of official record-keeping. While everyone knew that Josh Gibson had hit more home runs in a season than Babe Ruth, and many watched him hit four home runs out of Griffith Stadium in a single game, no record bureau stood behind this great slugger. Major-league baseball ultimately did recognize some of the great players of the black leagues by admitting them to the Hall of Fame (after some testy prodding by Ted Williams), but the harsh realities of baseball apartheid remained. It is indicative that the Yankees did not play a black until eight years after Jackie Robinson's breakthrough in 1947, and the Red Sox waited 12 years. Not until the end of the 1974 season was Frank Robinson, the first black manager, chosen to be skipper of the Cleveland Indians, signalling the downfall of the last barrier to blacks in the world of baseball.

ABOVE: *James 'Cool Papa' Bell slides into third base. Bell played from 1922 to 1946, mostly with the Homestead Grays. He started out as a pitcher, but was soon moved to the outfield so that he could play every day. He was not a power hitter, but was one of the fastest base runners in history, on occasion scoring from first on a sacrifice bunt. A switch hitter, he batted in the high .300s, and was eventually elected to the Hall of Fame.*

BELOW: *The Chicago American Giants of 1941 who dominated the Negro National League – one of the few teams to have been organized by a black man, Andrew 'Rube' Foster, in 1911.*

LEFT: *John Henry Lloyd, the greatest black shortstop of all time. Nicknamed 'The Black Wagner,' a reference to the great shortstop Honus Wagner, he played for several teams, but was mostly a star for the Lincoln Giants. A consistent .400 hitter, he batted an amazing .475 in 1911.*

RIGHT: *William J 'Judy' Johnson played in the Negro Leagues from 1921 to 1938. This third baseman batted around .300 for the Hillsdale club in the 1920s and the Pittsburgh Crawfords in the 1930s. After his playing days were over, the star infielder managed the Homestead Grays.*

The House That Ruth Built

Few individuals in any profession and few players in any sport have ever had the impact on their game that George Herman Ruth had on baseball. As brash and expansive as the Roaring Twenties, Babe Ruth recreated baseball in his own image, and brought to it, as Wall Street did to the economy, an astonishing and transforming inflation, with both inflated home runs and inflated salaries. In the process he ushered in an unprecedented era of prosperity for baseball, and served as the seed around which the Yankees crystallized as a major force, announcing their presence by taking six pennants in ten years.

Babe Ruth was already famous as a Red Sox pitching star and outfielder before he came to the Yankees, having set an all-time major-league record of 29 home runs in 1919. In 1920, when he hit 54 home runs in his first season with the Yankees, Yankee attendance doubled, American League attendance rose by one and a half million, and the American League became the first league to top the five million attendance mark.

To take advantage of Ruth's rising popularity and the overwhelming public response to his exciting new style of home run baseball, the ball was made much livelier. Despite official protests to the contrary, the statistics speak for themselves. Combined major-league batting averages for 1920 were almost 30 points higher than in 1915; by 1925 they were 45 points higher. In terms of home runs, of which Babe Ruth hit 467 during the twenties, major leaguers as a whole hit 384 in 1915, 631 in 1920, 1167 in 1925, and 1565 in 1930. The number of major leaguers hitting over .300 also rose astronomically.

To turn the game even more in the direction of hitters, in February

ABOVE: *Herbert Jefferis 'Herb' Pennock, 'The Knight of Kennett Square,' in his Yankee uniform. Herb pitched from 1912 to 1934 for the Philadelphia Athletics, the Red Sox, the Yankees and then back to the Red Sox.*

LEFT: *Carl William Mays pitching for the Yankees. His career lasted from 1915 to 1929 with the Red Sox, the Yankees, the Reds and the Giants.*

OPPOSITE: *Perhaps the greatest player ever – George Herman 'Babe' Ruth. Although he started as a pitcher for the Red Sox (and some of his hurling records still stand), he was soon shifted to the outfield, where he could play every day. Traded to the Yankees in 1920, he ended his career with a single season with the Braves in 1935.*

of 1920 both leagues outlawed all tampering with the ball, banning forever the application of sandpaper, emery, licorice, mud, and particularly spit to the baseball's surface, although 17 major-league pitchers who used the spitball as their primary weapon were permitted to continue to do so. In addition, after popular Cleveland shortstop Ray Chapman was hit on the head and killed by a pitch thrown by Yankee Carl Mays on 16 August 1920 (the only on-the-field fatality in major-league history), new balls were substituted whenever the one in play became even slightly scuffed or soiled. New balls are harder for the pitchers to get stuff on and easier to see and hit. As a result of these changes, hitters were favored over pitchers for the first time since the early days, when batters could call for their pitches.

The opening year of the decade saw landmarks set in several areas. Babe Ruth accompanied his 1920 record of 54 homers – twice what anyone else had ever hit – with a .376 batting average and the all-time slugging record of .847. The White Sox became the first team ever to have four 20-game winners. This was the last year an American League home run leader would hit fewer than 20, and the first year George Sisler hit over .400, turning in a .407 season.

Beginning in 1921, with the first of three consecutive pennants, the Yankees took 29 pennants and 20 World Series championships in the next 44 years. The players who formed the backbone of the first winning teams came almost entirely from the Boston Red Sox, whose owner, Harry Frazee, seeking cash for his Broadway productions,

ABOVE: *A parade across the field on the Yankees' opening day in 1923. New York Governor Alfred E Smith (third from right in the front row) marches with Colonel Jacob Ruppert, the beer baron and owner of the Yankees, and his wife.*

LEFT: *The 1921 New York Yankees won the American League pennant but were beaten in the World Series, 5 games to 3, by the New York Giants.*

found a ready buyer in wealthy Yankee owner and brewery scion Jacob Ruppert. The series of purchases which eventually became known as the 'Rape of the Red Sox' began in July 1919 with New York's acquisition of fastballer Carl Mays for two players and $40,000.

In December 1919, Babe Ruth was sold to New York for $125,000 and a loan to Frazee of $300,000, for which Fenway Park was mortgaged as security. Over the next four years, Frazee gradually liquidated his loan by sending a steady stream of outstanding players from Boston to New York. By 1923 seven of the thirteen Yankee front-line players were former Red Sox players. The Yankees even acquired general manager Edward G Barrow from the Red Sox. Making good use of field manager Miller Huggins and Ruppert's bucks, Barrow deserves much of the credit for New York's success. Not surprisingly, the 'Dead Sox' spent eight of the next nine years in the cellar.

After the Yankees finished three games out of first place in 1920, Babe Ruth led his team to the pennant in 1921 behind the greatest all-around season he ever had. That year the Big Guy set another home run record with 59 – more than most major-league teams hit – got 170 RBI's on 204 hits (including 16 triples and 44 doubles), batted .378, slugged .846, scored 177 runs and walked 144 times.

Combining with Ruth to establish the Yankees' first dynasty were the pitchers New York acquired from the Red Sox. In 1921 Carl Mays won 27 games and Waite Hoyt won 19; in 1922, Joe Bush won 26 and Hoyt won 19; and in 1923, when the Yankees finished 16 games ahead

of second-place Detroit, Sam Jones won 21, Hoyt won 17, Joe Bush won 19, and Herb Pennock won 19. Babe Ruth hit his best average ever in 1923, batting .393, set the league record for walks with 170, and most appropriately of all for the game's all-time leader in dramatic appeal, hit a game-winning home run at the inaugural game of New York's brand new Yankee Stadium.

The new park was built largely from the proceeds of Ruth's success (his own salary increases led to an increase in ball players' salaries by 15 to 45 percent across-the-board). When the Yankees, who had for years rented the Polo Grounds from the Giants, faced eviction, Ruppert constructed the 65,000-seat plus stadium in full view of the Polo Grounds, calling the biggest, most modern park in baseball, '. . . a mistake. Not mine, but the Giants'.'

Suitably tagged 'The House That Ruth Built,' the name 'Ruth Field' was ultimately rejected in favor of 'Yankee Stadium,' although the right field bleachers, towards which most of Ruth's hits went, were soon dubbed 'Ruthville.' These bleachers were located only 296 feet from home plate behind a fence 43 inches high: designing a park to benefit hitters was not uncommon in this era.

Located in baseball's biggest market, Yankee Stadium, with its state-of-the-art seating capacity and arrangement, insured, like the style of play Babe Ruth perfected, that the American League in general and the Yankees in particular would gain an edge on attendance and profits for some time to come.

ABOVE: *Yankee Stadium in 1923 – its maiden year.*

LEFT: *Samuel Pond 'Sad Sam' Jones when he was with the Yankees. In his 22-year career, 1914-35, he pitched for several clubs in the American League, and won 229 games.*

RIGHT: *Miller Huggins came from the St Louis Cardinals to manage the Yankees from 1918 to 1929 – their first set of glory years – winning six pennants and three World Series.*

BELOW: *Waite Hoyt, the great Yankee pitcher (1921-30). This Hall of Famer also played for several other clubs, and ended his career with 237 victories. He then broadcast the games of the Cincinnati Reds for years.*

The Giant Dynasty

Skippered by feisty John J McGraw, the New York Giants took four pennants in a row beginning in 1921 to become the first major-league club in history (and the only National League club) ever to take four consecutive pennants. McGraw, one of the most influential managers in history (in 31 years of managing his teams took 10 pennants, 11 second places, and finished in the first division 27 times), had been one of the great stars of the Orioles teams of the 1890s, stealing as many as 78 bases in a season and compiling a .334 lifetime batting average. As a manager, this master tactician, known as 'The Little Napoleon,' exercised extremely close control over his players, calling pitches and giving signs to his batters on every pitch.

Paradoxically, although McGraw resented the change the lively ball had brought to the game and insisted that dead-ball players such as Honus Wagner were far superior to Babe Ruth, his dynasty of the early twenties, which by his own estimation included his greatest teams, was built on batting. Art Nehf, Fred Toney, Jesse Barnes, Rosy Ryan and Jack Bentley supplied competent pitching, but during the four pennant years only Nehf recorded a 20-game season (1921). By contrast, McGraw had seven future Hall of Fame sluggers on his teams during those years – Frank Frisch, Bill Terry, George Kelly, Dave Bancroft, Ross Youngs, Travis Jackson and Hack Wilson – as well as sluggers Frank Snyder, George Burns, Irish Meusel and Heinie Groh.

Ross 'Pep' Youngs, a brilliant player with relentless hustle whose career was cut short by kidney disease in 1926, was one of McGraw's favorites. In the manager's later years, the only pictures on his office walls were of Youngs and Christy Mathewson. Even more fiery was Frank Frisch, a gifted infielder whose contemporaries considered him among the finest players in the league. Like Honus Wagner, Frisch was always the first pick for any All-Star team, but his uncompromising nature did not mix well with McGraw's authoritarian manner.

As much as McGraw respected Frisch's playing, after the 1926 season he traded him for Rogers Hornsby, the highest salaried player in the league, who was then earning $42,000 a year as the Cardinals' playing manager. During McGraw's 1921-1924 dynasty years, Hornsby had won the batting title all four seasons. Known as 'the Rajah,' Hornsby was a batting fanatic who refused to read or attend movies for fear it might weaken his eyes. With Babe Ruth and Ted Williams, he was one of those magical players who commanded full attention from everyone whenever he took a bat in his hands.

The Giants finished the 1921 season four games ahead of the second-place Pirates, and took the Series from the Yankees after dropping the first two games. In 1922, the year the Supreme Court

ABOVE: *Casey Stengel played for the Giants from 1921 to 1923, but he also played for several other National League teams during his career from 1912 to 1925. This outfielder, who later became an outstanding manager, had a career batting average of .284.*

LEFT: *Ross Youngs played his entire career with the Giants, from 1917 to 1926, and carried a lifetime batting average of .322. 'Pep' was elected to the Hall of Fame in 1972.*

OPPOSITE: *John Joseph 'Little Napoleon' McGraw has been referred to as 'the greatest manager ever.' After three years managing in Baltimore, he came to the Giants. From 1902 to 1932 he won nine pennants and three World Series, and ended with a winning percentage of .589.*

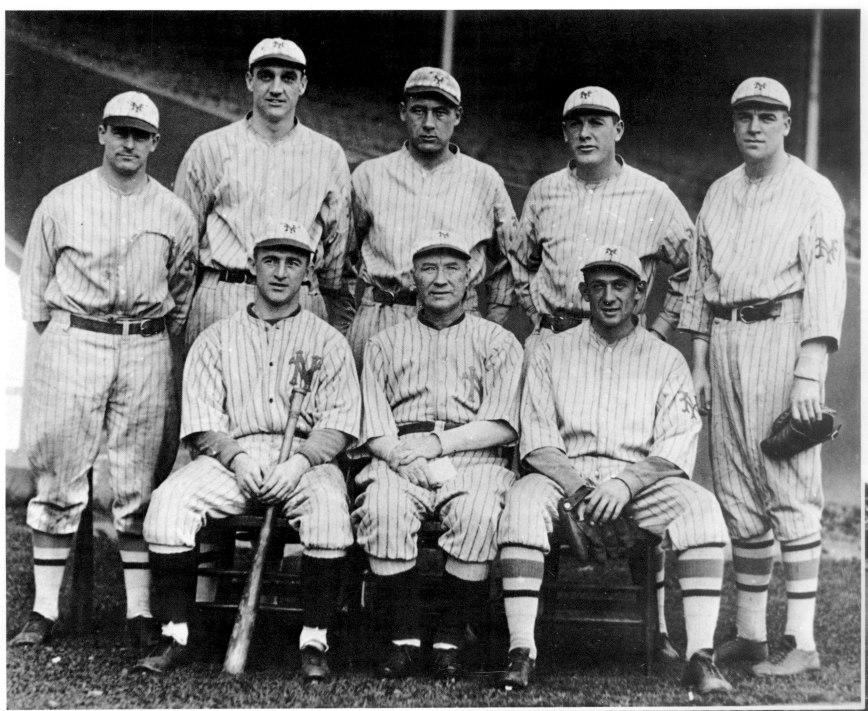

ABOVE: *Some of the New York Giants pose before the 1924 World Series – their last under McGraw. Seated left to right: Frankie Frisch, Hughie Jennings, Art Nehf. Standing left to right: Ross Youngs, George Kelly, Frank Snyder, Emil Meusel and Rosy Bill Ryan.*

ruled that baseball was not subject to the Sherman Anti-Trust laws, the Giants finished seven games ahead of Cincinnati, and took the Yankees in the Series in four games and one tie. As pitchers struggled to adapt to the lively ball, ERA's, batting averages and attendance rose throughout the league. In 1922 the National League composite batting average was .292, the Pirates leading the league with a .308 team average.

The 1922 season was marred by an unfortunate incident concerning talented but hard-drinking Giant pitcher Phil Douglas. After he received a particularly humiliating public reprimand from McGraw, Douglas wrote a letter to Leslie Mann of the Cardinals offering to 'go fishing' for the season, for a good price, to help the Cardinals take the pennant. He later called Mann to ask him to destroy the letter, but Mann had already passed it on to his manager Branch Rickey, who gave it to Commissioner Landis, and Douglas was banished from the game forever.

The Giants took the 1923 pennant four and a half games ahead of the Reds, but this time dropped the World Series to the Yankees, 4-2. In 1924, with Heinie Groh batting low man in the Giant starting lineup at .284, the Giants finished one and a half games ahead of Brooklyn to give McGraw his tenth and final flag. This fourth consecutive pennant victory was blackened by a scandal involving promising young outfielder Jimmy O'Connell, whose minor-league contract the Giants had

LEFT: *Jimmy O'Connell played for the Giants for only two years – 1923 and 1924, but the outfielder and utility infielder batted .270 in his 141 games, including two in the 1924 World Series.*

RIGHT: *Philips Brooks 'Shufflin' Phil' Douglas pitched for the Giants at the end of his nine-year career, from 1919 to 1922. He ended up all even – 93 wins and 93 losses during the regular season and two wins and two losses in the World Series. That sounds mediocre, but he had a respectable 2.80 earned run average.*

LEFT: *One Giant scores a run against the Yankees in the 1922 World Series while another slides into third. The Giants won four games, the Yankees won none, and one game ended in a tie.*

purchased for $75,000. Before the 27 September game, O'Connell had apparently offered the Phillies' shortstop Heinie Sand $500 if he would not 'bear down too hard.'

The affair eventually came before Commissioner Landis, at which time O'Connell implicated coach Cozy Dolan and star players Frisch, Kelly and Youngs. The other players were exonerated, but Dolan was banished forever, and O'Connell, who may have been the victim or the perpetrator of a tasteless practical joke, gained the distinction of becoming the last major-league player to be found guilty of suspected crookedness in this sordid era. The Giants lost the 1924 Series to the Senators in seven games.

1924 also saw the National League's inauguration of the Most Valuable Player Award. Despite Hornsby's batting .424 for the Cardinals and Cardinal first baseman Jim Bottomley setting an all-time record by driving in 12 runs with six hits in a single game, the award went to Brooklyn's pitcher Dazzy Vance. In an era when hitters terrorized pitchers, Vance proved it was still possible to strike batters out. He led the league in strikeouts for the seven years from 1922 to 1928, reaching his peak in 1924, when he also led the league in wins, ERA and complete games. Teammate Burleigh Grimes was the only pitcher who approached Vance's 262 strikeouts in 1924, fanning 134 in a year in which no other National League pitcher was able to strike out any more than 86.

The Cardinals Sparkle

In 1925 Rogers Hornsby, batting .403 and becoming that year's Most Valuable Player, took over as manager of the Cardinals in mid-season, bringing them in fourth. The next year, his last as their manager, the Rajah skippered the Cardinals to their first modern pennant. Every team in the National League had now won at least one flag. The last St Louis pennant had been in 1888, but beginning in 1926 the Cardinals became a major force in the league, winning nine flags and six World Series over the next two decades.

Their greatness during this period was unquestionably the result of the policies of general manager Branch Rickey. One of the finest intellects ever to come into the game, Rickey joined the impecunious Cardinals in 1919, and developed an idea that enabled his team to become a contender in a league in which rich clubs could maintain their success by outbidding poorer clubs for the best players. Rickey's idea was for the Cardinals to develop talented young players in their own minor-league clubs. Until then, most minor-league clubs were independently owned, and sold their better players to the major leagues.

Beginning in 1919 with the acquisition of part interest in the Houston club, the Cardinal farm system gradually grew to include 50 teams with more than 800 players under contract. Rickey's eye for talent was legendary, and his priority was on speed – he felt fielding and batting could be taught. His method proved so effective that after the Cardinals paid $10,000 for Jess Haines in 1919, more than 25 years passed before the club purchased another established star. The winning St Louis teams of those years were all products of Rickey's farm system; even in 1943 and 1946, the pennant-winning Cardinal teams

times. After winning the second and the sixth games, Alexander emerged from the bullpen with a legendary hangover in the seventh inning of the seventh game, Cardinals leading 3-2 and bases loaded, to face the Yankees' Tony Lazzeri, second in RBI's in the American League that year only to Babe Ruth. He struck Lazzeri out, and pitched two more hitless innings to clinch the game and the Series.

Over the winter Rogers Hornsby, an impossible human being despite his greatness, was traded to the Giants for Frank Frisch. Without Hornsby, the Cardinals failed to take the pennant in 1927, finishing one and a half games behind the league-leading Pirates. But they returned to the winners circle in 1928, with Frisch on second base, clinching their second pennant in three years on the next-to-last day of the season, and frustrating McGraw's hopes for an eleventh pennant by two games. Chick Hafey, a product of the St Louis farm system and one of the finest National League outfielders ever, hit .337 for the Cardinals, and teammate Jim Bottomley led the league in RBI's with 136, hit .325, and tied the Cubs' Hack Wilson for National League home run honors with 31.

Rogers Hornsby took his seventh and last league batting title with an average of .387 in 1928, playing for the Braves, his third team in three years. Apparently one year of his outspoken ways was all McGraw could handle from this outstanding slugger. The Cardinals once again skipped a year (Alexander ended his career in 1929 with 373 wins, equalling Christy Mathewson's lifetime mark), and were not to take another pennant until 1930, when they introduced a young pitcher named Jerome 'Dizzy' Dean.

LEFT: *Wesley Branch 'The Mahatma' Rickey, who later became probably the finest front-office mind in baseball, started out as a catcher-outfielder-first baseman for the Browns, the Yankees, and back to the Browns. He played four years, from 1905 to 1907, and then in 1917, batting .239 and hitting three home runs. His talents lay elsewhere.*

RIGHT: *Rogers 'Rajah' Hornsby, the Hall of Famer who played for the Cardinals from 1915 to 1926, and then for other clubs until 1937. His lifetime batting average was .358 and he hit an amazing 302 home runs.*

were still primarily his farm products. By then the farm system he invented had become standard operating procedure for almost every club in the majors.

The first crop of Rickey's farmers to make their mark did so in 1926, under Rogers Hornsby, taking the championship two games ahead of Cincinnati. Hornsby himself batted only .317, and one of the mainstays of the Cardinal pitching staff that year was not a farmer but Grover Cleveland Alexander. War-scarred, epileptic, alcoholic and 39, Alexander had been traded to the Cardinals by the Cubs in mid-season, partly because the Cubs thought he was burnt out, and partly because the Cubs' manager Joe McCarthy felt his unbridled drinking set a bad example for the rest of the team.

The aging pitcher won nine games for the Cards that half-season, and played a leading role in one of the most dramatic World Series of all

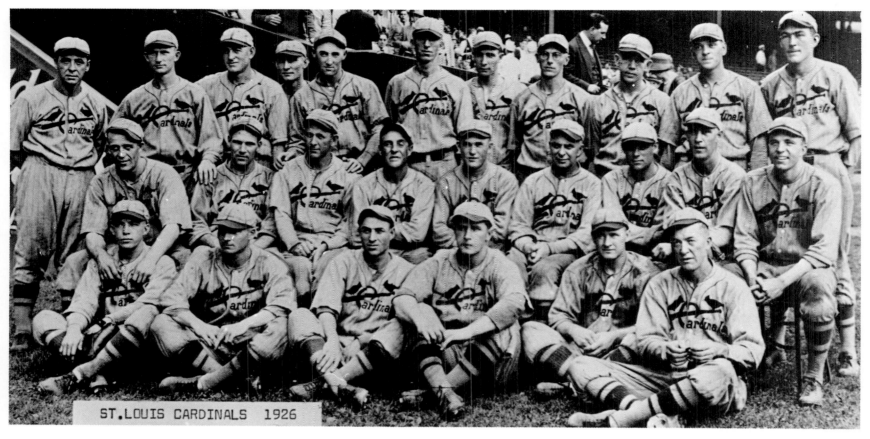
ST.LOUIS CARDINALS 1926

ABOVE: *The St Louis Cardinals' 1926 Gas House Gang. They won the pennant and beat the Yankees four games to three that year.*

RIGHT: *James LeRoy 'Sunny Jim' Bottomley, a first baseman and a .310 hitter.*

BELOW: *Frankie 'The Fordham Flash' Frisch, who hit .316 in his 19 years.*

ABOVE: *Leon Allen 'Goose' Goslin played for the Senators, the Browns and the Tigers during his 18-year career. This Hall of Fame outfielder carried a .316 lifetime batting average, and he hit 500 doubles, 173 triples and 248 home runs.*

LEFT: *The Waners with the Pirates – Lloyd and Paul (center and right). Lloyd James 'Little Poison' Waner played the outfield for Pittsburgh from 1927 to 1941. In 1941 he went to the Braves and then to the Phillies. In 1945, his last year, he returned to the Pirates. Elected to the Hall of Fame in 1967, he was a lifetime .316 hitter. Paul 'Big Poison' Waner also played the outfield in Pittsburgh, starting in 1926. In 1941 he was traded to Brooklyn and then to Boston. He returned to Brooklyn in 1943, went to the Giants in 1944, and finished his career with the Yankees in 1945. Elected to the Hall of Fame in 1952, he carried a batting average of .333.*

The Great Hitters
of the Golden Age

In 1920 baseball was a new game. The year before, a young slugger from the Boston Red Sox named Babe Ruth had shattered all existing records by hitting 29 home runs. Although the Red Sox were a mediocre team, finishing the season in a tie for fifth, enormous crowds came out to see Babe Ruth hit home runs wherever he appeared.

The lesson was not lost on the owners, as hitters were favored even further by pumping more life than ever before into the ball, and by outlawing all tampering with the ball. The introduction of the lively ball was an important factor in making the twenties the decade of the hitter. As Ring Lardner so eloquently put it "... the master minds that controls baseball says to themselves that if it is home runs that the public wants to see, why leave us give them home runs, so they fixed up a ball that if you don't miss it entirely it will clear the fence, and the result is that ball players which used to specialize in hump back liners to the pitcher is now amongst our leading sluggers."

Most of the outrageous slugging in the new hitters' game took place in the American League, but in the National League, Rogers Hornsby, the National League's greatest all-around hitter, epitomized the style of play that set the pattern for baseball for the next fifty years. In 1920, his first big year, Hornsby led the league in batting average, slugging, RBI's, doubles and hits. His 1920 average of .370, earning him the first of six consecutive batting titles (he took seven in all), was followed by averages of .397, .401, .384, .424 (the all-time major-league record) and .403. 'The Rajah' set all-time league lifetime records for batting average (.358) and slugging (.557), twice led the league in homers, four times in doubles, five times in runs scored, four times in RBI's,

and nine times in slugging. In 1922, the year the National League as a whole averaged .292, his 42 homers and 154 RBI's both set new league records. Hornsby was so impossible to pitch to that in 1924, his .424 year, he was walked so often that he got on base more than 50 percent of the time he came to bat.

The Pittsburgh Pirates, one of the hardest hitting National League clubs of the era, took the pennant with a team batting average of .307

LEFT: *Hall of Famer Sam Rice played the outfield for Washington for 19 years and Cleveland for one – 1915 to 1934, hitting .322.*

ABOVE: *George Harold Sisler, the Hall of Fame first baseman for the Browns, Senators and Braves, had a career batting average of .340.*

in 1925, and again in 1927 with a composite average of .305. This Pittsburgh club featured the hitting of the Waner brothers, Paul and Lloyd, who got more than 5600 lifetime hits between them. During the decade they so terrorized pitchers that they became known as Big Poison and Little Poison. In 1927 Paul led the league with a .380 average, and his younger brother Lloyd, in his rookie year, hit .355, the two adding a total of 460 hits toward that year's Pirate pennant. To put team and league batting averages in perspective, consider that while in 1930 the National League as a whole averaged .303, only six batters in the National League hit above .300 in 1968.

In this era of the new hitter, the great Babe Ruth stands out as the best of the best. Trying to write about Babe Ruth, journalist Arthur

Daley remarked, is like trying to paint a landscape on a postage stamp. Ruth followed his incredible 29 home runs in 1919 with an even more astonishing 54 home runs in 1920, more than any other major-league team except the Yankees. Of course he popped 59 homers in 1921, the year in which he slugged .846 and averaged .378. And in 1927 his 60 home runs represented 13.7 percent of all the home runs hit in the American League that season. During his career, he hit a home run every 11.7 times at bat. His lifetime home run total of 714 stood until 1974, and his lifetime batting average of .342 has been surpassed by only a handful of players.

1920 saw the Brown's George Sisler hit a league-leading .407, followed in 1922 by .420. Veteran Ty Cobb, as much as he disliked the new hitting game, hit .401 in 1922, placing second to Sisler. Outstanding American League sluggers of the era also included Philadelphia's Al Simmons; Heinie Manush, who recorded a .330 lifetime average; Hall of Famers Sam Rice and Goose Goslin of Washington; and Detroit's 'Mechanical Man' Charley Gehringer, who hit a lifetime average of .320 and played a nearly flawless second base. Tutored by Ty Cobb, Harry Heilmann of the Tigers traded four batting titles in the twenties with Sisler, Ruth and Manush, taking league honors in 1921 with .394. Topping four clubs that batted over .300, Detroit set the all-time American League team average of .316 in 1921.

Babe Ruth's Yankee teammate Bob Meusel led the league in homers in 1925 with 33 and in RBI's with 138. Tony Lazzeri joined the Yankees in 1926, seconding Ruth's American League-leading RBI total that year. Lou Gehrig, also newly arrived at the Bombers, smashed 47, 27 and 35 homers in the closing years of the decade. Hitting behind Ruth in the lineup and followed by Meusel and Lazzeri, Gehrig, whose greatest accomplishments were yet to come, was part of the legendary lineup known as 'Murderers' Row.'

Gordon 'Mickey' Cochrane, who holds the majors' highest lifetime average for a catcher (.320), was followed in the Athletics' lineup by Al Simmons and Jimmie Foxx, a combination almost as lethal as the Yankees'. In 1929 Foxx hit .354, drove in 118 runs, and launched 33 homers, the first of 12 consecutive seasons in which he would hit at least 30 round-trippers. That same year in the National League, the fifth-place Pirates hit .309 as a team, Lefty O'Doul led the league with .398 and set a new league high of 254 hits, and teammate Chuck Klein set a new league home run record of 43. The league as a whole hit 144 more home runs than it had the previous season. But all the exploits of all the teams and all the hitters of the twenties were only a prelude to what was to come in 1930. Then after that season, some of the juice was actually taken out of the ball.

RIGHT: *Harry Heilmann was an outfielder-first baseman-sometimes second baseman for the Detroit Tigers (1914-29) and the Cincinnati Reds (1930-32). This Hall of Famer, nicknamed 'Slug' – for his slugging, not his speed – had a lifetime batting average of .342, ending with 876 extra-base hits. After his career was over he became the respected radio voice of the Detroit Tigers, and was elected to the Hall of Fame in 1952.*

OPPOSITE TOP LEFT: *Henry Knight 'Heinie' Groh played mainly third base during his 16-year career from 1912 to 1927, hitting .292.*

OPPOSITE TOP RIGHT: *Joe (left) and Luke Sewell when they were both with the Cleveland Indians. Joseph Wheeler Sewell was a shortstop-third baseman for the Indians from 1920 to 1930, ending his career with the Yankees in 1933 and carrying a .312 average. He was elected to the Hall of Fame in 1977. His brother, James Luther Sewell, caught for Cleveland from 1921 to 1932, and then went on to play for the Senators, the White Sox and the Browns until 1942.*

OPPOSITE BOTTOM: *Francis Joseph 'Lefty' O'Doul began as a pitcher, but was later moved to the outfield so that he could play every day because of his fine batting eye – his career batting average was .349. O'Doul played for several teams – the Yankees, Red Sox, Giants, Phillies and Dodgers.*

Great Pitchers of the Twenties

Even more than the lengthening of the distance from pitcher to batter in 1893, the advent of the lively ball in 1920 changed the way the game was played, particularly for pitchers. With even weak hitters able to hit the ball out of the park on occasion, pitchers could no longer afford to take it easy through the lower part of the batting order. The toll on the pitcher's arm was therefore much greater. Nine innings today equal at least the effort a pitcher had to expend in seven innings during the era of the lively ball. Old strategies had to be replaced, creating, among other changes, the role of the relief pitcher as we know it today.

All trick pitches, particularly the spitball, were also outlawed in 1920, throwing the balance of power even further in the direction of the batters. However, 17 major-league pitchers who had built their careers on the spitter were permitted to continue to use it. In the American League this included five-time 20-game winner Stanley Coveleski, Red Faber of the Red Sox, and veteran Jack Quinn. In the National League, sanctioned spitballers included Bill Doak, Phil Douglas, and Brooklyn's Burleigh Grimes.

OPPOSITE: *Burleigh Grimes, the spitballer whose career spanned 19 years, from 1916 to 1934. He was relying on the spitter when its use was outlawed by professional baseball, but was permitted to use it until retirement.*

Grimes, the most famous spitballer of the era, continued to pitch until 1934, compiling 270 wins and earning a spot in the Hall of Fame. Although he held the ball tightly, instead of loosely, like most contemporary moisteners he combined his own saliva with slippery elm, and used the spitter to keep the batter guessing, as often as not throwing something else. He had a terrible temper, and made a point of not shaving when he was scheduled to pitch in order to intimidate the batter as much as possible.

Grimes' 23 wins helped the Dodgers take their second pennant, in 1920. Pitching for the Giants that year, Art Nehf, Jesse Barnes and Fred Toney all recorded 20-game seasons. In the American League, the White Sox became the first major-league team in history to have four 20-game winners, and that same year Cleveland's Ray Chapman was tragically struck and killed by a pitch thrown by Yankee Carl Mays. The beaning was unquestionably unintentional, and fastballer Mays came back in 1921 to win 27 games for the Yankees.

During a decade in which landmark hitting contributed to ballooning ERA's, one pitcher stood out among all others in the National League. Brooklyn's Clarence 'Dazzy' Vance, who came to the majors in 1922, when he was 31, led the league in strikeouts his first seven years, earning a niche in the Hall of Fame with 197 lifetime wins. In 1924, his best year, Vance led in wins (28-6), ERA, complete games and strikeouts (262). The only other pitcher in the league to strike out more than 86 batters that season was teammate Burleigh Grimes, who fanned 135.

The heavy-drinking and epileptic Grover Cleveland Alexander, shattered from his experiences in World War I, nevertheless continued to pitch effectively in the twenties, three times winning at least 21 games, the last time in 1927. His historic seventh-game seventh-inning strikeout of Tony Lazzeri and save of the World Series in 1926 (he won two other games that Series as well) after he had been traded to the Cardinals in mid-season by a Cubs manager who thought he was hopeless, insures Alexander a permanent place in baseball lore. When he retired in 1929, his 373 regular season wins equalled the National League record set by Christy Mathewson.

ABOVE: *Grover Cleveland Alexander, the Hall of Fame pitcher who won 373 games in his 20-year career.*

RIGHT: *Hall of Fame pitcher Walter Johnson – 'The Big Train.' He won 416 games in 21 years with Washington.*

LEFT: *Urban Shocker was born Urban Jacques Schockeor, but quickly simplified the spelling. Shocker won 188 games in his 13-year pitching career with the Yankees, Browns and Yankees again.*

ABOVE: *Jack Quinn played with many teams – the Yankees, Braves, Baltimore of the Federal League, White Sox, Red Sox, Athletics, Dodgers and Reds – during his 23-year career.*

In 1924 when the Yankees, staffed by the excellent pitchers they had acquired from the Red Sox – including Carl Mays, Waite Hoyt, Joe Bush, Sam Jones and Herb Pennock – were stopped by two games from taking a fourth straight pennant, it was by none other that the Senators' Walter Johnson, still going strong at 36. That year Johnson led his team to victory with a 23-7 season, and led his league in strikeouts, shutouts and ERA. In 1925, his twelfth and last 20-game year, Johnson led the Senators to a second consecutive pennant behind his 20-7 season (teammate Coveleski contributed a 20-5 year). But Johnson proved he was human in 1926, throwing 15-16 in his last full season. Cleveland's righthander George Uhle, completing 32 of 36 starts that year, recorded a 27-11 season of his own. One of the greatest of all American League pitchers, Walter Johnson retired after the 1927 season with 416 lifetime wins.

The Yankees began their second dynasty of the decade in 1926, repeating in 1927 with what many consider the greatest team in baseball history. Supporting their amazing sluggers – Ruth, Gehrig, Lazzeri, Meusel – was one of the strongest pitching staffs of the era.

RIGHT: *Robert Moses 'Lefty' Grove won an even 300 games in his 17 years in the American League from 1925 to 1941 – first with the Athletics and then with the Red Sox. He was elected to the Hall of Fame in 1947 because of his phenomenal .682 winning percentage.*

BELOW: *George Uhle – 'The Bull.' Uhle won 200 games in his 17 years with the Indians, Tigers, Giants and Yankees from 1919 to 1936.*

Waite Hoyt threw 22-7 in 1927, Herb Pennock 19-8, spitballer Urban Shocker 18-6, Dutch Ruether 13-6, George Pipgras 10-3, and rookie Wilcy Moore, the league's leading relief pitcher, who also set the ERA pace with 2.28, threw 19-7.

Robert Moses 'Lefty' Grove, purchased from Baltimore's Jack Dunn for $100,600 (Dunn wanted more than the $100,000 he'd received for Babe Ruth), joined Connie Mack's Athletics in 1925. Possibly the best lefthander in history, Grove soon established himself as heir to Walter Johnson as the league's greatest pitcher. As for Johnson, Grove's one pitch was a fastball. Some of his contemporaries said it looked like 'a piece of white thread coming to the plate,' and some said they couldn't describe its motion because they couldn't see it. Beginning in 1926, Grove led the league in strikeouts for seven straight years. With George Earnshaw, who also came from Dunn's Baltimore club, Grove formed the backbone of the pitching staff of the Athletics club that dominated the league from 1929 through 1931.

'The Greatest Team'
– the 1927 Yankees

Futile as it may be to try to decide which was the greatest baseball team of all times, few would fail to agree that the Yankee club of 1927 was one of the greatest baseball teams the world has ever seen. Repeating their championship of 1926, in 1927 the Yankees were so hot that there was no American League pennant race. Philadelphia, with seven Hall of Famers aboard, batted .303 as a team and won 91 games, but the Yankees never fell from first place, and ended the season a league-record 19 games ahead of the second-place Athletics. Their 110 wins and .714 percentage remained the best in league history until the amazing Cleveland victory of 1954. Their team total of 158 home runs was almost three times that of the 56 round trips slammed by the Athletics, the next best.

The 1927 Yankees, essentially the same personnel as the 1926 club, were the product of some serious team rebuilding. For the 1926 season, Hall of Famer Earle Combs, an outstanding center fielder and the team's leadoff batter, replaced aging veteran Whitey Witt, and rookie Mark Koenig replaced shortstop Everett Scott, who ended his record 1307 consecutive games in May. At second base, Tony Lazzeri earned the nickname 'Push 'Em Up Tony' because of his ability to hit with men on base, and recorded a rookie RBI total second only to Babe Ruth's in his first year. Babe Ruth and Bob Meusel continued their outstanding slugging and fielding, and third baseman Joe Dugan was also in top form, although his participation was somewhat limited due to injuries. Future Hall of Famers Waite Hoyt and Herb Pennock led one of the finest pitching staffs of the era with 22 and 19 wins, respectively.

The final element in this powerful equation was 24-year-old native New Yorker Lou Gehrig, one of the greatest first basemen and finest sluggers of all times. Gehrig got his start as a Yankee regular on 2 June 1925, when veteran first baseman Wally Pipp, who had hit .295 and led the league in triples the year before, complained of a headache. From that day on, 'Iron Horse' Gehrig compiled the unsurpassed record of playing in 2130 consecutive games, not once returning to the bench until, 14 years later, as captain he took himself out of the lineup when

72

RIGHT: *Earl Combs, the Hall of Fame outfielder who played for the Yankees from 1924 to 1935. His .325 batting average and .462 slugging average included an amazing 309 doubles. He batted .350 in the four World Series he played in.*

OPPOSITE TOP: *The 1927 New York Yankee team – there are those that contend that this was the finest baseball club in the history of the game.*

OPPOSITE BOTTOM: *Lou Gehrig, one of the many stars on the 1927 Yankees. He hit .373 that year and had a .765 slugging average. 'The Iron Horse' played for the Yankees from 1923 to 1939 – mostly at first base – and hit .340 during his career. He was elected to the Hall of Fame (by special dispensation) the year he retired.*

the onset of a fatal illness weakened his play.

What distinguished the 1927 Yankees from the 1926 Yankees was that in 1927 each member of a superb team turned in an outstanding personal performance. Harry Heilman, in an exciting race with Al Simmons that was not decided until the final day of the season, took the league batting title with a .398 average, and George Sisler led the league with 27 stolen bases, but a Yankee took top honors in every other offensive category. In fact, the Yankees not only had the top man in most categories, but often the second and third best as well.

Babe Ruth hit a record 60 home runs, four more than any team in the league except the Yankees, and drove in 164 runs for a .772 slugging percentage and a .356 average. Lou Gehrig was second to Ruth in league home runs with 47, second in slugging with .765, first in league RBI's with 175 (Ruth was second), second to Ruth (Combs was third) in league runs scored with 149, and averaged .373. Between them, Ruth and Gehrig accounted for nearly 25 percent of the homers hit in the American League that year. Lazzeri was third in home runs with 18, and drove in 102 runs for a .309 batting average. Lazzeri, Meusel,

LEFT: *Bob Meusel played mainly the outfield for the Yankees from 1920 to 1928, ending his career with the Reds in 1930. He hit .309 and carried a .497 slugging average.*

FAR LEFT: *Tony Lazzeri played the infield (mainly second base) for the Yankees from 1926 to 1937, ending his career in the National League in 1939. 'Poosh 'Em Up' was a flashy glove man, and hit .292 during his 14 years in the majors.*

BELOW: *Wilcy Moore pitched for the Yankees from 1927 to 1933, with a year and a half off (1931-32) with the Red Sox. His best year was his first, when he won 19 games while losing only seven. In his two World Series appearances, he won both games and posted a phenomenal 0.56 ERA.*

Ruth and Gehrig all drove in over 100 runs each. On a team with a collective batting average of .307, the batting order featuring Ruth, Gehrig, Meusel and Lazzeri became known as 'Murderers' Row.'

Combs, batting .356, led the league in hits (Gehrig was second) with 231; was third after Gehrig and Ruth in total bases; and led in at bats and triples. Gehrig was second in triples and league leader in doubles. In addition to his other honors, Babe Ruth led in walks and strikeouts. With the championship never in doubt, Yankees fans focused on a home run contest between Ruth and Gehrig that as late as 15 August saw Gehrig leading Ruth 38-36.

The Yankee pitching staff, one of the finest of the era, led the league in ERA, shutouts, fewest bases on balls, and was second in complete games. In addition to Hoyt's 22 wins and Pennock's 19, Wilcy Moore, who led the league with a 2.28 ERA, compiled a 19-7 record in his only great season, Urban Shocker was 18-6, Dutch Ruether was 13-6, and George Pipgras was 10-3. Only the Yankees' catching, which was average, was less than outstanding in 1927.

The Yankees met a strong Pittsburgh team in the Series, and by flattening the Pirates four straight became the first American League club to take a Series without a loss. Pittsburgh's Waner brothers, Big Poison and Little Poison, turned in excellent performances in the Series, as did their great third baseman Pie Traynor, but proved no match for Ruth's two homers, six hits, seven RBI's, and .400 Series average; and Gehrig's two doubles, two triples, five RBI's, and .308 average. Legend has it that the Pirates were so awestruck when Ruth, Gehrig, Meusel and Lazzeri knocked ball after ball into the bleachers at batting practice before the Series that they never recovered.

The Athletics Shine

In 1928 Connie Mack's rebuilt Athletics made the mighty Yankees sweat, even briefly pulling ahead of the Ruth-Gehrig machine before finishing two and a half games behind the team that had stopped them by 19 games the year before. The Athletics, the last dynasty formed exclusively from players purchased from minor-league clubs – Branch Rickey's farm system was well on its way to becoming accepted practice – finished second in 1925, third in 1926, and second in 1927 and 1928 before putting it all together. Beginning in 1929 they swept to three consecutive pennants by margins of 18, 8, and 13 and a half games.

Mack's winning teams of those years are always remembered for Hall of Famers Lefty Grove, Mickey Cochrane, Jimmie Foxx and Al Simmons, but like all dynasties it was solid throughout. Outfielders Bing Miller and Mule Haas were .300 hitters, and with Al Simmons in left formed one of the outstanding outfields of the era. Lefty Grove was assisted on the mound by George Earnshaw and Rube Walberg, both of whom, like Grove, were products of Jack Dunn's Baltimore club. Ed Rommel's pitching was important too.

Starters Max Bishop at second and Joe Boley at short (he was replaced in 1931 by the younger Dib Williams) were also products of Dunn's club. The nearly-faultless Jimmy Dykes had replaced veteran Sammy Hale at third by 1926. With Mickey Cochrane behind the plate and Jimmie Foxx at first, the Athletics' lineup remained intact for their three dynasty years.

Robert Moses 'Lefty' Grove, who led the league in strikeouts for seven straight years beginning in 1926, won 83 games during the Athletics' dynasty and lost only 15. A fierce competitor, he had no

LEFT: *George Earnshaw pitched for nine years in the majors and was with the Athletics from 1928 to 1933. He won 127 games plus four in the World Series.*

ABOVE: *Jimmie 'Double X' Foxx was primarily a first baseman during his 20-year career. The Hall of Famer hit .329 and slugged .609.*

compunction about throwing at opposing batters, including Babe Ruth, and even at his own teammates in batting practice. He did claim he never aimed for the head, and had learned through experience never to shave Lou Gehrig: 'It was best not to wake him up.'

In 1929 Grove was 20-6 (Earnshaw won 24), and led the league with a 2.81 ERA and 170 strikeouts; in 1930, he was 28-5 with a 2.54 ERA (next best was 3.37) and 209 strikeouts; and in 1931, as the league's Most Valuable Player, Grove was 31-4 with an ERA of 2.06 and 175 strikeouts, leading the league in wins, ERA, strikeouts, complete games (27) and percentage.

Catching for Grove in his heyday was Gordon 'Mickey' Cochrane. Considered by many the best catcher of all times, Cochrane holds the all-time record lifetime batting average for a catcher (.320). He was fast enough to bat third and often first on a team of great hitters, winning three of his nine .300-plus seasons during the A's 1929-1931 dynasty (.331, .357 and .349, respectively). Like Grove, Cochrane was a fierce competitor who could not accept defeat gracefully. He and his pitcher were known for smashing up the locker room and throwing anything that wasn't tied down on days when Grove's pitching was a little off. Fortunately for the rest of the team, there weren't many of those.

When Cochrane batted first, he was followed in the batting order by Al Simmons and Jimmie Foxx, a lineup almost as lethal as the Yankees' Murderers' Row. Foxx, a gifted natural athlete with a temperament and outlook on life much like Ruth's, was only 21 in 1929 when he became the Athletics' regular on first base and turned in his first great season. To kick off the dynasty, Foxx hit .354, drove in 118 runs, and

Hall of Fame catcher Mickey Cochrane making a play at home plate. Cochrane was one of the most agile of catchers and played for the Athletics from 1925 to 1933, finishing his career at Detroit in 1937. He also managed the Tigers from 1934 to 1938. His lifetime batting average was .320.

LEFT: *George William 'Mule' Haas started in the outfield for the Pirates in 1925, and then moved to the Athletics from 1928 to 1932, joined the White Sox in 1933 and ended his career back with the Athletics in 1938. He was a .292 hitter.*

BELOW: *Howard Ehmke broke in with Buffalo of the Federal League in 1915, then pitched for the Tigers (1916-22), the Red Sox (1923-26) and the Athletics (1926-30).*

launched 33 homers, the first of twelve consecutive seasons in which he hit at least 30 homers. Only twice in those twelve years did his batting average fall below .300. When he retired in 1945, his 534 career home runs were second only to Ruth's 714.

Al Simmons, a superb left fielder and one of the best righthanded hitters in baseball history, was in his prime during his nine years with the A's (1924-1932), four times topping .380 and averaging .364 overall. He was famous for his RBI's – he drove in over 100 during each of his first 11 years – and hit over 30 home runs three times between 1929 and 1931. By the book, Simmons' batting style was all wrong. He supposedly robbed himself of power by stepping away from the pitch instead of into it – 'putting his foot in the bucket' – but still managed two league championships and a respectable .334 lifetime average.

In 1929 the A's met the Cubs for the World Series. In a move that surprised everybody, Connie Mack started little-used pitcher Howard Ehmke in the first game. His slow balls kept the Chicago team so off

ABOVE LEFT: *Jimmy Dykes was a stellar infielder (mostly at third base) for the Athletics (1918-32) and the White Sox (1933-39), hitting .280. He also managed the Sox (1934-46, 1951-54 and 1958-61).*

ABOVE: *Hall of Fame outfielder Al Simmons, with his .334 batting average and 307 home runs, played for the Athletics from 1924 to 1932, then for various teams, only to return from 1940 to 1941 and 1944.*

balance that Ehmke set a record of 13 Series strikeouts that stood until 1953. In the fourth game, Al Simmons hit a homer that began a record-breaking Series inning in which 15 A's came to bat. In the same inning, Mule Haas hit an inside-the-park home run that accounted for three of the 10 runs the Athletics recorded before their three outs were up. Haas hit another homer in the Series' final game, helping the A's clinch the championship 4-1. With Dykes hitting .421 for the Series, Cochrane hitting .400, Miller hitting .368, and Foxx hitting .350 and slugging two homers, no one could doubt that the Athletics, fresh from their first pennant in 15 years and poised to take two more league championships, had finally arrived.

Great Players of the Late Twenties and Early Thirties

In 1927 founder and American League president Ban Johnson re-signed, marking the end of the autocratic league presidents. Power in organized baseball was now concentrated in the hands of the commissioner. That same year arguably the greatest pitcher the American League has ever seen, Walter Johnson, retired with 416 lifetime wins, and at the end of the following season Ty Cobb and Tris Speaker, both with the Athletics, ended their active careers. Cobb's 4191 lifetime hits was the record until 11 September 1985, and his lifetime batting average of .367 has still not been touched.

Although the dead-ball era of which he had been master really ended at the beginning of the twenties, the close of Cobb's career brought down the final curtain. As if to prove it, the year before Cobb's retirement, Babe Ruth, home run ball's greatest prophet, set a new home run record of 60 that was destined to stand for decades, and in 1928, Ruth and teammate Lou Gehrig, in a final fanfare to the old game, turned in a phenomenal display of slugging in the World Series that has yet to be equalled. While the Yankees flattened the Cardinals four straight, Ruth hit .625, still the highest average in Series history, launched three homers in a single game (for the second time in Series play), drove in four runs and scored nine. Gehrig hit .545, banged out four homers, drove in nine runs and scored five.

Babe Ruth, still the home run champion, was aging, but Lou Gehrig was just swinging into his prime. Known as the 'Iron Horse' for his strength, durability and consistency, Gehrig five times led the league in RBI's, twice in homers, and hit as many as 52 doubles and 18 triples a season. He averaged 39 home runs a season for the eleven years

ABOVE: *Babe Ruth being congratulated by fellow Yankee Lou Gehrig as he crosses the plate after hitting his 60th home run in 151 games in 1927, setting the home run record that would last for 34 years.*

OPPOSITE: *The great Yankee first baseman, Lou Gehrig.*

BELOW: *Ty Cobb at bat in 1922, the year he hit .401. This Hall of Fame outfielder played from 1905 to 1926 with the Tigers, finishing his career in 1927 and 1928 with the Athletics. He carried a lifetime batting average of .367, and his record of 4191 hits lasted for 57 years.*

from 1927 to 1937. When illness forced his retirement, his 493 career home runs and 1990 RBI's were second only to Babe Ruth's career totals. Only Ruth and Hank Aaron ever surpassed Gehrig's RBI's and only Ruth and Red Williams ever bettered his career slugging percentage of .632. Gehrig was an outstanding first baseman. His .340 lifetime batting average places him among the very best hitters in baseball history.

In 1930, with the American League batting .288, the Yankees batted .309 as a team. Gehrig averaged .379, Ruth .359, Combs .344, and catcher Bill Dickey .339. Ruth and Gehrig combined for 327 RBI's, and the Athletics' Jimmie Foxx and Al Simmons combined for 321. Gehrig was league leader with 174 RBI's, Simmons second with 165, Foxx third with 156, and Ruth fourth with 153.

Athletics pitcher Lefty Grove led the American League with 28 wins and a 2.54 ERA in 1930, on his way to an amazing 31 wins and only four losses with an ERA of 2.06 in 1931. Outdistancing and outclassing all the competition in 1931, Grove tied the record set by Wood and Johnson of 16 straight wins. Only one other pitcher in the league, Lefty Gomez, managed an ERA of under 3.00 in 1931.

Cleveland's Wes Ferrell, in the second of four consecutive 20-game seasons for the Indians, took 25 games in 1930, with a 3.31 ERA second to Grove's 2.54. Ferrell would have two 20-game seasons with the Red Sox as well. Elsewhere in the American League, Joe Cronin of the Senators distinguished himself as one of the hardest-hitting shortstops in history (.301 lifetime average). The son-in-law of the Senators' owner Clark Griffith, Cronin managed Washington to a pennant in 1933, and later became president of the American League. Charlie Gehringer, known as the 'Mechanical Man' for his years of near-flawless fielding at second base for the Tigers, distinguished himself by leading all second basemen in fielding eight times, and also recorded 13 .300 seasons and seven 200-hit seasons.

In the National League, the 1929 pennant-winning Cubs featured Kiki Cuyler, Hack Wilson and Riggs Stephenson in the outfield batting .360, .345 and .362 respectively. The great Rogers Hornsby, pur-

OPPOSITE TOP: *Chuck Klein receives his 1932 Most Valuable Player Award. The Hall of Fame outfielder played for 17 years, mostly with the Phillies, batted .320 and hit 300 homers.*

BELOW: *Hall of Fame shortstop Joe Cronin played for the Pirates (1926-27), the Senators (1928-34) and the Red Sox (1935-45), batting .301.*

ABOVE: *Hazen Shirley 'Kiki' Cuyler played the outfield from 1921 to 1938. This Hall of Famer batted .321 for the Pirates, the Cubs, the Reds and the Dodgers.*

LEFT: *Mel Ott played the outfield for the Giants from 1926 to 1947, managed the team from 1942 to 1948, and was elected to the Hall of Fame in 1951 for his fielding and .304 average.*

OPPOSITE BOTTOM: *First baseman and Hall of Famer Bill Terry played for the Giants from 1923 to 1936, batting .341 and amassing 2193 hits.*

chased from Boston for $200,000, was with the Cubs now, and batted .380, although Philadelphia's Lefty O'Doul led the league with .398 and logged 254 hits. His Phillies batted .309 overall, teammate Chuck Klein hitting .356 and slugging the new league high of 43 home runs.

As more and more life was pumped into the ball, the National League led the way in murderous slugging. In 1930, when six National League clubs had team batting averages of over .300, the Giants led the league with a .319 average, and the league as a whole averaged .303. After 1930 the ball was actually made less lively, but that was small consolation to pitchers who survived that murderous season. Grover Cleveland Alexander escaped the carnage by retiring with 373 lifetime wins in 1929, but in 1930, no pitching staff in the league gave up fewer than an average four runs per game, and the league ERA was almost five runs per game. Brooklyn's pitchers led the league with a composite ERA of 4.03, and their Dazzy Vance, at 2.61, was the only hurler in the league with an average of under three runs a game that year. Philadelphia's hurlers gave up nearly seven.

Giant first baseman Bill Terry, with an average of .401 in the midst of 10 consecutive seasons of batting over .300, became the last National Leaguer to hit .400. He also got 254 hits, tying O'Doul's 1929 mark, still the National League record. Terry's lifetime average of .341 places him first for National League lefthanders, and second among National League hitters only to Rogers Hornsby. Chuck Klein, whose Phillies averaged .315 overall, got 250 hits for a .386 average in 1930, racking up 59 doubles, 40 home runs, 170 RBI's and 158 runs scored. Incredible as it may seem, in a year in which 15 National Leaguers batted over .340 and 17 drove in over 100 runs, only Klein's doubles and runs-scored led the league.

Outstanding among National League sluggers in 1930 was Chicago's Lewis 'Hack' Wilson. In a never-repeated performance, the hard-drinking 5' 6" center fielder blasted 56 home runs, still the National League record, and 190 RBI's, a major-league record that has not been even remotely approached since Hank Greenberg batted in 183 runs in 1937. Hack originally came up with McGraw's Giants in 1923, but due to a clerical error that must have caused McGraw endless gnashing of teeth, he became available to the draft and was purchased by the Cubs for next to nothing in 1925. In 1931 the best Wilson could do was 13 home runs and 61 RBI's.

Chicago Cubs
of the Early Thirties

Under the stewardship of former minor-league infielder Joe McCarthy, the Chicago Cubs beat out the second-place Pirates by 10 and a half games in 1929. This was the first flag for the Cubs since 1918, and the first of nine pennants for manager McCarthy. The Cubs had good pitching, led by Pat Malone (22 wins), Charlie Root (19) and Guy Bush (18), but their real strength was in their hitting.

Rogers Hornsby, traded the previous November for five players and $200,000, hit 40 homers and got 149 RBI's for a .380 average in his last great season, receiving his second MVP Award. The Cubs' outfield of Kiki Cuyler, Hack Wilson and Riggs Stephenson hit .360, .345 and .362, respectively. Wilson hit 39 homers and batted in 159 runs, Stephenson batted in 110 and Cuyler batted in 102 runs and stole 43 bases. As a team, the Cubs batted .303 in 1929. They would take two more pennants and come in a tight second over the next five years.

The man responsible for the Cubs' return to a position of power, Joe McCarthy, was one of the great managers of all time. In 24 years with the Cubs, Yankees and Red Sox, he never finished out of the first division, and his teams won pennants nine times and World Series six times. A stern disciplinarian, McCarthy was not afraid to cut Grover Cleveland Alexander from the Cubs in mid-season when it became clear he could not discipline his troops with Alexander going his own way. He was one of the few managers who actually stressed the fundamentals, apparently accepting that physical errors were inevitable, and insisting on the importance of being mentally alert. A player who threw to the wrong base might soon find himself working elsewhere. When McCarthy came to the Cubs in 1926, a team that had

LEFT: *Guy Bush, 'The Mississippi Mudcat,' pitched for the Cubs from 1923 to 1934, then traveled around the league until 1945.*

RIGHT: *Outfielder Jackson Riggs 'Old Hoss' Stephenson began with the Indians and came to the Cubs in 1926. He retired in 1936 with a .336 average.*

OPPOSITE: *Hall of Fame manager Joe McCarthy led the Cubs from 1926 to 1930, winning the pennant in 1929, but losing the Series to the Athletics four games to one. He managed the Yankees from 1931 to 1946, winning eight pennants and seven World Series. He finished his career managing the Red Sox from 1948 to 1950.*

finished in the cellar the year before, he brought them in fourth. By 1929 the Cubs were in the Series for the first time in over a decade. Over the next decade, they would share domination of the National League with the Cardinals and the Giants.

The Cubs failed to repeat in 1930, trailing the pennant-winning Cardinals by two games, but in the first year of the Great Depression they set a new home attendance record with 1,463,264. More life than ever before was pumped into the ball that season, drawing National League crowds to the parks in record numbers. Many of the spectators who flocked to Wrigley Field undoubtedly came to witness Lewis 'Hack' Wilson blast his way to two National League records and one

all-time major-league slugging record. In 1930 Hack Wilson, who had led the National League in home runs in 1926, 1927 and 1928, hit an all-time league-leading 56 home runs and batted in 190 runs.

With one week to go in the 1930 season, Cubs owner William Wrigley fired Joe McCarthy because he wanted a manager who could bring him a world championship. Two years later McCarthy was to have his revenge when his Yankees whipped the Cubs in the Series. Meanwhile, without McCarthy and with Wilson slipping to 13 home runs and 61 RBI's, the Cubs were out of the race even though they led the National League with a team batting average of .289. A strong Cardinal team took the pennant in 1931, featuring the energetic play of total of 37 runs in the Series, averaging nine runs per game and batting .313 as a team.

Lou Gehrig turned in one of the greatest individual Series performances ever in 1932, batting .529 and getting nine hits, including three home runs and a double. He scored nine runs and drove in eight; teammates Ruth and Lazzeri launched two home runs each. Babe Ruth, in his tenth and last Series performance, created what remains one of the most famous moments in baseball history when he pointed to the most distant part of Wrigley Field, took two deliberate strikes, and then hit a home run into the bleachers to which he had pointed. Some, including Joe McCarthy, later insisted that Ruth had merely pointed to the Cubs dugout to silence hecklers. The Bambino himself never clarified the question, and the truth behind his legendary 'called shot' may never be known.

ABOVE: *Billy Herman played second base for the Cubs from 1931 to 1940, then played for various other teams until 1947. He batted .304.*

freshman John Leonard 'Pepper' Martin, manager Frank Frisch at second base, and Chick Hafey, winning the closest batting race in history with an average of .3489 (Bill Terry was .3486 and Cardinal Jim Bottomley was .3482).

Billy Herman, one of the greatest second basemen in National League history (lifetime average of .304), began his career with the Cubs in 1931. By the middle of the 1932 season, the Cubs were in second place. On 2 August, Rogers Hornsby, who had replaced McCarthy as manager, was fired by club president William Veeck after a series of policy disputes. First baseman Charlie Grimm replaced Hornsby, and under his inspired leadership the Cubs took the pennant four games ahead of Pittsburgh. Just to show how much they missed Hornsby, the Cubs did not vote the never-popular slugger any share of the World Series money.

The Cubs met the Yankees in an historic Series. For Joe McCarthy, who had been picked up by the Yankees as soon as he had been released from the Cubs, New York's demolition of Chicago in four straight games must have been particularly sweet. The Yankees also rode the Cubs hard because the Cubs had voted only a fraction of a share to former Yankee shortstop Mark Koenig, who had come to the Cubs late in the season and played well for them. New York scored a

The Cubs finished out of the picture in 1933 and 1934, but in 1935 tore off a 21-game September winning streak that carried them past the league-leading Giants and Cardinals and on to a shutout victory over Detroit in the first game of the World Series. Both pitcher Lon Warneke, who took that game from Detroit's Schoolboy Rowe, and fellow righty Bill Lee had been 20-game winners for Chicago during the regular season. Second baseman Billy Herman had batted .341. But Charlie Grimm and his men were only able to take one more game from Detroit in the Series, and the Cubs recorded their fifth Series loss in as many tries. 1935 was also the year (24 May, to be exact) in which the Reds' Larry MacPhail got major-league clubs to try night games. Dubious as the experiment seemed to many at the time, within 13 years every major-league club except the Cubs had installed lights in their parks.

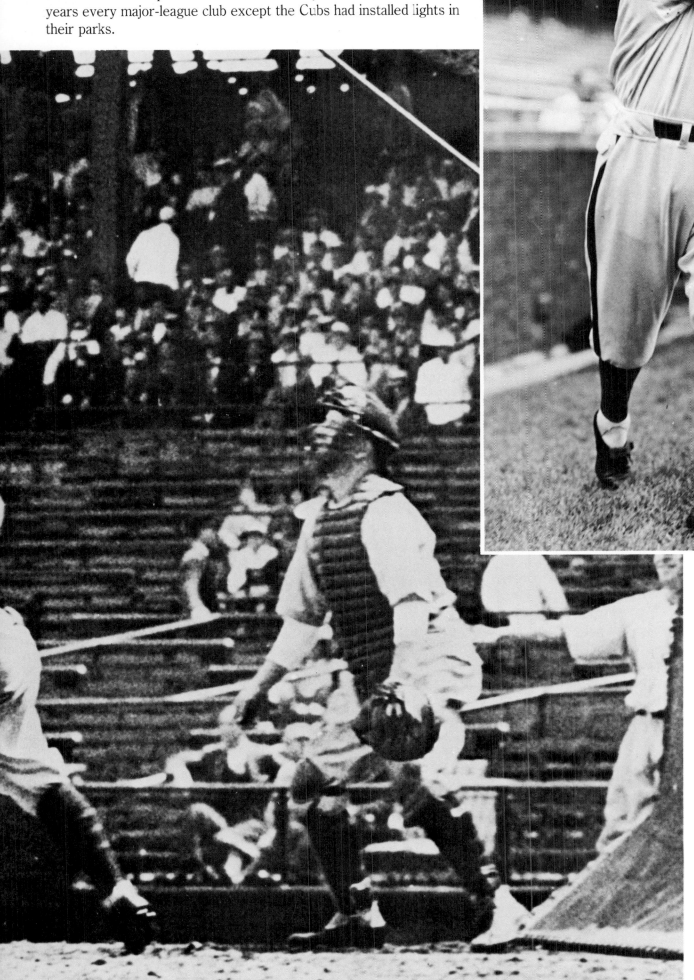

ABOVE: *Hall of Fame catcher Gabby Hartnett was the sparkplug of the Cubs from 1922 to 1940, and he ended his career in 1941 with the Giants. With a batting average of .297, he hit 236 home runs. Hartnett also managed the Cubs from 1938 to 1940.*

LEFT: *Hack Wilson, the Hall of Fame outfielder, watches one of his homers go out of the park in 1930, the year he set the still-standing National League record of 56. That was also the year he hit .356 and set the major-league baseball record of 190 runs batted in.*

The Gashouse Gang

Cardinals finished in a sixth-place tie with the Giants in 1932 (Giant manager McGraw retired on 3 June), but distinguished themselves by adding slugger Joe Medwick and hurler Dizzy Dean to their regular lineup.

Known as 'Muscles' for his build or 'Ducky Wucky' for his walk, Medwick became the National League's premier slugger of the thirties. He was called up from the Cardinals' farm system Houston club at the end of the Texas league season, and made his mark by batting .349 in 26 games. Dizzy Dean, in his first full season, led the league in strikeouts (191), shutouts and innings pitched, throwing 18-15.

The son of an Arkansas sharecropper, Jerome Dean (or Jerome Herman or Jay Hanna – at least he was always 'Dizzy') was a pitcher of uncanny natural ability. Throughout the Depression his fastballs, curves, fractured English, endearing homespun personality, and amazing antics delighted the American public, and earned him the distinction of replacing Babe Ruth as the greatest draw in baseball. Among other quirks, Dean sometimes predicted shutouts and other

LEFT: *Joe 'Ducky' Medwick, the St Louis Cardinals' outfielder, played for the club from 1932 to 1940, then appeared with various National League teams until 1948, batting .324 and hitting 205 home runs. He appeared in two World Series and hit .326. Medwick was elected to the Hall of Fame in 1968.*

The Cardinals, with eight .300 hitters in their regular lineup and four more on the bench, took the 1930 pennant two games ahead of the Cubs. They repeated in 1931, and the 'Gashouse Gang,' specialists in unbridled horseplay, went on to set the tone for an era. By their 1934 pennant year, St Louis had flowered with a spirit achieved by only a handful of clubs in the history of the game. Although not the greatest Cardinals edition, the Gashouse Gang established itself as what would be one of the National League's best-remembered teams and the most colorful since the Orioles of the 1890s.

Sparking the 1931 Cardinals to victory was John Leonard 'Pepper' Martin, a product of the Cardinals' bottomless farm system and a player of such unorthodox fielding and grubby appearance that he reminded at least one sportswriter of a refugee from a gasworks. Belly-diving into bases, stopping balls by blocking them with his chest or diving at them like rabbits, the unfettered Pepper used to hop freight trains to get to spring training so he could pocket the expense money. His colorful and seemingly clumsy style was effective, as he lead the National League in stolen bases three times.

Pepper followed up a .302 rookie season (he averaged .298 for 13 seasons) by capturing the national imagination in the Series, getting 12 hits off the Athletics and averaging .500 on his route to stardom. He told A's catcher Mickey Cochrane that if he got to first base he would steal second, and did so five times. Although the Cardinals lost the 1930 Series to the Athletics 4-2, they returned the favor in 1931, taking the A's by one game in a thrilling seven-game Series. Such was the mood of the nation and such was Martin's appeal that President Herbert Hoover's presence at the Series was greeted with boos, while Martin, the 'Wild Horse of the Osage,' was greeted with tumultuous applause and screams of appreciation.

The Cardinals won 101 games in 1931, besting the second-place Giants by 13 games. The 1931 season also witnessed the closest batting race in history, with the Cardinals' Chick Hafey emerging as league leader by a fraction of a point, with a .3489 average. The

BELOW: *Johnny Leonard Roosevelt 'Pepper' Martin – 'The Wild Hoss of the Osage' – tries a head-first slide. Martin played the outfield and third base (he even pitched in two games, for the Cardinals from 1928 to 1944, with three years off in World War II. His career batting average was .298.*

LEFT: *Three members of the St Louis Cardinals' Gashouse Gang clown before a game.*

pitching feats in advance, maintaining, 'It ain't braggin' if you go out and do it after sayin' it.' In 1934, for instance, after his brother Paul joined the team, Dizzy pitched a three-hitter in the first game of a double-header and Paul pitched a shutout in the second game. Remarked Dizzy, 'If I'd known Paul was going to do that, I'd have pitched a no-hitter too.'

Dizzy Dean won 120 games in his first five years in the league, and was also the undisputed king of the zany collection of unkempt characters known as the Gashouse Gang. He, Pepper Martin and Joe Medwick led the way, and were joined in mid-season 1933 by Leo Durocher, known less for his pranks than for his creative vocabulary and belligerence. A weak hitter with a career average of .247, short-stop Durocher was nevertheless a brilliant fielder, a born leader and apparently just what the Cardinals needed to win in 1934.

Bouncing back after finishing in the second division in 1932 and 1933, the Cardinals took the pennant in 1934 two games ahead of the Giants. With fiery Frank Frisch managing, the Gashouse Gang bloomed in full splendor. Dizzy Dean became the first National League pitcher since Alexander in 1917 to win 30 games, in true Gashouse style taking his 30th win and seventh shutout in the last day of the season in a game which also clinched the pennant. In his best year

ever, Dizzy Dean lost only seven games in 1934, and led the league in strikeouts (195), shutouts (7), and complete games (24). His brother Paul, a quiet man nicknamed 'Daffy' for no particular reason, added 19 wins in his first year up from the Cardinal farms, bringing the Dean family win total to 49. Before the season, Dizzy had predicted that 'me and Paul' would win 45, and for once his achievement surpassed his prediction. Joe Medwick turned in a solid .319 average with 106 RBI's, and Durocher held down short, apparently with his mouth. For added personality, Ripper Collins and Pepper Martin played first and third.

Both Dean brothers won two games in the Series against the Tigers, Dizzy taking the seventh and last (a shutout) after telling Tiger manager Cochrane before the game that his chosen starter, Eldon Auker, 'won't do.' In the sixth inning of the same game, Joe Medwick slid forcefully into third baseman Marv Owen, and a brief altercation between the two ensued. When Medwick returned to his defensive position, he received such a barrage of vegetables and similar throw-ables from Detroit fans that Commissioner Landis, in attendance, had him removed from the game as a safety precaution. The Cardinals won the game (11-0) and the Series anyway, sparing Landis any possible embarrassment, but Medwick had to eat his victory dinner in his hotel room, protected by two plainclothesmen, safe from rabid Detroit fans.

RIGHT: *Paul 'Daffy' Dean (left) and brother, Jay Hannah 'Dizzy' Dean, the pitching stars for the Gashouse Gang. Daffy played for the Cardinals from 1934 to 1939, then for the Giants and the Browns, retiring in 1943. His best two years were his first two, when he was 19-11 and 19-12. Dizzy was with the Cardinals from 1930 to 1937, then moved to the Cubs and the Browns, retiring in 1947. In his 12 years he had a .644 winning percentage and made the Hall of Fame in 1953. He ended his career as a baseball broadcaster.*

BELOW: *The 1934 St Louis Cardinals won the National League pennant and beat the Tigers four games to three in the World Series.*

Great Hitters of the Thirties

ABOVE: *Johnny Mize clobbers another one. 'The Big Cat' hit 359 homers in his 15-year career on the way to the Hall of Fame. Mize played for the Cardinals, Giants and Yankees and carried a .312 batting average.*

BELOW: *Hall of Fame second baseman Charlie Gehringer played for the Detroit Tigers from 1924 to 1942. His batting average was .320 to go along with a slugging average of .480.*

The 1930 season was the most prosperous baseball had ever seen, particularly in the National League, which saw attendance rise by half a million over the preceding year. Everywhere fans flocked to see the liveliest ball the game had ever seen get knocked out of the park by the most prodigious hitters any single season had ever produced. The American League batted .288 overall, with teams averaging five runs per game. The National League, whose Hack Wilson challenged Babe Ruth with 56 homers and a record 190 RBI's, sported six clubs with team averages over .300, 71 individuals with averages over .300, and a league batting average of .303.

Babe Ruth, hitting .359 and launching 49 homers, was still the American League home run king. Lou Gehrig hit .379 (Combs hit .344 and Dickey hit .339) and led the league with 174 RBI's, followed by Al Simmons with 165, Jimmie Foxx with 156 and Ruth with 153. Simmons led the Americans with a .381 average. Bill Terry of the Giants became the last National Leaguer to hit over .400, leading the league with .401 and tying Lefty O'Doul's still-standing National League record of 254 hits. The Phillies, who averaged .315 as a team but finished in the basement, featured O'Doul with .383, and Chuck Klein with a .386 average, 250 hits, 59 doubles, 40 home runs, 170 RBI's and 158 runs scored. Babe Herman of the Dodgers hit .393, and Fred Lindstrom of the Giants hit .379.

For 1931 the ball was deadened, the owners fearing fans might have had enough of home runs. There would never be another year like 1930. Reflecting the change in the ball, the National League composite average for 1931 was 29 points off the previous year. Cardinal Chick Hafey's .3489 average gave him the league batting title over teammate Jim Bottomley and Giant Bill Terry. The Cubs led the National League

Hank Greenberg made the Hall of Fame in 1956. He played for the Detroit Tigers from 1930 to 1946 (with four and a half years off in the service) and finished his career with the Pirates in 1947. Here he is hitting one of his career 331 home runs. He was a power hitter who managed to hang up a career batting average of .313.

with a team average of .289, 30 points below the Giants' record of 1930. In the American League, Al Simmons took top honors for the second straight year with a batting average of .390. Ruth and Gehrig tied for home run honors at 46, and Gehrig set the all-time American League record of 184 RBI's.

In 1932 Babe Ruth, now 37, managed 41 home runs and a .341 average. Lou Gehrig continued to hit away with consistent excellence, but Jimmie Foxx established himself as the American League slugging king, blasting 58 home runs in the first of his MVP years. He also got

213 hits, led the league in both runs (151) and RBI's (169), and recorded a .364 average which stood only three points below league-leading Dale Alexander's figure. The next year Foxx repeated as MVP and took a triple crown, hitting 48 home runs, logging 163 RBI's and scoring 125 runs for an average of .356. Former teammate Al Simmons became the last American Leaguer to record five consecutive 200-hit seasons. 1932, of course, was the year Lou Gehrig turned in the greatest individual Series performance on record, and also the year of Babe Ruth's famous Series 'called shot.'

In the National League, 1932 saw the modest debut of the Gashouse Gang's Joe Medwick, destined to become the league's premier Depression slugger, who checked in by batting .349 in 26 games. Chuck Klein was the league's top hitter in 1933, taking the triple crown with 28 home runs, 120 RBI's and a .368 average. In Series play, the Giants' Mel Ott hit two homers and averaged .389. His 511 career homers were the National League record until Willie Mays improved upon them.

The Detroit Tigers introduced young first baseman Hank Green-

berg in 1933. Never more than adequate at his defensive position, Greenberg nevertheless realized his boyhood ambition to become one of baseball's all-time great sluggers. He hit .300 or better for each of the first seven years of a career interrupted by four and a half years of military service, in 1934 knocking in 26 homers and 63 doubles, only four below the major-league record. In 1935 he led the league with 170 RBI's, tied Foxx for home runs with 36, and averaged .328. Greenberg four times led the league in home runs, socking 58 in 1938. In 1937, his best year, he got 200 hits for a .337 average, including 40

homers, 14 triples, 49 doubles, 137 runs scored and 183 of the RBI's for which he was famous (one less than Gehrig's league record).

Gehrig took the American League triple crown in 1934 with 49 homers, 163 RBI's and a .363 average. Teammate Babe Ruth was beginning to show his age. His 22 homers, 84 RBI's and .288 average could hardly be criticized, except by his standards, but 1935 found him playing for the Boston Braves. The Bambino retired on 2 June 1935, having hit three out of Forbes Field on 25 May for a long-time major-league record lifetime total of 714 home runs.

The Chicago Cubs' second baseman Billy Herman hit .341 in 1935, and the Cardinals' Joe Medwick hit .353, but Pittsburgh's Arky Vaughan led the league with .385, still the record average for a National League shortstop. The Giants' 1936 and 1937 pennants were facilitated by Mel Ott, who led the league in homers both years with 33 and 31. After belting a still-standing league-high record of 64 doubles in 1936, Joe Medwick had his greatest year in 1937, leading the league in average (.374), RBI's (154), home runs (31), runs (111), slugging (.641), at-bats (633), hits (237) and doubles (56). Medwick took 1937's triple crown and was voted MVP. Teammate Johnny Mize, whose lifetime slugging average is second only to Rogers Hornsby's in the National League, batted .364 with 25 home runs and 113 RBI's.

In 1936 Yankee manager Joe McCarthy put together a team that had six men batting over .300 and five men hitting over 100 RBI's. Rookie Joseph Paul DiMaggio got 206 hits – including 44 doubles, 15 triples, 29 home runs – scored 132 runs and batted in 124. He averaged .323 and, revealing his defensive grace, led all American League outfielders in assists. In 1937 DiMaggio improved, batting .346 with 46 homers, 167 RBI's and 151 runs scored.

Hitting was heavy throughout the American League in 1936, with five teams batting over .290, and 18 men driving in over 100 RBI's. Lou Gehrig, 1936's MVP, led the league with 49 home runs and 130

ABOVE: *Hal Trosky was a slugging first baseman for the Indians (1933-41) and the White Sox (1944 and 1946). He ended with a lifetime batting average of .302 and 228 home runs in his 11 years.*

BELOW: *Luke Appling, the Hall of Fame shortstop for the Chicago White Sox from 1930 to 1950. Luke, who played until he was 43 years old, had a lifetime batting average of .310 and was famous for fouling off pitches until he got one he could turn into a base hit.*

LEFT: *Chick Hafey, who made the Hall of Fame in 1971, played the outfield for the Cardinals (1924-31) and the Reds (1932-37). A .315 hitter, he carried a .526 slugging average.*

OPPOSITE TOP: *Red Rolfe scores a run in the 1939 World Series, in which the Yankees beat the Reds four games to none. Joe DiMaggio is holding the bat. Rolfe played third base for the Yankees from 1931 to 1942.*

OPPOSITE BOTTOM: *Arky Vaughan was a good-hitting shortstop for the Pirates (1932-41) and the Dodgers (1942-48). His career batting average of .318 was accompanied by a slugging average of .453.*

RBI's. Teammate Tony Lazzeri batted in 109 runs, George Selkirk knocked in 107, and catcher Dickey chalked up 107 RBI's while posting an average of .362, the American League season record for a catcher. Chicago's Luke Appling led the league with .388, the highest average by a shortstop this century, and Cleveland's Hal Trosky led the league with 164 RBI's, while teammate Earl Averill led in hits and seconded Appling in batting.

Detroit's MVP Charlie Gehringer took league honors with a .371 average in 1937, but otherwise it was the Yankees again, all the way. Gehrig turned in his last great year with 37 homers, 159 RBI's and a .351 average, and sophomore Joe DiMaggio led the league with 46 home runs. New arrival to the outfield Tom Henrich hit .320 in 67 games and became a regular.

In 1938 Hank Greenberg rivetted attention by compiling 58 home runs, two short of Babe Ruth's record. Jimmie Foxx, now with the Red Sox, blasted 50 homers, leading the league in average (.349), RBI's (175) and in slugging (.704) to take his third MVP title. Lou Gehrig managed 29 homers and 114 RBI's with a .295 average, not bad for the average player but for the Iron Horse it indicated that something was very wrong. Gehrig was to end his career one year later, on 2 May 1939, when illness closed out a record 2130 consecutive games. Two years later, at 38, on 2 June 1941, Lou Gehrig died from the effects of amyotrophic lateral sclerosis.

The arrival of Charlie 'King Kong' Keller, hitting .334 in his rookie season, helped replace the gap left by Gehrig. With DiMaggio in center and Henrich in right, Keller became part of one of the great outfields in baseball history. In 1939, as the Yankees repeated, DiMaggio led the league with .381, his lifetime best, to become the last righthanded batter to clear .380. Jimmie Foxx led the league with 35 homers, averaged .360, and racked up 105 RBI's; and a 20-year-old rookie Red Sox teammate named Ted Williams batted .327, launching 31 homers and leading the league in RBI's with 145.

With sluggers like this, by the first year of the next decade the American League out-homered the National League by almost 200 runs, out-scored it by over 700 runs, and out-batted it by an average of seven points. It would take a second world war and a social revolution called Jackie Robinson before American League supremacy at the plate would slacken.

Great Pitchers of the Thirties

In 1930, with batting averages commonly ranging from .330 to .340, ERA's rose correspondingly. In the National League the last-place Phillies yielded 7.7 runs per game (while batting .315 as a team). The Dodgers, in fourth, had a relatively low ERA of 4.03, due largely to Dazzy Vance, now 39, who led the league with an ERA of 2.61. The league as a whole averaged an ERA of almost five runs per game, New York's young Carl Hubbell coming in second to Vance with 3.76. For 1930 both these ERA's were remarkable. Grove's league-leading mark was seconded in the American League by Cleveland's Wes Ferrell, who posted 3.31 and won 25 games on his way to setting a record by winning over 20 games in each of his first four years in the majors.

The Cardinals, with twelve .300 batters on their team, broke ground by starting 19-year-old Dizzy Dean once their flag was secure, in the last game of the season. Dean won his game, allowing only one run and three hits in nine innings. In 1932, his first full season, Dean led the league in strikeouts (191), shutouts and innings pitched, winning 18 and losing 15.

Jerome Dean, best known as Dizzy, was as colorful a performer as the National League has ever produced. Like teammate Pepper Martin, he was an ideal hero for the Depression, just as his club, the Cardinals of Gashouse Gang fame, was the perfect antidote for the nation's economic winter. His fiery fastball and snapping curve earned him 120 wins in his first five years in the majors, and his native wit and fantastic prognostications endeared him to the public and won the hearts of baseball fans.

In 1934, his greatest season, Dean became the first National Leaguer since Alexander in 1917 to win 30 games. He also led the league in strikeouts, shutouts and complete games. This was the year that Dizzy Dean and his brother Paul 'Daffy' Dean, up to the Cardinals through their farm system, would win 49 games together.

In 1935 Dean was 28-12, but two years later his effectiveness was permanently hampered when he was hit in the toe by a line drive in an All-Star game for which he was the National League's starting pitcher. Dean returned to action too soon, and in favoring his painful broken toe, changed his pitching motion and ruined his arm. After that he was only moderately successful, but continued to excel on the banquet

ABOVE: *Johnny Allen pitched for the Yankees (1932-35), the Indians (1936-40), the Browns (1941), the Dodgers (1941-43) and the Giants (1943-44). In his 13 years, he had a .654 victory percentage and won 20 games in 1936.*

LEFT: *Lefty Grove and Dizzy Dean shake hands before an All-Star game.*

OPPOSITE: *Bob 'Rapid Robert' Feller, the kid pitcher from Van Meter, Iowa. Feller, who entered the Hall of Fame in 1962, pitched for the Indians from 1936 (when he was 17 years old) to 1956, with three years off for duty in the Navy. During his career he won 266 games and lost 162, for a .621 winning percentage. In his 18 playing years, he led the league in wins six times.*

circuit and as a radio announcer whose fractured English kept his listeners in stitches.

The Giants' quiet, thoughtful, publicity-shy pitcher Carl Hubbell – in every way the antithesis of Dizzy Dean – helped his club to the pennant with 23 wins in 1933, beginning a string of five consecutive years in which he won at least 21 games, averaging 23. Henceforth he was known as 'Meal Ticket' for his dependability. Hubbell's 1933 season included 10 shutouts (46 consecutive shutout innings), and a league-leading 1.66 ERA, the best in the National League since Alexander's 1.22 in 1915. On 2 July 1933, in what was perhaps the finest game of his career, the great screwball master shut out the Cardinals 1-0 in 18

innings. Then in the All-Star game, Hubbell struck out Babe Ruth, Lou Gehrig, Jimmie Foxx, Al Simmons and Joe Cronin in order, and kept the Americans scoreless for the innings he pitched. His best year was 1936, when he hurled 26-6, and ended the season with 16 straight wins, good enough to get him voted MVP. He began the 1937 season with eight wins in a row, compiling a total of 24 consecutive wins before he was stopped. He was 22-8 for the season. The second Giant pennant in a row also saw a contribution of 20 wins from rookie lefthander Cliff Melton. A big man, Melton turned in a 2.61 ERA and hurled seven saves as well.

Lefty Grove won 31 games and lost only four for the Athletics in 1931, tying the American League record with a 16-game winning streak. Outdistancing and outclassing all the competition, he led the league in wins, percentage (.886), complete games (27), strikeouts and ERA (2.05). New York's Vernon 'Lefty' Gomez, who with Red Ruffing formed the backbone of the Yankees' pitching staff, was at 2.63 the only other pitcher in the league to post an ERA under 3.00 that year. In 1932, Grove, who was 79-14 for the previous three years, actually lost 10 games, but won 25, and once again posted the only league ERA under 3.00. Seven years later, in 1939, pitching for the Red Sox, Grove turned in a 15-4 season and took his record ninth ERA title.

The Yankees' 1932 pennant was secured with the help of Lefty Gomez's 24-7 record, and Red Ruffing's 18-7. Gomez, a gifted comedian who attributed his success to 'clean living and a fast outfield,' led the league with a 26-5 season in 1934, and was also tops in ERA (2.33), strikeouts, shutouts, complete games, innings pitched and winning percentage. Teammate Ruffing took 20 games in 1936, the first of his four consecutive 20-game seasons that not accidentally coincided with the Yankees' four consecutive pennant years.

On 23 August 1936, a promising young pitcher for Cleveland named Bob Feller made headlines when he struck out 15 players in his first major-league game. Less than a month later, he struck out 17 players in a game against the Athletics, setting a new league record and tying the all-time record set by Dizzy Dean. Said Feller, '. . . I guess that's when people began to realize I was for real.' After his second game, Feller went home to finish school in Iowa.

Feller, the only real prodigy in baseball history, was mid-America personified, a product of the Iowa corn belt and a former semipro father who tutored him on a baseball diamond carved out of their farm. In a sequence of events that has since become legendary, Cleveland general manager Cy Slapnicka gave in to months of pestering by Feller fans, took one look at the boy, and made an on-the-spot deal sweetened by an autographed baseball and a one dollar bill.

In 1938 Feller set a new major-league record by striking out 18

ABOVE: *Mel Harder pitched for the Cleveland Indians from 1928 to 1947, winning 223 and losing 186 for a .545 percentage. His best year was 1935, when he won 22 and lost 11.*

LEFT: *Paul 'Oom Paul' Derringer won 223 games in 15 years with the Cardinals (1931-33), the Reds (1933-42) and the Cubs (1943-45). His winning percentages of .692 in 1931 and .781 in 1939 led the league.*

RIGHT: *Red Ruffing, the Hall of Fame pitcher, played for the Red Sox (1924-30), the Yankees (1930-46) and the White Sox (1947). He three times led the league in wins, and his World Series record of seven wins and two losses was phenomenal.*

batters in one game. His fastball was called by many better than Johnson's, and he had a curve which moved nearly as fast. He won 107 games by the time he was 22, including his first no-hitter. Although four years in the service robbed him of spectacular career statistics, no one ever recorded more low-hit games than Feller. He tied Cy Young's record of three no-hitters, and threw 11 one-hit games, seven more than any other hurler. He set then major-league records for most strikeouts in a season and most strikeouts in a single game. Although some considered him on a par with Johnson and Grove, most fellow players considered him in a class by himself. Feller was one of the most exciting players since Babe Ruth, and almost as big a draw.

The Yankee Dynasty of the Late Thirties

New York manager Joe McCarthy was a perfectionist who rankled under his club's three consecutive second-place finishes beginning in 1933. In 1936 his hard work paid off, and he put together a team that had six men batting over .300, five men batting in more than 100 runs, and was propelled by the first of four consecutive 20-game seasons from pitcher Red Ruffing. McCarthy had helped form a four-year Yankee dynasty so powerful it finished 19 and a half, 13, 9 and a half, and 17 games ahead of the runners-up. Beginning in 1936 Yankee domination extended to seven pennants and four consecutive World Series victories over the next eight years.

To the solid lineup of Lou Gehrig, Tony Lazzeri, Frank Crosetti and Red Rolfe in the infield, catching great Bill Dickey behind the plate, and George Selkirk and Ben Chapman in the outfield, in 1936 McCarthy added a young outfielder named Joseph Paul DiMaggio. It is no accident that the Yankees' precedent-setting four consecutive pennants and four consecutive World Series victories began with his arrival.

In his rookie year with a club that averaged seven runs per game and clinched the pennant on the earliest date in American League history (9 September), the fisherman's son batted .323, got 206 hits (including 44 doubles, 15 triples and 29 home runs), 124 RBI's and scored 132 runs. His virtuoso performance in center field earned him top place among all American League outfielders in assists, a rare accomplishment from that position, and revealed a style and grace that were soon to create a following and a mystique second only to that of Babe Ruth. While DiMaggio's chemistry with the crowd was completely different from the Bambino's, and he had nothing of the common touch, he rapidly

LEFT: *Joe McCarthy (shown in his Yankee uniform) won more games than any manager except for Connie Mack, John McGraw and Bucky Harris — 2126. He was elected to the Hall of Fame in 1957.*

ABOVE: *Joe DiMaggio, the Hall of Fame Yankee outfielder, played for New York from 1936 to 1951, with three years out for World War II. He batted .325 and hit 361 home runs.*

became the object of a hero worship such as very few ball players and statesmen ever receive.

Also turning in solid performances for the Yankees in 1936 was Lou Gehrig, that year's Most Valuable Player, who led the league with 49 home runs and 130 RBI's; Tony Lazzeri, in his last big year, pushing in 109 runs; and right fielder Selkirk, knocking in 107. Hurler Monte Pearson added 19 wins to Ruffing's 20, and catcher Bill Dickey knocked in 107 runs and hit .362, the American League season record for a catcher.

The Yankees lost the first and the fourth World Series games to the Giants, but came out on top to take the first of their four straight world

LEFT: *Spurgeon Ferdinand 'Spud' Chandler pitched for the Yankees from 1937 to 1947. He had an excellent record of 109 wins and 43 losses for a winning percentage of .717. He led the league in 1943 with 20 wins and a percentage of .833, losing only four games.*

OPPOSITE: *Charlie 'King Kong' Keller played the outfield for the Yankees (1939-49) and Detroit (1950-51), returning to the Yankees in 1952, his last year. His .286 lifetime batting average included 189 homers.*

BELOW LEFT: *Ben Chapman was an outfielder for the Yankees (1930-36), the Senators (1936-37), the Red Sox (1937-38), the Indians (1939-40), the Senators again (1941), the White Sox (1941), the Dodgers (1944-45) and the Phillies (1945-46). He hit .302.*

BELOW: *Tommy 'Old Reliable' Henrich played the outfield for the Yankees from 1937 to 1950, with three years off in the service. He hit .382 and had a slugging average of .491.*

championships. In the second game Tony Lazzeri became the second player ever to hit a home run with bases loaded in the Series. The Yankees would lose only one more game in the remaining three world championship contests.

McCarthy and DiMaggio, who eventually joined Ruffing, Gomez, Gehrig and Dickey in the Hall of Fame, revamped the Yankee style from one of Ruthian brute strength to one of cool, efficient dominance. McCarthy expected his Yankees to win, but he expected them to be dignified as well, on and off the field, and he canned outfielder Ben Chapman, for instance, because of his emotional outbursts.

The Yankees repeated in 1937 with 102 wins, finishing 13 games ahead of the Tigers. Gehrig turned in his last great year with 37 homers, 159 RBI's and a .351 average, and DiMaggio, improving in his second year, led the league with 46 home runs, batted in 167 runs, scored 151 and averaged .346. Outfielder Tom Henrich was added to the club after a fierce bidding war. 'Old Reliable' personified the solid Yankee players who stood behind their superstars and gave the team its depth. He hit .320 in 67 games in 1937, and played through 1950.

The Giants took only one game from the Yankees in the '37 Series, one of the easiest Series wins ever for an American League team. The 4-1 victory made the Bombers the first club ever to take six world championships. Tony Lazzeri led both leagues with a .400 Series average and got one homer, and Lou Gehrig hit his tenth and last home run in World Series play. Contributing to his legend as a cool player, Lefty Gomez paused on the mound to observe a plane pass overhead.

The 1938 Yankees, in manager McCarthy's opinion the best team he ever fielded, finished nine and a half games ahead of a strong Red Sox club. The Yankee farm system, started a few years earlier under the gifted administration of George M Weiss, added Joe Gordon, one of the many excellent players it would generate, as a replacement for Lazzeri at second. In his rookie year Gordon hit 25 homers and established a great double play combination with Frankie Crosetti. Lou Gehrig hit 29 homers, got 114 RBI's and averaged .295, a weak year by his standards, but pitching was solid throughout. Ruffing won 21, Gomez 18, Pearson 16 and farmer Spud Chandler 14. The Yanks

swept the Cubs in the Series, making McCarthy the first manager in history to win three consecutive world championships. Joe Gordon drove in six runs, and he and Bill Dickey both hit .400 for the Series.

Lou Gehrig was clearly a sick man at spring training in 1939. After eight games, for which he averaged .143, on 2 May 1939 he asked McCarthy to take him out of the lineup, ending his record of 2130 regular season appearances. Two months later he learned he was suffering from an incurable neuromuscular disease, amyotrophic lateral sclerosis. A 4 July 1939 doubleheader at Yankee Stadium served as the occasion for Lou Gehrig Appreciation Day. The Iron Horse received a bear hug from former teammate Babe Ruth, and announced, '... I consider myself the luckiest man on the face of the

earth.' Two years later he died, a member of the Hall of Fame and the first Yankee to have his number retired.

Charlie Keller, up from the Yankees' Newark farm team in 1939, took up position in left field, and with DiMaggio in center and Henrich in right formed one of the great outfields in baseball history. Hitting over .300 in his rookie year, 'King Kong' Keller helped to replace the slugging gap left by Gehrig, and the Yankees ended the season with 106 wins and a finish 17 games in front of the Red Sox. The 1939 Yanks had five .300 hitters, and four players – DiMaggio, Dickey, Gordon and Selkirk – who hit more than 20 homers and had more than 100 RBI's. DiMaggio, 1939's Most Valuable Player, led the league with a .381 average, his lifetime best, and became the last righthanded hitter

to clear the .380 mark. Ruffing contributed 21 games, and although Gomez was limited by a sore arm to 12, Yankee farm system products Spud Chandler and Atley Donald took up the slack.

Sweeping Cincinnati 4-0 in the Series, the unstoppable Yankees became the first and only club ever to win four consecutive world championships. Charlie Keller batted .438 for the Series, drove in six runs, and got three home runs, a triple and a double. The Yankees missed the next pennant by two games before resuming their hegemony and taking the next three, 1941-1943. Perhaps the most striking measure of Yankee dominance in the thirties is that in none of their dynasty years was there ever any question of who would take the pennant after mid-season.

PART III

The War Years and Baseball Comes of Age

1940-1959

Into the Forties

Few decades since the 1880s have brought as many changes to baseball as the 1940s. After climbing slowly out of the pit of the Depression and achieving something like normal prosperity, the game was totally disrupted by the Second World War. Within the same decade, organized baseball would have to deal with the player-raiding tactics of the Mexican League, the near-organization of a players' union, and the long-overdue opening of the game to black Americans.

The night games of the thirties were now accepted practice. In 1946 the Braves became the seventh National League team to install arc-lights, leaving the Cubs as the last hold-outs. Perhaps most significant of all, regular radio broadcasts, which had definitely been shown not to hurt live attendance, continued to add a new dimension to the game, as well as a new source of income. In the American League total receipts from radio broadcasts climbed from $11,000 in 1933 to $420,000 in 1939. Figures for the National League were similar.

On 27 August 1939, the first televised major-league game, a doubleheader at Ebbets Field in Brooklyn between the Dodgers and the Reds, was viewed enthusiastically by those with the sets to receive it. Television would have to wait until after World War II to make its full impact felt on baseball, but when it did its impact would be considerable. By the late forties television and the ease of commercial air travel made it possible for clubs to consider new locations, and created the potential for the revolution of franchise shifts.

In 1940, however, most people just expected the Yankees to win again. As it happened, in the American League Joe DiMaggio led with a .352 average, but he was the only Yankee regular to hit over .300 on a team that batted as a whole 28 points below their previous year's mark. Cleveland joined the tight race behind a superb season from Bob Feller, who won 27 games, led the league in virtually every pitching category, and pitched the only opening day no-hitter in the history of baseball. When the dust settled, a Detroit team, spirited by Hank Greenberg's .340 average and league-leading 41 home runs and 150 RBI's, carried the day. Cleveland finished second, one game behind, and New York was third, two games out.

The team that derailed the Yankees' bid for a fifth consecutive pennant in 1940 also featured 33 homers, 134 RBI's, and a .316 average from backup catcher Rudy York, whom manager Del Baker had moved to first base (Greenberg went to left field) to keep in the starting lineup. Outfielder Barney McCosky batted .340, and the ageless Charlie Gehringer hit .313. Schoolboy Rowe was 16-3, demonstrating his recovery from a sore arm, and Norman Louis Newsom, called 'Bobo' because that is what he called everyone else, demonstrated the pitching skill that kept him in the majors for 20 years through nine teams, throwing 21-5 in his finest year.

In the National League, the Cincinnati Reds, still displaying the effects of Larry MacPhail's team-building, repeated in 1940, finishing 12 games ahead of second-place Brooklyn. Bucky Walters and Paul Derringer again added 20-game years, Walters with 22 wins and

BELOW: *Joe DiMaggio getting a hit in his 42nd consecutive game in 1941. He ended up with hits in 56 consecutive games – a record.*

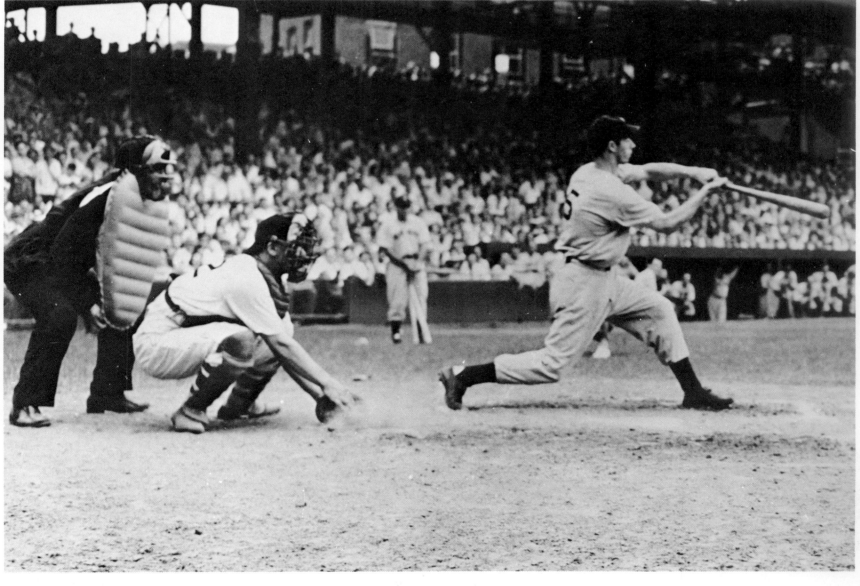

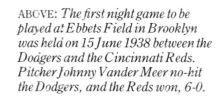

ABOVE: *The first night game to be played at Ebbets Field in Brooklyn was held on 15 June 1938 between the Dodgers and the Cincinnati Reds. Pitcher Johnny Vander Meer no-hit the Dodgers, and the Reds won, 6-0.*

LEFT: *Bobo Newsom pitched for 20 seasons in the majors for nine different clubs (1929-53, with a few years off). Although he won 211 games while losing 222, he three times led his league in victories – 1935, 1941 and 1945.*

RIGHT: *Rudy York was a first baseman who could also double as catcher or in the outfield. He played for the Tigers (1934-45), the Red Sox (1946-47), the White Sox (1947) and the Athletics (1948), hitting 277 home runs.*

Derringer with 20. First baseman Frank McCormick, voted 1940's Most Valuable Player, led the league in hits for the third straight year. The Red's second consecutive victory was marred when backup catcher Willard Hershberger, depressed after 'making a bad call,' slashed his throat with a razor in the club's Boston hotel, but Cincinnati vindicated its Series loss of the year before to the Yankees by defeating the Tigers 4-3, giving the National League its first World Series victory since 1934.

The war in Europe was still far away from America in 1941, and though Hank Greenberg, the first major star to go, was drafted on 7 May, most of baseball's biggest stars would remain in place through the next season as well. As if to emphasize business as usual, the Yankees took the pennant again in 1941, clinching it on 4 September, the earliest date in history, their fifth flag in six years and the first of three more consecutive wins.

1941 will always be remembered in the American League for two numbers: 56 and .406. Beginning with a single on 15 May, Joe DiMaggio riveted the attention of the baseball world by hitting safely in 56 consecutive games, passing George Sisler's American League record of 41, and Wee Willie Keeler's all-time mark of 44, set in 1897. While DiMaggio was hitting away, 22-year-old Ted Williams, in his third year with the Red Sox, hit 37 home runs, and came into the last day of the season with a .400 batting average. Manager Cronin told Williams he could sit out their doubleheader with the Athletics to preserve his average, but Williams declined. By going 4 for 5 in the first game and 2 for 3 in the second, he ended the season with a .406 average. DiMaggio's '56' still stands as an all-time record, and Williams' .406 mark has not been equalled since he set it.

In the National League, 1941 saw a tight race between the Brooklyn Dodgers and the Cardinals, the lead changing 27 times during the season. Despite the loss in effectiveness of newly purchased slugger Joe Medwick when he was beaned by former Cardinal teammate Bob Bowman on 19 June, a strong Dodger team, rebuilt by general manager Larry MacPhail and managed by 'Lippy' Leo Durocher, moved up from a second place in 1940 to first place in 1941. For Brooklyn, this was the first flag since 1920.

MacPhail had purchased hurler Kirby Higbe from the Phillies to strengthen the squad (he took 20 games in 1941), catcher Mickey

ABOVE: *Larry MacPhail at the radio microphone studies the Detroit Tigers' player roster.*

LEFT: *Ted Williams at batting practice. 'The Splendid Splinter,' who was elected to the Hall of Fame in 1966, played for the Red Sox from 1939 to 1960, with three years off during World War II and almost two years for service in Korea. His lifetime batting average of .344 included one year with a .406 average (1941) and six years when he led the American League in hitting. He also led the league in slugging nine times, in home runs four times and in RBI's four times. This outfielder ended his career by hitting his 521st homer.*

OPPOSITE LEFT: *Harold 'Pee Wee' Reese, who played shortstop for the Dodgers from 1940 to 1958, with three years off in service. 'The Little Colonel' was a fast, scrappy player who hit a lifetime .269.*

OPPOSITE RIGHT: *Fred 'Dixie' Walker – 'The Peepul's Cherce.' This outfielder played for the Yankees (1931-36), the White Sox (1936-37), the Tigers (1938-39), the Dodgers (1939-47) and the Pirates (1948-49). His career batting average was .306.*

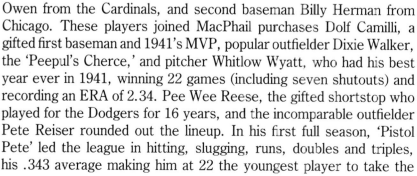

Owen from the Cardinals, and second baseman Billy Herman from Chicago. These players joined MacPhail purchases Dolf Camilli, a gifted first baseman and 1941's MVP, popular outfielder Dixie Walker, the 'Peepul's Cherce,' and pitcher Whitlow Wyatt, who had his best year ever in 1941, winning 22 games (including seven shutouts) and recording an ERA of 2.34. Pee Wee Reese, the gifted shortstop who played for the Dodgers for 16 years, and the incomparable outfielder Pete Reiser rounded out the lineup. In his first full season, 'Pistol Pete' led the league in hitting, slugging, runs, doubles and triples, his .343 average making him at 22 the youngest player to take the

National League batting title.

In the Series, the first for these two New York rivals, the Yankees led two games to one going into the fourth game, but it was still considered anybody's Series. The Dodgers were leading in the top of the ninth, 4-3, with two out. Relief pitcher Hugh Carey got a full count on Yankee slugger Tom Henrich. On the next pitch Henrich swung and missed, but ace catcher Mickey Owen let the ball get away from him, and Henrich got safely to first. The Yankees went on to take the game, 7-4, and took the fifth game, 3-1, recording their own eighth consecutive world championship.

A Season on Hold: 1942-1943

For most Americans, World War II began in December 1941. By the beginning of the 1942 season, American participation in the war was in full swing. Hank Greenberg re-enlisted, although his age could have exempted him from further service, and Bob Feller joined the Navy shortly after Pearl Harbor; but most major stars remained in place for one more year, and the war was slow to make its effects felt on organized baseball. Baseball, as in World War I, was classified as a non-essential industry. However, in sharp contrast to the 'work or fight' order of World War I, the official government policy was to encourage the game. Early in 1942, in response to a query from Commissioner Landis, President Franklin Delano Roosevelt wrote his famous 'green light' letter, praising baseball for its contribution to sustaining national morale. 'I honestly feel that it would be best for the country to keep baseball going. . . . Carry on to the fullest extent consistent with the primary purpose of winning the war.' In 1943 ball players were even permitted to leave essential winter factory jobs to report for training.

The provisions notwithstanding, there was a war going on, and players were slowly siphoned off to fight. Most of the superstars were in the armed forces by the end of 1943, and by the end of 1944, 60 percent of all major-leaguers – more than 1000 players – were in uniform. As the largely male baseball public declined in numbers and time available for sports, attendance and receipts gradually declined, reaching their nadir in 1942-1943, when several teams found themselves in financial straits.

Joe DiMaggio's batting average dropped from .357 to .305 in 1942,

but the Yankees, with strong support from veterans Bill Dickey, Red Ruffing and Lefty Gomez, and particularly fine seasons from Charlie Keller and Joe Gordon, had little trouble taking their sixth pennant in seven years. Ernie Bonham, winning 21 games, and Hank Borowy, winning 15, were fresh up from the Yankee farm system, as was shortstop Phil Rizzuto. Forty-one-year-old Ted Lyons of the White Sox, 14-6 for the season, led the league with an ERA of 2.10, and Ted Williams took the triple crown with 36 homers, 137 RBI's and a .356 average. Both these players entered the service at the end of the year.

In the National League, the Dodgers were 10 and a half games up in mid-August, and despite a warning from Larry MacPhail that they ought to be 20 games up, expected an easy pennant repeat for 1942. Unfortunately for Brooklyn, MacPhail's misgivings were born out when the second-place Cardinals, in the best National League pennant performance since Pittsburgh in 1909, put on the greatest stretch run in history, taking 43 of the last 51 games to nose Brooklyn out by two games. Contributing to the Dodgers' defeat was an accident suffered by Pete Reiser, who was batting .390 when he ran into an outfield wall chasing a ball in St Louis. His average dropped to .310 as he finished out the season playing through headaches, dizzy spells and double vision, and was never quite the same again.

Twenty-two of the Cardinals twenty-five-man roster in 1942 came from their own farm system. This team, which was to take four pennants in five years, is considered by many among the great National League teams of all times. Heading the strong pitching staff was Mort Cooper, 1942's Most Valuable Player, taking 22 games and

LEFT: *A big league reunion is held by three former major-league baseball players at a camp in the Pacific. Left is Marine PFC James 'Big Jim' Bivin, a former Phillies pitcher. Center is Army Lieutenant Thomas 'Long Tom' Winsett, a former outfielder for the Red Sox, Cardinals and Dodgers. Right is Marine Corporal Calvin Leavell 'Preacher' Dorsett, a former pitcher with the Indians.*

OPPOSITE TOP LEFT: *Ted Lyons, who pitched for the White Sox from 1923 to 1942, and was called back for the 1946 season. He was elected to the Hall of Fame in 1955.*

OPPOSITE TOP RIGHT: *Rip Sewell demonstrates his 'eephus' pitch to catcher Al Lopez. Sewell was famous for this blooper pitch when he played for the Tigers (1932) and the Pirates (1938-49).*

OPPOSITE BOTTOM: *Bob Feller and Walker Cooper were an All-Star battery at the Great Lakes Naval Training Center during the War.*

LEFT: *Walker Cooper was a star catcher for 18 years with the Cardinals (1940-45), the Giants (1946-49), the Reds (1949-50), the Boston (later the Milwaukee) Braves (1950-53), the Pirates (1954), the Cubs (1954-55) and the Cardinals again (1956-57).*

BELOW LEFT: *Larry McPhail (left), the ex-Dodger boss who served as a lieutenant colonel in the US Army during World War II, gets the lowdown from his successor, Branch Rickey.*

BELOW: *Stanley Frank 'Stan the Man' Musial was a star in the outfield and at first base for the Cardinals from 1941 to 1963 (with service time off in 1945). He had 3630 hits, 475 homes runs and a batting average of .331. He made the Hall in 1969.*

ABOVE: *Big leaguers in a service game: Hugh Casey, Tom Ferrick, Vern Olsen, Walt Masterson and Jack Hallett.*

RIGHT: *Joe 'Flash' Gordon who played for the Yankees (1938 to 1946, with two years off for service) and Cleveland.*

leading the league with an ERA of 1.77. Johnny Beazley won 21 games, and Ernie White, Howie Pollet and Max Lanier all contributed to a team ERA of 2.55. Mort Cooper's brother Walker played behind the plate, and Marty Marion held down short. Beefing up the Cardinals' strong outfield of Enos Slaughter and Terry Moore was rookie Stanislaus Musial.

Stan Musial batted .315 in his first full season, and batted well over .300 for the next fifteen seasons to dominate league hitting for more than a decade. A strong defensive player and an excellent base-runner, he was so well-liked that his popularity transcended team loyalties – it was Brooklyn fans, in fact, who gave him the title 'Stan the Man.' When he retired, the city of St Louis placed a statue of him outside the Cardinals' stadium, Sportsman's Park.

The Cardinals lost the first game of the Series to the mighty Yankees, but in one of the major upsets since the miracle Braves of 1914, St Louis swept the next four games to take the Series 4-1 and end the Yankees' own string of eight consecutive Series victories.

After the 1942 season, Larry MacPhail left the Dodgers for the military and was replaced by Branch Rickey. Pee Wee Reese and Pete Reiser followed their former general manager into the service in 1943. Johnny Sturm and Tommy Henrich of the Yankees had entered the service during the 1942 season, and were followed in 1943 by Joe DiMaggio, Phil Rizzuto, Red Ruffing and Buddy Hassett. The Cardinals lost many of their regulars, including John Beazley and Terry Moore, but all the other teams were losing players too. Mort Cooper was still on hand, and Stan Musial, kept out of the service by his children until 1945, hit his stride in 1943, leading the league in batting (.357), hits (220), doubles (48), triples (20), total bases (347) and slugging (.562).

With more depth in their farm systems than any other teams, in a world where civilian life was rapidly going on hold, it came as no surprise to anyone that the Yanks and the Cardinals both repeated in their leagues, the Yankees finishing 13 and a half games ahead of the Senators and the Cardinals 18 games ahead of the Reds. In the Series, the Yankees took quick revenge on the Cardinals for their defeat of 1942, this time dropping only one game, the second, before sweeping to a 4-1 victory, their tenth world championship and their seventh under manager McCarthy.

The War Ends

By 1944 the ranks of baseball were drained by the call to arms. Only a few outstanding players remained, and the major leagues, filled with 4-F's, overage players and youngsters, were no longer playing major-league ball. Cincinnati sent 15-year-old Joe Nuxhall to the mound. The Waner brothers (Paul got his 3000th hit in 1942), Pepper Martin and Debs Garms were among the elderly who returned to the diamond during what is often charitably referred to as the caretaking era.

Lack of available talent was compounded by transportation restrictions which temporarily ended spring training in the South. Everyone knew that this was not really baseball, but the fans gave no sign of deserting the game. Attendance, after slumping considerably in 1942-1943, picked up rapidly in 1944-1945, topping all records since 1930. Significantly, during the war every major-league team except the Yankees stepped up radio broadcasting, a development which almost certainly increased interest in the game. In 1944, the nadir as far as talent was concerned, American League attendance topped five million for the first time since 1940. The World Series of 1945, which one sportswriter said he didn't think either team could win, set a new all-time record for attendance and profit.

Mort Cooper, chalking up his third 20-game season in a row, won 22 games for the Cardinals in 1944. George Munger won 11 of 14 before his induction in July, and Ted Wilks, released from the army because of a stomach ulcer, was 17-4. The Cards' great shortstop Marty Marion was voted Most Valuable Player, and Billy Southworth became the first National League manager to win three consecutive pennants since McGraw in the early 1920s. The Cardinals became the first

ABOVE: *Vern 'Junior' Stephens played shortstop for the Browns (1941-47), the Red Sox (1948-52), the White Sox (1953), the Browns again (1953), the Orioles (1954-55) and the White Sox (1955).*

LEFT: *Joe Nuxhall appeared as a pitcher for the Reds in 1944 at the tender age of 15, then returned to pitch for them from 1952 to 1960.*

He also played for the Kansas City Athletics (1961) and the Angels (1962) before returning to the Reds (1963-66). He won 135 games in those 16 years.

OPPOSITE: *Baseball Commissioner A B 'Happy' Chandler (made the Hall of Fame), the former governor of Kentucky, throws out the first ball of the World Series in 1947.*

National League club to win over 100 games in each of three straight seasons (106 in 1942, and 105 in 1943 and 1944). Stan Musial contributed a .347 average in 1944. Boston's Jim Tobin, in the outstanding pitching achievement of the season, pitched two no-hitters, blanking the Dodgers on 27 April and the Phillies on 22 June.

With all the great players off to war, the Tigers and the Yankees found themselves struggling for American League top honors, only to be overtaken by the St Louis Browns, who won the first and only pennant the club would win in St Louis since it joined the league in 1902. Managed by Luke Sewell, the Browns had a couple of veteran hitters, Mike Kreevich and Vern Stephens, and a couple of pitchers, Jack Kramer and Nelson Potter, and managed to clinch the pennant by one game on the last day of the season.

Both the Browns and the Cardinals used the same stadium, their shared home field of Sportsman Park, for the first World Series played entirely west of the Mississippi. In a contest distinguished by excellent pitching by both clubs and inept fielding by the Browns, the Cardinals pulled themselves together after losing the first and third games and took their second world championship in three years, 4-2. In November 1944, Judge Kenesaw Mountain Landis, baseball's first commissioner, died five days after his 78th birthday, after 44 years of service. He was replaced the following spring by Albert Benjamin 'Happy' Chandler, former governor and United States senator from Kentucky.

In 1945 the Chicago Cubs, aided by Stan Musial's induction into the Navy and spearheaded by MVP Phil Cavarretta, finished three games ahead of the second-place Cardinals and put an end to the Redbirds' three-year dynasty. The Cubs would not come close to a pennant again until 1984, when they won their division. Cavarretta hit .355 to take the league batting championship, and righthander Hank Borowy, purchased from the Yankees at the end of July for $100,000, threw 11-2 for the Cubs, becoming the first pitcher ever to win 20 games while dividing a season between two leagues (he was 10-5 for the Yankees). The batting achievement of the season came from the Boston Braves' outfielder Tommy Holmes, who established a National League record by hitting safely in 37 consecutive games.

ABOVE: *Virgil 'Fire' Trucks pitched for Detroit (1941-52), the Browns (1953), the White Sox (1953-55), the Tigers again (1956), the Athletics (1957-58) and the Yankees (1957).*

OPPOSITE: *Phil Cavaretta played first base and outfield for the Cubs (1934-53) and the White Sox (1954-55). He had a .293 batting average, was the National League's Most Valuable Player in 1945 and managed the Cubs from 1951 to 1953.*

LEFT: *Tommy Holmes played the outfield for the Braves (1942-51) and the Dodgers (1952). He batted .302.*

As the war was winding down, first in Europe, then in the Pacific, several players were able to rejoin their teams. Hank Greenberg returned to the Tiger lineup on 1 July, and pitcher Virgil 'Fire' Trucks got out of the Navy after the Japanese surrender in August in time to pitch the final game of the season. A grand slam homer from Hank Greenberg sunk the Browns and clinched the pennant for the Tigers that day.

Playing for the Browns in that last pennant race of World War II was one-armed outfielder Pete Gray. Although he lost his right arm in a childhood accident, retaining only a stub above the elbow, Gray learned to excel at baseball, and perfected a method of catching the ball and getting it out of the glove so that his throw was only slightly slower than an average outfielder's. Gray played in 77 games in 1945 – he was a great draw – and ended his major-league career on 30 September 1945, the day the Tigers took the pennant.

The Tigers took the last World War II Series from the Cubs in an exciting seven-game battle that drew record numbers of fans. With it ended baseball's oddest era. A very few knew that the new one had already begun. During the 1945 season, Branch Rickey had signed three blacks to the Dodgers: pitchers Ray Partlow and John Wright went to Three Rivers for seasoning, and shortstop Jackie Robinson, signed on 28 August 1945, was sent to the Dodgers' top farm club in Montreal, in the International League. Two years later he would become the first black American to play major-league baseball in the twentieth century.

The Mexican League and Integration

1946 saw the return of almost all the pre-war stars to the diamond. Major-league baseball once again expressed the spirit of the country, and fans turned out in record-breaking numbers to cheer on their teams. But with the nation just beginning to adjust to a peace-time economy, organized baseball faced two separate but related precedent-setting challenges. In the spring, the fabulously wealthy Mexican millionaire Jorge Pasquel and his four brothers decided to start a league that would compete with the two in the United States, and began with the time-honored method of offering players more money.

Pasquel succeeded in enticing away a few excellent players from among those who were dissatisfied with the domestic pay scale. Most came from the National League, including such stars as Sal Maglie, Max Lanier and Mickey Owen. Stan Musial, just back from a year in the Navy, considered a $65,000 advance, but decided to stay with the Cardinals. The new commissioner, Happy Chandler, immediately outlawed the Mexican League and blacklisted any players who jumped, vowing they would be barred from playing in the States for five years if they ever returned.

As it happened, the Mexican League never got off the ground. Mickey Owen, the first of the returnees, came back to the States in August. But American players and the Mexican government were furious at the blacklisting and the declaration of illegality. Danny Gardella, one of seven players who jumped from the Giants, took his blacklisting to the courts. Baseball executives retreated from their weak legal position and granted amnesties to jumping players, and Gardella was awarded an out-of-court settlement to drop his suit.

LEFT: *Ralph Kiner, the Hall of Famer, played for the Pirates, the Cubs and the Indians (1946-55).*

ABOVE: *Sal Maglie pitched for ten years in the majors, with time off for the Mexican League.*

In the spring of 1946 attorney Robert Murphy, a former examiner for the National Labor Relations Board, formed the American Baseball Guild to represent players against owners. Players across the leagues were remarkably united in their grievances, and the Pirates came very close to striking against owner Bill Benswanger. With the Mexican League checkbook ready to snap up dissatisfied players, the owners were not in a strong position.

Hoping to outflank the formation of a serious players' union, Commissioner Chandler invited the players to send delegates to discuss their grievances. In September the owners finally agreed to a $5000 minimum salary, limits on annual salary cuts, a pension fund and other benefits. Player organization was stopped short of unionization, but the incident led in time to the formation of the powerful Major League Baseball Players' Association.

Hank Greenberg hit 44 homers for the Tigers in 1946, and Bob Feller, back from four years in the Navy, set a new strikeout record of

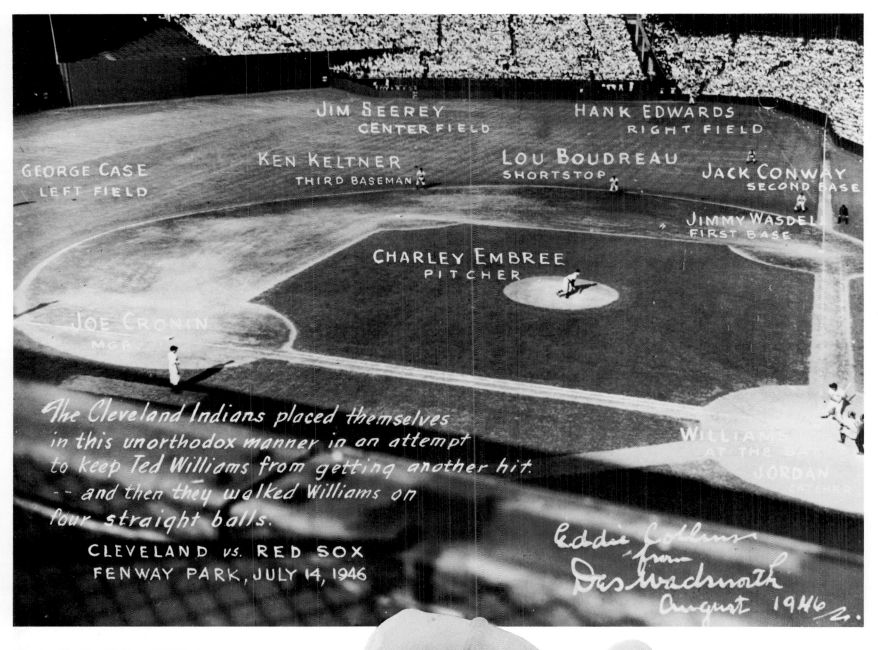

JIM SEEREY
CENTER FIELD

HANK EDWARDS
RIGHT FIELD

GEORGE CASE
LEFT FIELD

KEN KELTNER
THIRD BASEMAN

LOU BOUDREAU
SHORTSTOP

JACK CONWAY
SECOND BASE

JIMMY WASDELL
FIRST BASE

CHARLEY EMBREE
PITCHER

JOE CRONIN
MGR.

The Cleveland Indians placed themselves
in this unorthodox manner in an attempt
to keep Ted Williams from getting another hit.
-- and then they walked Williams on
four straight balls.

CLEVELAND vs. RED SOX
FENWAY PARK, JULY 14, 1946

WILLIAMS
AT THE BAT

JORDAN
CATCHER

Eddie Collins
from
Des Wadsworth
August 1946

ABOVE: *The Ted Williams Shift that
was invented by player-manager Lou
Boudreau of the Indians.*

RIGHT: *Johnny Pesky played shortstop
for the Red Sox, the Tigers and the
Senators (1942-54).*

348 (research eventually established that Rube Waddell had struck out 349 in 1904). But it fell to another returned serviceman, Ted Williams, to lead his team to the pennant 12 games ahead of the second-place Tigers, the first flag for the Red Sox since 1918. Williams hit 38 homers and batted in 123 runs for a .342 average, receiving plenty of help from Johnny Pesky (.342), Dom DiMaggio (.316), Rudy York and Bobby Doerr.

In the National League, Stan Musial helped his team to the pennant with a league-leading .365 average, and also led in doubles, triples, hits, runs, slugging and total bases. A rookie outfielder with Pittsburgh, Ralph Kiner, led the league in homers with 23 – he would lead the league in home runs for the next six seasons. The Cardinals and the Dodgers ran a tight and exciting pennant race, ending the season in a tie which necessitated the first pennant play-off in major-league history. The Cardinals took the play-off in two games (out of three), and went on to greater glory by defeating the heavily-favored Red Sox in the World Series, 4-3.

During the spring training exhibition season of 1947 in Havana, Dodger manager Leo Durocher heckled former boss Larry MacPhail, then with the Yankees, for associating with gamblers, and soon after claimed that MacPhail had offered him the management of the Yankees. MacPhail, who was already involved in an acrimonious dispute with Dodger general manager Branch Rickey over former Dodger coach Chuck Dressen, whom the Yankees had hired, denied Durocher's charge and filed a bill of particulars with Commissioner Chandler accusing Durocher of 'conduct detrimental to baseball.' After a couple of hearings and fines all around, Durocher was suspended from baseball for one year. Burt Shotton was called out of semi-retirement to replace him.

At the height of the commotion, about one week before the opening of the 1947 season, Branch Rickey announced that the Dodgers had purchased Jackie Robinson's contract from Montreal. Major-league baseball was now officially reintegrated, but not without a flood of racial incidents. The Cardinals threatened to strike rather than appear on the same field with a black man. League President Ford Frick, vowing to suspend any player who struck, announced, 'I do not care if

BELOW: 'Joltin' Joe' DiMaggio, the Hall of Fame outfielder for the New York Yankees, being congratulated by the batboy as he crosses the plate after hitting a homer.

OPPOSITE: Hall of Fame infielder-outfielder Jackie Robinson at the plate for the Brooklyn Dodgers. Robinson was the courageous player who broke the color line in major-league baseball in 1947.

half the league strikes. Those who do will encounter quick retribution. All will be suspended and I do not care if it wrecks the National League for five years. This is the United States of America, and one citizen has as much right to play as another.'

Despite a hellish season that included abuse from some of his own teammates, Robinson played better than competent ball, batting .297 and stealing 29 bases. His Rookie of the Year performance undoubtedly helped his team to take the pennant, and he became a mainstay of a Dodgers club that was to win six pennants in the next ten years. Elsewhere in the league, the Pirates' Ralph Kiner, in his second season, hit 51 home runs, tying Johnny Mize of the Giants for the title.

The fourth-place Giants, with Mize hitting 51 homers, Willard Marshall 36, Walker Cooper 35 and Bobby Thomson 29, set a new team home run record with 221. Pitching for Cincinnati, Ewell Blackwell had a 22-8 season that included 16 wins in a row and a no-hitter.

Ted Williams became the first American League batter to take a second triple crown in 1947, but the pennant went to the Yankees, who turned in a 19-game winning streak (surpassed by the 1916 Giants, who had a 26-game winning streak). Joe DiMaggio and Tom Henrich turned in excellent seasons, as did a new young pitching staff featuring Allie Reynolds (19-8) and reliever Joe Page.

The Yanks met the Dodgers in a dramatic Series, highlighted in the fourth game, when the Yankees were leading two games to one. Floyd Bevens had held the Dodgers hitless into the ninth inning when, with the score 2-1 Yankees, two outs and two men on, pinch hitter Cookie Lavagetto hit a double to drive in the winning run and tie up the Series. The Yankees lost one more game, but clinched the Series 4-3 for their eleventh championship in a period of 25 years.

The 1947 Series was the first to be televised (rights sold for $65,000) and the first to produce total receipts of over $2 million; the same year, the National League became the first league to pass the 10 million attendance mark. No crystal ball was necessary to see that postwar baseball had entered a lucrative period.

The End – and Beginning – of an Era

Baseball's blossoming prosperity reflected that of American society in general as it entered the final years of the forties. With the war a thing of the past, baseball would find its customary place as both a diversion from, and reflector of, society's larger issues. As for the latter, for instance, Jackie Robinson's first season with the Dodgers (and Larry Doby's with the Indians) had begun to pave the way for all black players. Not that the teams exactly rushed for the opportunity. Even by the end of 1949, there were only five other black players, in addition to Robinson and Doby, on major-league teams. One of these was the legendary Leroy 'Satchel' Paige, hired by the Cleveland Indians in the 1948 season. Long recognized as a pitcher who could have held his own with the best in any league, Paige was now well into his forties and past his prime, but even as a symbol his appearance in the majors was worth applauding.

Whether Paige contributed that much to the Indians of 1948 is debatable, but the fact is that they moved ahead to take the pennant in the American League. Other teams might have looked stronger on paper – the Red Sox, for instance, had not only Ted Williams, but Bobby Doerr, Vern Stephens and Johnny Pesky as well – but the Indians were led by one of the most successful player-managers ever, Lou Boudreau, and by the last day of the season they had a tie for first place with the Red Sox. Then, in a one-game playoff, and with Boudreau himself hitting two home runs, the Indians defeated the Red Sox, 8-3. (Boudreau batted .355 for the season and was voted the league's Most Valuable Player.)

In the National League, there was a classic case of the diversion that baseball has always been: Leo 'The Lip' Durocher. After his year's suspension, Durocher returned in 1948 to manage the Dodgers, and then, in one of the most astonishing 'doubleplays' in baseball history, he suddenly went over on 16 July to manage the Dodgers' arch enemies, the New York Giants. (This came about simply because the Giants' owner, Horace Stoneham, was impatient with Mel Ott as manager and when he went to negotiate with Branch Rickey of the Dodgers about hiring Burt Shotton, Rickey, equally frustrated by Durocher, offered to sign over 'The Lip.') Burt Shotton, who had filled in for Durocher in 1947, took over the Dodgers, while Mel Ott was 'kicked upstairs' to the Giants' front office. In any case, neither team gained much from such diversionary tactics. Instead, the Boston Braves – a team almost forgotten by baseball fans, since it had not won a pennant in 34 years – ended up in first place in the National League. Although the Braves had some fairly solid hitters in such as Eddy Stanky, everyone agreed that they owed most to the superlative pitching of Johnny Sain (who won 24 games) and Warren Spahn (the future Hall of Famer); as a ditty of the day went, 'Spahn and Sain/Then pray for rain.'

In the end, though, the Braves didn't have enough depth and they lost the World Series to the Indians, four games to two. But Warren Spahn would go on to play many more seasons and victories, as would another National Leaguer who enjoyed a banner year in 1948, Stan Musial. Musial had the best season of his 22-year career, leading the league in eight categories and falling just one short of that year's league home run record of 40, set by Ralph Kiner and Johnny Mize.

OPPOSITE: *Larry Doby of the Cleveland Indians was the first black player in the American League. This great outfielder played in the league from 1947 to 1959.*

ABOVE: *Managers Burt Shotten (left) of the Dodgers and Mel Ott of the Giants.*

RIGHT: *The legendary Hall of Fame pitcher Satchel Paige.*

RIGHT: *Lou Boudreau while he was with the Cleveland Indians. Boudreau, who was elected to the Hall of Fame in 1970, was the shortstop for the Indians (1938-50) and the Red Sox (1951-52). He also was the player-manager of the Indians from 1942 to 1950, the manager and sometimes player of the Red Sox (1952-54) and the manager of the Kansas City Athletics (1955-57) and the Cubs (1960). He later became the broadcaster of the Cubs' games.*

OPPOSITE: *Hall of Famer Roy Campanella caught for the Dodgers (1948-57), hit 242 home runs and batted in 856 runs in those nine years.*

The Red Sox might have figured to come back and take the pennant in 1949 – often the way with a second-place team the following year – and indeed, coming into the final weekend with a two-game series against the Yankees, the Red Sox held first place. But the Red Sox lost both of those games, and the Yankees once again came up with the pennant. These Yankees were a mixture of some veteran talents – Joe DiMaggio and Yogi Berra (although both missed much of the season to injuries) Tommy Henrich and Phil Rizzuto – and some new faces: Hank Bauer, Jerry Coleman, Bobby Brown. But the man who was both an old veteran of the baseball wars and the freshest Yankee ever was their new manager, Charles Dillon 'Casey' Stengel. He had played with National League teams from 1912 to 1925 and then managed Dodgers and Braves teams in the 1930s, but nothing had prepared the baseball world for his phenomenal success as the manager of the Yankees in the years ahead.

His first test came in the 1949 World Series, in which the Yankees came up against their old rivals, the Dodgers. The Dodgers now had three black players – Roy Campanella and Don Newcombe, in addition to Robinson – who joined such stalwarts as Pee Wee Reese, Gil Hodges, Duke Snider and Carl Furillo to start a dynasty that would continue to challenge the Yankees. These '49 Dodgers had only taken the pennant by winning in the tenth inning of the season's last game and thus edging out the Cardinals. The Dodgers won the first and fifth games of the World Series, but with fine pitching from Allie Reynolds, Eddie Lopat and reliever Joe Page, the Yankees took the four they needed to win the Series.

In the 1940s Americans had survived the greatest war in history. The major leagues had stifled the challenge of a Mexican league (and all defecting players were accepted back in 1949). Now organized baseball faced only two threats: the Yankees and the Dodgers.

The Fifties:
Tradition and Change

After the euphoria that followed the end of World War II, Americans turned some of their pent-up energies and enthusiasm onto all kinds of activities, including major-league baseball. But in the 1950s, several new forces would be at work that would eventually change the relationships between Americans and many of their pastimes such as baseball. One of the most obvious of these new forces was television, which would profoundly affect the ways Americans looked at sporting events and simultaneously change the ways these sports were financed. Teams, for instance, that had depended largely on the support of the home city and the immediate region would now find themselves competing for a national audience; this would both stimulate new interest in baseball throughout the country and free the teams from total dependence on ticket sales. The upshot of such changes was that the major-league clubs no longer felt they were so confined to their traditional hometowns: the 1950s would witness the first shifts since the two leagues had divided up the territory early in the century. And perhaps a harbinger of this new attitude came when the owners of the major-league clubs refused to renew the contract of Happy Chandler, Baseball Commissioner since 1945. Instead the owners gave a three-year contract, starting in 1951, to Ford Frick, President of the National League; it was no secret that the owners wanted to change the autocratic nature of the commissioner's office. Another sign of the changing times was that Cornelius McGillicuddy, otherwise known as Connie Mack, retired at the end of the 1950 season after managing the Philadelphia Athletics for fifty consecutive years – a record that just in its naming evokes an almost ancient era.

ABOVE: *Carl Furillo was a Dodger outfielder from 1946 to 1960. 'Skoonj' or 'The Reading Rifle' hit .299 during his career.*

LEFT: *Ford Frick, the president of the National League.*

OPPOSITE TOP: *Charles Dillon 'Casey' Stengel when he was manager of the Yankees. From 1949 to 1960, 'The Old Professor' won ten pennants and seven World Series. He had been the manager of both the Dodgers and the Braves and went on to become the manager of the new-born Mets.*

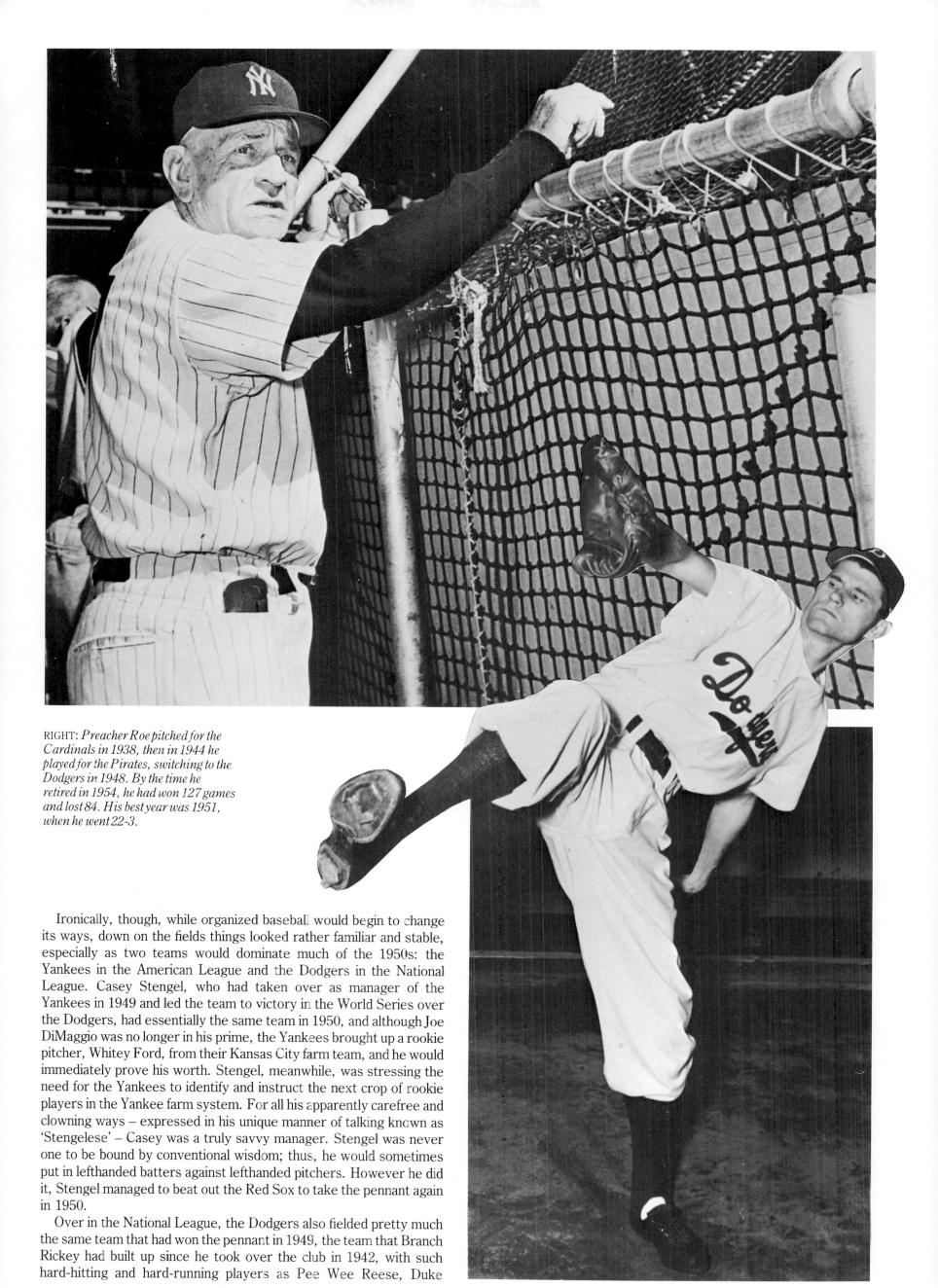

RIGHT: *Preacher Roe pitched for the Cardinals in 1938, then in 1944 he played for the Pirates, switching to the Dodgers in 1948. By the time he retired in 1954, he had won 127 games and lost 84. His best year was 1951, when he went 22-3.*

Ironically, though, while organized baseball would begin to change its ways, down on the fields things looked rather familiar and stable, especially as two teams would dominate much of the 1950s: the Yankees in the American League and the Dodgers in the National League. Casey Stengel, who had taken over as manager of the Yankees in 1949 and led the team to victory in the World Series over the Dodgers, had essentially the same team in 1950, and although Joe DiMaggio was no longer in his prime, the Yankees brought up a rookie pitcher, Whitey Ford, from their Kansas City farm team, and he would immediately prove his worth. Stengel, meanwhile, was stressing the need for the Yankees to identify and instruct the next crop of rookie players in the Yankee farm system. For all his apparently carefree and clowning ways – expressed in his unique manner of talking known as 'Stengelese' – Casey was a truly savvy manager. Stengel was never one to be bound by conventional wisdom; thus, he would sometimes put in lefthanded batters against lefthanded pitchers. However he did it, Stengel managed to beat out the Red Sox to take the pennant again in 1950.

Over in the National League, the Dodgers also fielded pretty much the same team that had won the pennant in 1949, the team that Branch Rickey had built up since he took over the club in 1942, with such hard-hitting and hard-running players as Pee Wee Reese, Duke

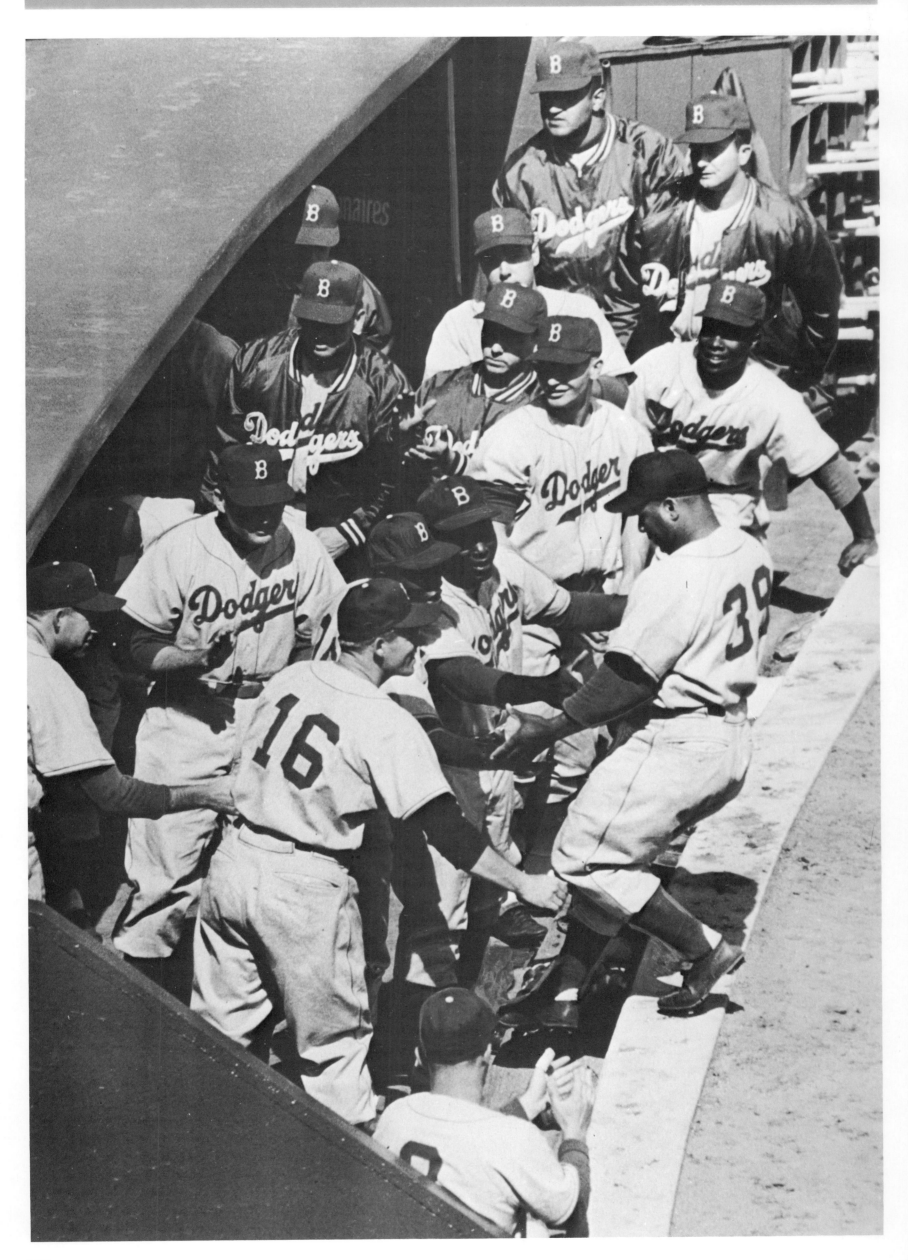

Snider, Jackie Robinson, Gil Hodges, Roy Campanella and Carl Furillo. But as it happened, the Dodgers came up against the so-called Whiz Kids of 1950, the Phillies, a team that had been built up in the previous few years by its new owner, a Delaware millionaire, Robert Carpenter. Led by the pitching of Robin Roberts, Curt Simmons and Jim Konstanty, the Phillies held first place with only 11 games left to play. Then the fizz went out of the kids and they lost 8 of 10 of these, and as the chance of scheduling had it, they came into the last game of the season against the Dodgers and needing a win to take first place. Robin Roberts, starting his third game in five days, went up against Brooklyn's ace, Don Newcombe, and through nine innings the teams battled to a 1-1 draw. Then, in the 10th inning, the Phillies' Dick Sisler, son of the great George Sisler, blasted a three-run homer to give the Phillies their first pennant since 1915.

After that, the World Series was bound to be something of an anticlimax, as it definitely was for the Phillies, who lost four straight to the Yankees. But it was hardly an overwhelming display of Yankee power: the Phillies lost the first three games by only one run each – 1-0, 2-1, 3-2 – and the fourth game only by a 5-2 margin.

In 1951 the Yankees once again took the American League pennant – their third straight – clinched by Allie Reynolds' second no-hitter of the season. But 1951 would go down in Yankee history as one of those pivotal years, as it was Joe DiMaggio's final season and Mickey Mantle's first (Mantle having been called up during the season from a Yankee farm team). At least as much excitement was caused by another Yankee rookie in 1951, Gil McDougald, who would end up leading the team in batting with his .306 average and then go on to become the only rookie to hit a grand slam home run in the World Series. Joe DiMaggio tied another record by becoming the first player since Babe Ruth to play in 10 World Series.

In the National League, another rookie came up from another farm club (Minneapolis), and would go on to become one of the all-time great players, noted not only for his hitting but for his fielding and base-running. Willie Mays joined the Giants in May, spearheading the team's rush to the finish line against the Dodgers. By 9 September the Dodgers' lead was cut to five and a half, but as the Dodgers lost six of

ABOVE: *Yankee manager Casey Stengel (left) and Yankee vice-president Dell Webb (right) bid farewell to Joe DiMaggio on his retirement in 1951.*

RIGHT: *Mickey Mantle took over where Joe DiMaggio had left off. He played outfield for the Yankees from 1951 to 1968, batting .298 and hitting 536 home runs. Mantle was elected to the Hall of Fame in 1974.*

OPPOSITE: *The Dodgers greet Roy Campanella after one of his towering home runs.*

their final 10 games and the Giants won 16 of their final 20, they ended up in a dead heat. The teams then went into a best-of-three playoff, and the Giants took the first game, 3-1, but the Dodgers came back and took the second, 10-0. In the deciding game, the Dodgers went into the bottom of the ninth with a comfortable 4-1 lead; with Don Newcombe on the mound, the Giants' dash for glory seemed about to end. Then Alvin Dark singled, Don Mueller singled, Monte Irvin pop-fouled out, and Whitey Lockman doubled, driving Dark home and putting the tying runs on second and third. Ralph Branca came in to relieve Newcombe and found himself facing Bobby Thomson, a respectable but hardly powerful batter. Thomson took a called strike on the first pitch, then sent the second one into the left field stands to give the Giants the game and the pennant – and baseball fans one of the most-often recalled moments in the history of baseball.

But after that the Giants seemed to run out of steam, and although they beat the Yankees in two out of the first three World Series games, the Yankees pulled themselves together and went on to take the next three to clinch their third consecutive World Championship.

BELOW: *Willie Mays turns on the speed and scores. The Hall of Fame outfielder played for 22 years, batting .302, with 660 home runs, 338 stolen bases and a .557 slugging average.*

RIGHT: *Alvin Dark played mainly shortstop for the Braves (1946-49), the Giants (1950-56), the Cardinals (1956-58), the Cubs (1958-60) and the Braves (1960), hitting .289.*

ABOVE: *Bobby Thomson hits his 'shot heard round the world' – the home run that won the National League playoff for the Giants over the Dodgers in 1951.*

RIGHT: *Allie 'Superchief' Reynolds pitched for the Indians (1942-46) and the Yankees (1947-54). He had a lifetime winning percentage of .630, but in the World Series he was almost unbeatable. In six Series he won seven and lost two, for a .778 percentage. His best year was his last year, when he went 13 and 4 for a .765 percentage.*

Players in the Service,
Teams on the Move

If professional baseball needed any reminder that it was not totally divorced from forces in the world beyond it, this came in 1952. War had broken out in distant Korea in June 1950 and at first only America's regular forces had participated, but as the war dragged on increasing numbers of American men found themselves called up either through their reserve units or by a draft. Professional sports figures were not exempt, and by 1952, many baseball players were in uniform – Whitey Ford, the Yankee pitcher, and Don Newcombe, the Dodger pitcher, being only two among the many. One of the more dramatic departures came on 30 April 1952, when Ted Williams, in his final game before he was to go off to Korea as a Marine Corps jet pilot, hit a game-winning two-run homer. Meanwhile, the Giants had been holding the lead in the National League, but when Willie Mays was drafted on 29 May, the team lost 8 of the next 10 games and never could recover.

The fact is that all teams lost players. But although the Dodgers lost Newcombe, they came up with a rookie knuckleballer, Hoyt Wilhelm, who would pitch 1070 games over the next 21 years, and they also had a rookie relief pitcher, Joe Black, whose 1952 season saw him with a 15-4 record plus another 15 saves. It was in 1952 that the Dodgers set a modern major-league record by scoring 15 runs in the first inning of a game, against the Reds; and Dodger pitcher Carl Erskine missed a perfect game by giving up one walk to the opposing pitcher, Willard Ramsdell of the Cubs. Still, the Dodgers managed to take the pennant in 1952, only to come up against their old nemesis, the Yankees.

The Yankees, despite losing several solid players to the draft, still had the 20-year-old switch-hitter, Mickey Mantle, and his .311 batting

RIGHT: *Carl Erskine pitched for the Dodgers from 1948 to 1959, moving with them from Brooklyn to Los Angeles. He led the league in pitching in 1953, with a 20 and 6 mark for a .769 percentage.*

OPPOSITE: *Phil Rizzuto (left) and Billy Martin polish up their techniques of reeling off twin killings during a Yankee infield practice session.*

FAR RIGHT: *Edwin Donald 'Duke' Snider, also known as 'The Silver Fox,' played outfield for the Dodgers (1947-62), the Mets (1963) and the Giants (1964). This Hall of Famer's batting average was .297 and he hit 407 homers.*

ABOVE: *Mickey Mantle scores on a slide.*

LEFT: *Hall of Famer Warren Edward Spahn pitched for the Braves from 1942 to 1964 – first in Boston and then in Milwaukee – before spending 1965 with the Giants. He won 363 games and had an ERA of 3.09.*

TOP LEFT: *Edwin Lee 'Eddie' Mathews played third base for the Braves in Boston and Milwaukee (1952-65) and then went with them to Atlanta (1966). The Hall of Famer went to Houston in 1967 and then switched to the American League, playing for the Tigers (1967-68), hitting 512 home runs with a .271 batting average.*

average and 23 homers helped spark the team, although they nosed out the Cleveland Indians by only two games. In the World Series the Dodgers put up a stiff fight, taking the Yankees to seven games, but a Mantle homer clinched the final game, 4-2, and the Yankees had their fourth consecutive World Championship.

1953 was marked by the first of the various franchise shifts that would change the map of organized baseball in America. The Boston Braves, having dropped from their peak attendance of 1,455,439 in their pennant-winning season of 1948, to 281,000 in 1952, were moved to Milwaukee in 1953. There attendance jumped to 302,667 for the first 13 home games. The 1953 total would be 1,826,397, and for four years, 1954-57, Milwaukee home attendance would top two million. Other club owners could see the effect of such a move as quickly as anyone. And not only did the move boost the Braves' attendance, it lifted them from near-bottom in the league to first or second place from 13 May on. Warren Spahn had a 23-7 year with a 2.10 ERA; on 25 May, Braves righthander Max Surkant struck out eight consecutive batters for a modern record; Eddie Mathews hit 47 homers to lead the league; and Lew Burdette pitched for 15 wins. In the end, though, the Braves couldn't match the experienced Dodgers, who won the pennant with a 13-game lead.

In the American League, despite Ted Williams' return to the Red Sox lineup on 6 August – and his subsequent 13 homers with a .407 average – the Yankees won yet again. With Mickey Mantle now beginning to hit his stride, the Yankees at one point had an 18-game winning streak and they ended up with an eight and a half game lead over the Cleveland Indians. In the Series the Yankees won four games to two, but some Dodgers set personal records: Gil Hodges hit .364 for the Series while Carl Erskine struck out 14 Yankees in the third game, a new Series record. The most exciting moment came in the sixth game, bottom of the ninth when the score was tied at three all; Billy Martin – later to be known for his highjinks as a Yankee manager – singled home Hank Bauer for the tie-breaking run, the game and the Series.

When the 1953 season ended on the field, there were two significant developments elsewhere. Charlie Dressen, who had managed the Dodgers to two consecutive pennants, tried to force the club to give him a three-year contract; he was dropped, and Walter Alston, manager of the Montreal (International League) farm club, came up to the first of his 23 years with the Dodgers. And Bill Veeck, after his first three seasons as owner of the St Louis Browns, faced such financial problems that he got permission to sell his franchise to a syndicate that moved the team to Baltimore, where the team appeared in 1954 as the Orioles. Definitely, the major leagues were on the move.

New Cities, Old Rivalries

By the start of the 1954 season, virtually all the ballplayers who had gone into the military for the Korean War were back with their teams and with no apparent loss of skill. Willie Mays, for instance, returned with the Giants and hit 41 homers, batted in 110 runs and led the league with his .345 average, all of which won him the National League's Most Valuable Player Award and not coincidentally helped the Giants take the pennant, beating out the Dodgers by five games. Obviously Mays didn't do it all by himself; teammate Don Mueller had a batting average second only to Mays' in the league, while Johnny Antonelli pitched away to end up with a 21-7 season. Other National League players who would remember 1954 included Stan Musial, who set a new major-league record by hitting five homers for the Cardinals in a doubleheader; Joe Adcock of the Braves, who tied a record by hitting four homers in one game; and a player who hit his first homer in the majors on 23 April but would go on to hit quite a few more – Henry Aaron.

In the American League, the Orioles began their new existence with a spectacular opening day parade – graced by the presence of then Vice-President Richard M Nixon – and then went on to lose the first of 100 games they dropped in 1954. The Yankees, on the other hand, won 103 – more than they ever had before under Casey Stengel. But as it happened, the Cleveland Indians were winning 111, thus beating out not only the 1954 Yankees but also the 1927 Yankees, which had held the American League's record of 110 games won in a season. The Indians were managed by Al Lopez (who had played under Stengel in the National League back in the 1930s), and he relied less on the

ABOVE: *Hall of Famer Bob Lemon pitched for the Indians from 1941 to 1958, with three years out for service. He ended his career with 207 wins and 128 losses. Three times he led the American League in wins.*

LEFT: *Pee Wee Reese forces Willie Mays at second and gets his throw off in midair to complete the double play.*

OPPOSITE TOP: *Vice-President Richard N Nixon throws out the first ball at the Orioles' opener in 1954.*

OPPOSITE BOTTOM: *Joseph Wilbur Adcock played outfield and first base for 17 years in the majors – with the Reds (1950-52), the Braves (1953-62), the Indians (1963), the Dodgers (1964) and the Angels (1965-66). He hit 336 homers and had a .277 batting average. He also managed Cleveland in 1967, coming in eighth.*

LEFT: *Al Rosen played mainly third base from 1947 to 1956 with the Cleveland Indians, batting .285 and hitting 192 home runs. He led the league in homers in 1950 and 1953, banging out 37 and 43 respectively. He also led the league in RBI's in 1952, with 105, and in 1953, with a phenomenal 145.*

OPPOSITE TOP: *Hall of Fame catcher Lawrence Peter 'Yogi' Berra played for the Yankees from 1946 to 1963, ending his career with the Mets in 1965. He hit .285 while knocking 358 home runs. He later became a manager of both the Yankees and the Mets, winning pennants in both leagues.*

OPPOSITE BOTTOM: *Ted Kluszewski of the Reds is welcomed at the plate after his 14th home run of the 1955 season by (left to right) outfielder Wally Post, catcher Wes Westrum and the batbay. Ted ended up with 17 homers that year – his second best.*

respectable hitting of such as Al Rosen and Bobby Avila than on the superb pitching of Bob Lemon and Early Wynn, both with 23 victories, and the solid pitching of Mike Garcia (19-8) and now aging Bob Feller (13-3).

In the 1954 World Series, although the Indians were favored to beat the Giants, the Giants took the Series in four straight games, ending the American League's seven-year dominance of the Series. Undoubtedly the most inspiring and unforgettable play of the Series came in the first game in the top of the eighth, with the score tied at two all. Vic Wertz, who was to prove to be the Indians' best hitter for the

Series, came to bat with two runners on and slammed one way out across center field. Willie Mays simply turned and dashed and then at the last second caught the ball as it came across his left shoulder at about the 440 foot mark and just as he appeared to go crashing into the barrier. The fans, and the Indians, would never forget that spectacular catch.

The 1954 Series happened to be played in the two largest stadiums of both leagues, the Giants' Polo Grounds and the Cleveland Municipal Stadium. The attendance record for four games (251,507) inevitably reminded the club owners of the money that was to be made, or lost,

from ticket sales (as television was yet to come up with the astronomical sums it would eventually pay the leagues). One team in particular had to take notice, the once-proud Philadelphia Athletics, who had been slipping drastically in standings, attendance and receipts. The Athletics were still owned by Connie Mack's sons, but in 1954 they sold out to Arnold Johnson, who moved the franchise to Kansas City, Missouri, where none other than the 92-year-old Connie Mack appeared for the opening home game of the 1955 season. Although Lou Boudreau, the Athletics' new manager, could only get the team to finish sixth in 1955, it was at least a start.

The American League's pennant race in 1955 was a fairly close one among four teams – the Yankees, Indians, White Sox and Red Sox – but despite some heroic pitching for the Indians by Herb Score, the Yankees finally took the pennant, at one point winning 15 games in a row. In the National League the pennant race was anything except close: the Dodgers won 22 of their first 24 games and by the end of the first month of the season had a nine and a half game lead. The Dodgers never lost first place and clinched the pennant by 8 September, the earliest date in National League history.

So it was that for the third time in four years, the Dodgers found themselves confronting the Yankees in the World Series; the Dodgers had lost to them in 1952 and 1953 – indeed, they had yet to win a World Series. The exciting Series seesawed back and forth and went into the seventh game. Then in the bottom of the sixth, with the Dodgers leading 2-0 behind the pitching of Johnny Podres, Billy Martin and Gil McDougald got on base and Yogi Berra hit one along the left-field line. Sandy Amoros, who had just been put into left field, went sprinting toward the railing where he managed to snag the ball and relay it to Reese, who in turn snapped it to Gil Hodges at first, where Gil McDougald was caught off base. That did it for the Yankees, and the Dodgers had their first World Championship.

New Talents, Old Talents

Two major developments off the field in 1956 would have far-reaching effects on major-league baseball – one universally praised and the other more controversial. The former was the adoption by the National League of the rule making it compulsory for all their players to wear protective headgear when batting. Although there had been only one fatality in major-league history – Carl Mays' pitch on 16 August 1920 that had killed Cleveland's Ray Chapman – everyone would agree that there was no need to flirt with the odds any longer. The second development came at the end of the 1956 season, when the Major League Baseball Players' Association was formally organized; although there had been previous attempts at 'unionizing' the players, this would become the only one that would produce significant results over the years.

On the field, in the American League's pennant race, the Yankees were in first place by the All-Star Game but right on their heels came the Chicago White Sox. The White Sox were a younger and more aggressive team on the bases than the Yankees, with such players as Luis Aparacio, Minnie Minoso, Jim Rivera, Nellie Fox, Larry Doby and Sherman Lollar. Also in contention this year were the Cleveland Indians, powered by Rocky Colavito, while the Red Sox couldn't be entirely written off so long as Ted Williams continued to hit as he did. (This was also the year that Williams, expressing his contempt for jeering fans, spit in the general direction of the box seats – and was fined $5000.) In the end, though, the Yankees prevailed, led by Mickey Mantle, who now seemed to be in high gear after his first seasons of promise. Mantle ended up 1956 with 53 homers, 130 RBIs

LEFT: *Don Larsen pitched from 1953 to 1967 for nine different teams in both leagues, but is best remembered as a Yankee. He is the only pitcher ever to throw a perfect game in the World Series.*

OPPOSITE: *Rocky Colavito as an Indian. He played for six different teams from 1955 to 1968, hitting 374 homers.*

ABOVE: *The young Henry Aaron. Hank played mainly the outfield for the Braves (1954-74) both in Milwaukee and Atlanta. He went back to Milwaukee to finish his career with the Brewers (1975-76). This Hall of Famer ended up hitting 755 home runs, a record that should last for decades, if not forever, while hitting .305.*

and an average of .353 to lead both major leagues in all three categories, only the fourth time this has been accomplished.

In the National League the race was even tighter, going right down to the last day of the season. In that final game, the Dodgers' Don Newcombe won his 27th of the season (and also became the first winner of a Cy Young Award as the year's best pitcher), and the Dodgers just managed to snatch the pennant away from the second-place Milwaukee Braves. Also threatening in 1956 were the Cincinnati Reds. With such sluggers as Frank Robinson, Ted Kluszewski, Wally Post and Gus Bell, the Reds ended up tying the Giants' major-league record for the club total for home runs with 221.

The World Series thus saw those perennial rivals pitted against each other, the Dodgers and the Yankees, and it took all seven games for the Yankees to emerge on top yet again. But what will always be remembered about the 1956 World Series is the fifth game, when Don Larsen was pitching against the Dodgers' Sal Maglie. It was a scoreless pitchers' duel going into the fourth inning when Mantle hit a homer off Maglie. As the game proceeded, it soon became apparent that Larsen not only had a no-hitter going – he was pitching a perfect game. As he came into the ninth inning, Larsen still had faced only 24 batters.

ABOVE: *Jacob Nelson 'Nellie' Fox, the Hall of Fame second baseman, played for the Athletics (1947-49), the White Sox (1950-63) and the Astros (1964-65). A great fielder, he also led the league in hits four times.*

OPPOSITE: *Lew Burdette pitched from 1950 to 1967, winning 203 games with a 3.66 ERA.*

ABOVE: *Don 'Newk' Newcombe pitched for the Dodgers (1949-58), the Reds (1958-60) and the Indians (1960). He twice led the National League in pitching, in 1955 and 1956.*

RIGHT: *Hall of Famer Frank Robinson played the outfield from 1956 to 1976, but is best remembered for his years with Cincinnati and Baltimore. He was MVP in both leagues and became the first black manager in 1975, with Cleveland.*

Carl Furillo flied out and the excitement grew as Roy Campanella grounded to Billy Martin who threw him out at first. Dale Mitchell then came in as a pinch hitter for Maglie. Larsen worked him to a 1-2 count; on the next pitch, Mitchell began to swing and checked it, but umpire Babe Pinelli called a strike (although many spectators would agree that this was a generous interpretation). Don Larsen had pitched the first and only perfect game in the history of the World Series.

1957 was a classic instance of the 'Wait till next year!' aspect of baseball. The Braves, who had lost to the Dodgers in 1956, came back to take first place in the National League. The Dodgers, in fact, had to settle for third, with the Cardinals coming in second. The Braves, who had only been in Milwaukee five years, had assembled an impressive team. There was the veteran pitcher Warren Spahn, who got his eighth 20-game season, and two other solid pitchers, Lew Burdette and Bob Buhl. For hitting, the Braves could come up with old reliables such as Red Schoendienst and Joe Adcock, and the newer talents of Eddie Mathews and Henry Aaron. Aaron's 44 homers, 132 RBIs and average of .322 were good enough to earn him the league's Most

Valuable Player Award.

In the American League, the Yankees seemed in serious trouble during the early weeks, but by 30 June they had pulled themselves into first place, with their chief threat coming from the Cleveland Indians. One of the sad moments in baseball history came, by chance, in the Yankees-Indians game on 7 May 1957, when the Indians' promising young pitcher, Herb Score, was struck in the right eye by a line drive from Gil McDougald. Although Score would eventually return to baseball, he never showed the stuff that had gained him 16 wins in his first year and 20 in his second.

In the World Series, it was the experienced Yankees against the upstart new team, the Braves. The Series went back and forth into the seventh game (for the third consecutive year), but thanks in large part to the superb pitching of Lew Burdette – who won three games, two of them shutouts – the Braves became the World Champions. But in case anyone thought the veterans were all washed up, Stan Musial took his seventh National League batting title with .351 while Ted Williams won the American League's with .388.

The Minor and Farm Leagues

The story of 'the natural' – the isolated and untutored farmboy who is discovered accidentally and can pitch or hit better than any pro – is fun and may have occurred a few times in the history of organized baseball, but it is hardly sufficient to explain how the major-league teams obtain the steady stream of young players they need, year in and year out. And from the very beginnings of the major leagues, the main tributary has been 'the minors.' Like so much with the sport of baseball, the minor leagues did not develop according to any master plan: they were simply the teams that did not make it into the major leagues. By and large they were teams in smaller cities and particularly those cities outside the northeast quarter of the United States where the two major leagues were first based. Over the decades, of course, many new minor-league teams have been formed, but meanwhile they have also all been evolving in their relationship to the major-league teams. At first, the minor-league teams were totally independent clubs whose players would be under contract to them; to obtain these players, the major-league teams had to negotiate with the minor-league teams. Gradually, more and more of the minor-league teams came to be bought outright by the major-league teams, or at least to have a working agreement under which the major-league team gave some support in return for top priority in acquiring players. And it is because of this that the minor leagues have come to be regarded as 'farm teams,' nurturing the young talents for the great harvest of the major leagues.

The individual usually credited for first recognizing the value of the minor leagues as a resource for the majors is Branch Rickey, who as

LEFT: *A jubilant Casey Stengel, manager of the Oakland Oaks, during the 1948 victory parade celebrating his team's first place finish in the Pacific Coast League after rolling up a 114-74 record and winning the playoffs.*

OPPOSITE TOP: *Branch Rickey, the baseball genius who invented the modern baseball farm system.*

OPPOSITE BOTTOM: *Jackie Robinson gets to second base safely when he played for the Montreal Royals in a game with the Havana Cubans in the International Association.*

BELOW: *The Oakland Oaks Pacific Coast League team of 1948. Top row: Cookie Lavagetto (second from left), Ernie Lombardi (seventh from left). Middle row: Casey Stengel (fifth from left). Bottom row: George Metkovich (second from left), Billy Martin (fourth from left).*

ABOVE LEFT: *University of Texas standout pitcher Roger Clemens made it to the Red Sox after two years in professional baseball.*

ABOVE: *John Fishel (#12), the third baseman-outfielder from Fullerton State who was MVP of the 1984 College World Series, gets a 'high-five' from a teammate.*

LEFT: *An exciting moment from an Oneonta Yankees game in the Eastern League.*

the general manager of the St Louis Cardinals in the 1920s and 1930s began to seek out young raw talent, sign them on with fairly cheap contracts, and then place them on minor-league teams until they were ready to come up to the Cardinals or to be sold to other teams. As other major-league teams realized what was going on, they, too, began to purchase or start minor-league teams where they could 'season' their own young discoveries (or 'send down' players who for

whatever reason didn't seem to be doing that well in the majors).

The minor leagues were at one time divided into seven classes, but in 1963 they were reorganized into four: AAA (or Triple A), AA (Double A), A and Rookie (limited to players in their first or second season of professional play). And by the 1970s, the many minor-league teams were organized into various leagues: Class AAA has the International, Pacific Coast, American Association and Mexican; Class AA

LEFT: *An exciting moment in a 1983 American Association game. Joe Carter clouts one for the Iowa Cubs as Carmelo Martinez waits on deck.*

BELOW LEFT: *A Denver Zephyrs' hitter takes a swing during a 1985 American Association game with the Omaha Royals.*

BELOW: *John 'Boog' Powell, when he played for the Rochester Red Wings in the International Association. He went on to become a star outfielder for Baltimore (1961-74), Cleveland (1975-76) and Los Angeles (1977), hitting 339 home runs.*

BELOW: *Keith Moreland, former All-American third baseman at the University of Texas, is now a star for the Chicago Cubs.*

has Eastern, Southern and Texas; Class A has California, Carolina, Florida State, Western Carolina, Northwest, Midwest, New York-Pennsylvania and three Mexican leagues; while the Rookie leagues are the Appalachian, Gulf Coast and Pioneer. Note that there are minor-league teams in Canada and Mexico; there had also once been such teams in Cuba, but these were expelled when the United States broke off diplomatic relations with Cuba in 1961. All this organizing and classifying has been intended to make sure that young players get a chance to compete at their own level yet also to move up (and it also has to do with controlling the salaries). Each season, teams are allowed to 'draft' players from the class below, and the major-league teams are also allowed to 'bring up' players at set times in the year.

The minor leagues enjoyed their heyday in the 1930s and 1940s, by which time there were some 60 leagues with teams in over 400 cities in the USA, Canada, Mexico and Cuba. But in the 1950s they went into decline, until in the 1980s there are only about 100 teams. The televised broadcasts of so many major-league games and the expansion of the major leagues across North America (from 16 teams in 1960 to 26 by 1977) contributed to this decline. In addition, it became increasingly expensive to operate a minor-league team and young men were no longer so willing to put in the time in such low-paid jobs.

But if the minor leagues went into decline, another 'tributary' for the major leagues has emerged in the 1970s and 1980s – college baseball teams. For long all but ignored as a sport at colleges and universities, where hundreds of thousands of fans turned out each season for football and basketball games, college and university baseball teams have begun to attract increasing numbers of serious players and spectators – and scouts from the major-league teams. Especially in the south and southwest, where the climate allows virtually year-round time for training and playing, these college teams have begun to replace the minors as nurturing grounds for professional players. In 1947 the National Collegiate Athletic Association established a 'World Series' for college baseball teams (and it is now televised nationally); and since 1963, organized baseball has supported summer leagues for promising college undergraduates.

One way or another, the major leagues are going to make sure that if there are promising 'naturals' out there, they must first perspire a bit before becoming inspired superstars.

Perfect Climax to a Decade

Major-league baseball had been enjoying a renaissance by the late fifties, at least as measured by the record-breaking numbers of fans showing up at the ball parks. Nowhere was this more true than in the new host cities, Baltimore, Kansas City and Milwaukee: the Braves, for instance, led the league in attendance in 1957. Television, meanwhile, had created a continental-wide new public, while airplanes had done away with the excuse that the transcontinental distances were too great for teams to traverse during a season. It was only a matter of time, then, before the major leagues would have to consider expanding to the West Coast – and that is just what happened with the end of the 1957 season. First the Giants announced they were going to leave New York City for San Francisco, then the Dodgers announced they were leaving Brooklyn for Los Angeles. Their excuses were, respectively, declining attendance and inadequate facilities, but there was no hiding the simple fact that the club owners were eyeing greener-backed publics. (Asked if he didn't feel badly about taking the Giants away from New York kids, the club president Horace Stoneham retorted, 'I feel bad about the kids, but I haven't seen too many of their fathers lately.')

But if the Dodgers expected to rise to new heights with their move, they were immediately disappointed (justly punished, some of their angry fans in Brooklyn contended) by plunging into seventh place in 1958, only two games out of last. The Giants managed a bit better, coming in third, despite the fine performances by veteran Willie Mays and rookie Orlando Cepeda. The Pirates took over second place, while in first for the second year running were the Braves, thanks once again

ABOVE: *Orlando Cepeda played first base for the Giants (1958-66), the Cardinals (1966-68), the Braves (1969-72), the A's (1972), the Red Sox (1973) and the Royals (1974), with 379 homers and a .297 average.*

BELOW: *New York fans chase their Giants into the clubhouse after the game of 30 September 1957 as the Pirates trot up the steps at left. This was the Giants' last appearance at the Polo Grounds.*

to the 20-game seasons of Warren Spahn and Lew Burdette.

In the American League's pennant race, the Yankees won for the fourth straight year (their ninth in ten years). Ten games behind were the White Sox, with their heavy-hitting Rocky Colavito tying a record by hitting four homers in four consecutive times at bat on 10 June 1958. But it was the 40-year-old Ted Williams who took the league's batting crown, his sixth, with his .328 average (and beat out his own record as the oldest player to take the crown). The Yankees thus went into the World Series to meet their opponent of the previous year, the Braves, and this time the Braves worked up a lead of three games to one that must have moved all the smart money to the Braves again. But Gil McDougald came through with homers in the fifth and sixth games to give the Yankees two wins, and in the seventh game Bill Skowron hit a three-run homer that clinched the game and the Series for the Yankees.

But the Yankees could not maintain the pace in 1959, probably to the good of the game – for some people were really beginning to believe that the Yankees were just too 'damned' good to be explained by natural means – and the American League's pennant race ended up between the White Sox and the Indians. The White Sox were managed

OPPOSITE: *Bill Skowron played first base for 14 years in the majors – nine of them with the Yankees. He carried a .282 batting average and a .459 slugging average.*

RIGHT: *Richie Ashburn played the outfield for 15 years, batting .308.*

BELOW: *Harvey 'The Kitten' Haddix pitched for 14 years in the big leagues, winning 136 games with a 3.63 ERA.*

by Al Lopez, who had as it chanced once managed the Indians. Combining solid pitching, speedy base-running and a tight defense, the White Sox beat out the Indians by five games. The National League had a three-way race among the Giants, Braves and Dodgers; the Giants took a two-game lead into the final week, but came out of the last day to see a tie between the Dodgers and Braves, who went into the third pennant playoff in National League history. The Dodgers then took the first two games and won the playoffs and pennant.

In the 1959 World Series, the Dodgers beat the White Sox, four games to two, and broke all attendance records for single Series games, with 92,796 at the third game in the Los Angeles Coliseum. But the real record-breaker of 1959 came on 29 May when Harvey Haddix was pitching for the Pirates against Lew Burdette of the Braves. With the likes of Aaron, Mathews and Adcock, the Braves were regarded as the hardest hitting team in the majors, while Haddix had only a mediocre record after 14 years in the majors. Yet somehow Haddix managed to retire the 27 Braves he faced in nine innings. Because his teammates couldn't score against Burdette, however, the

game went into extra innings – in which Haddix continued to set the Braves down, 1, 2, 3, for three more innings. Then, in the 13th, the Pirates' third baseman, Don Hoak, made a bad throw after fielding a grounder by Felix Mantilla. Mantilla moved to second on a sacrifice by Mathews, Aaron was given a walk, and Joe Adcock proceeded to hit a home run: there went Haddix's 12 innings of perfect pitching, his no-hitter and the ballgame (which because of some confused base-running ended up with two runs voided and the score 1-0, in favor of Braves).

But if this was a personal disaster for Harvey Haddix, major-league baseball came out of the fifties stronger than ever. So strong that a group of men decided to try to get a piece of the action by forming a third league, the Continental. Although they failed in their immediate aim, they ended up forcing the two major leagues to expand in the 1960s. And when the Boston Red Sox finally hired their first black player, Elijah 'Pumpsie' Green in 1959, it meant that all the teams in the majors had at last integrated since Jackie Robinson joined the Dodgers in April 1947. Now it was on to the sixties.

PART IV
The Game Goes On
Since 1960

The 1960s Commence with a Bang

The 1960s would prove to be one of the most tumultuous and divisive decades in American history – what with the assassination of President Kennedy and other major public figures and the violence that attended the Vietnam War abroad and at home – yet in most respects organized baseball remained isolated from these all-but devastating forces. Whether it is because baseball is too removed from reality or just plain resilient might be debated; perhaps it is one of the functions of sports to remain an island of stability when society around it is in turmoil.

In any case, the traditions of baseball held steady as the 1960s began. Ted Williams took over third place, from Mel Ott, in career home runs with his 512th. Williams continued to fire away throughout 1960 but when he hit his 29th of the season in the next-to-last game, he chose to make that his last at-bat and retired with his career of 521 homers. But there were powerful young hitters coming up now – Mickey Mantle with the Yankees and Henry Aaron with the Milwaukee Braves. Veteran Warren Spahn continued to pitch away for the Milwaukee Braves, while 1960 was also the year that the young Sandy Koufax, pitching for the Dodgers, began to gain control of his game.

In the end, the Yankees took the American League pennant for Casey Stengel's 10th win in 12 years with the team (tying him with John McGraw's record for the most league championships). Over in the National League, the Pittsburgh Pirates surprised everyone except their loyal fans by beating out the Braves and the Dodgers to take the pennant. But only their most die-hard fans probably gave them a chance in the Series. Here were the Yankees, veterans of more

OPPOSITE TOP: *The big righthander Ralph Terry pitched for about half of his 12-year career for the Yankees, appearing in a New York uniform for five consecutive Series. During the 1960 World Series Terry served up the fateful pitch that Pirate Bill Mazeroski belted over the fence.*

OPPOSITE BOTTOM: *Bill Mazeroski jubilantly crosses the plate after slamming the home run that won the 1960 World Series for the Pirates.*

ABOVE: *Elston Howard, the first black player drafted by the Yankees, played outfield, then catcher, for them from 1955 until 1967, ending his career with the Red Sox the following year. Howard's 14-year career included ten World Series.*

RIGHT: *Righthander Camilo Pascual led the league in strikeouts for three consecutive seasons, beginning in 1960. Pascual turned in 20-win seasons for the Twins in 1962 and 1963.*

World Series than the rest of the majors cared to think about. And the Pirates hadn't appeared in a Series since 1927, when they had been defeated four straight by – who else – the Yankees. And when it came to simple statistics, the Yankees apparently did win the 1960 Series: getting 91 hits to the Pirates' 60; scoring 55 runs to the Pirates' 27; batting .338 to the Pirates' .256.

But games are played on the field, not in the record books, and the Pirates took the Yankees into the seventh game, where in the ninth inning one of the Grand Eternals of Baseball occurred. The Pirates had taken a 9-7 lead into the ninth, but the Yankees managed to get two runs and tie it up. Ralph Terry was pitching for the Yankees when the Pirates led off the bottom of the ninth with Bill Mazeroski, a respectable but hardly record-setting hitter. He went for Terry's high fast ball and sent it over the left-field fence of Forbes Field – winning the game, the Series and immortality. (And costing Casey Stengel his job as manager of the Yankees.)

The 1961 season was a turning point in modern major-league base-ball, for it saw the first expansion in the number of teams in a league since they were fixed at eight in 1901. The pressures to expand were several: for one, the population of America was not only growing larger, a greater percentage of Americans were living in the West and the Southwest. And although television was allowing people to stay home and look at sporting events, it was also creating a new public. The more immediate pressure had come from the threat of a third league, the Continental, in 1959, which had never got a team on a field, but had shown the two major leagues the handwriting on the wall. In 1961 the Washington Senators moved to Minneapolis and emerged as the Minnesota Twins, while a new franchise took over in Washington and retained the name of Senators. At the same time, a brand new franchise was begun in Los Angeles, the Angels (to become the California Angels in 1966). And in expanding to 10 teams, the American League also added eight games to the season – from 154 to 162. (The National League would follow suit when it expanded in 1962.).

And as it chanced, the 162-game season immediately became controversial, for 1961 was the year that Roger Maris made his assault on Babe Ruth's season record of 60 home runs. Jimmie Foxx and Hank Greenberg had come the closest, with 58, in the 1930s, and now in 1961 both Mickey Mantle and Maris got hot. Mantle got his 54th but then was stifled by injuries; Maris hit his 60th by the 154th game and then got his 61st on the final, or 162nd, game. Maris would be honored, but as with his record in the book, there would always be a qualifying asterisk, for many fans felt that Ruth's record was sacrosanct.

The Yankees, under their new manager, Ralph Houk, dominated the American League in 1961, and went into the Series to face the Cincinnati Reds, who had beat out the Dodgers. But this was the year of the Yankees, who took the Series, four games to one. Yankee pitcher Whitey Ford surpassed Babe Ruth's record of 29 and two-thirds consecutive scoreless innings pitched in the World Series when he picked up where he had left off in 1960 and ended up with 32 consecutive scoreless innings.

ABOVE: *Yankee lefthander Whitey Ford led the league in games won and in winning percentage three times, and twice in games started and innings pitched. After 16 years with the Yankees (1950-67) Ford retired with a career 236-106 record for a spectacular .690 lifetime winning percentage. Winner of ten World* *Series games as well, Ford was elected to the Hall of Fame in 1974.*

BELOW: *Yankee slugger Roger Maris blasts his 61st homer to break Babe Ruth's landmark single-season record of 60 home runs. Maris managed this feat on the last day of the season.*

The Leagues Expand

1962 was the year that the National League fielded its two new teams, the Mets in New York City and the Colt 45s in Houston. (This latter name soon struck everyone as inappropriate and it was changed to the Astros in 1965.) The Mets were managed by none other than Casey Stengel, who had been dropped after the Yankees lost the World Series in 1960, and it did not take the Mets long to become record-breakers: they lost 120 games in their first season, a major-league record that no one intends to emulate. This was somewhat expected from an expansion team, although over in the American League this year, two new teams – the Los Angeles Angels and Minnesota Twins, both playing only their second season – gave the Yankees a run for the pennant of the American League.

The Yankees took the pennant and sat back to wait the results of the three-game playoff series between those arch rivals, the Dodgers and Giants, who had ended the regular season tied for first. They split the first two games, and the Dodgers went into the ninth inning of the third game leading 4-2. First place seemed theirs, but the Giants exploded for four runs and snatched away the pennant. Going into the Series, the Giants and Yankees seemed evenly matched, and they proved to be so by going into seven games. (Along the way, Whitey Ford had his record of consecutive scoreless World Series innings stopped at 33 and two thirds.) Even going into the bottom of the ninth, the Yankees were leading only 1-0 when the Giants got runners on second and third; there were two out when Willie McCovey came to bat to face none other than the same Ralph Terry who only two years earlier had given up that fateful pitch to Mazeroski in a similar situation. McCovey

ABOVE: *Yankee rightfielder Roger Maris poses at bat. Before joining the Yankees in 1960, Maris played for Cleveland and Kansas City. Maris won the MVP Award in 1960 and 1961, and when he batted next to Mickey Mantle in the lineup the 'M&M Boys' were renowned for their brutality to pitchers. Maris ended his 12-year career in 1968 with the St Louis Cardinals.*

LEFT: *Willie Lee 'Stretch' McCovey played first base for the San Francisco Giants from 1959 to 1973 and from 1977 to 1980, playing for San Diego and Oakland in the interim. The big slugger led the league in home runs three times and in RBI's twice.*

OPPOSITE: *Casey Stengel as manager of the rag-tag New York Mets – 'Can't anybody here play this game?' 'The Old Professor' ended his 25-year managerial career in 1965 after four seasons with the Mets.*

RIGHT: *Juan Antonio Sanchez 'Manito' Marichal hurled six 20-win seasons in his 13 years with the San Francisco Giants, leading the league in wins twice. He ended his career with Los Angeles in 1975 after one year with the Red Sox. 'The Dominican Dandy' was elected to the Hall of Fame in 1983.*

BELOW: *'Stan the Man' Musial is greeted by teammates in the dugout after getting his 3431st hit on 19 May 1962. Outfielder Musial played for the Cardinals for 22 years, and was elected to the Hall of Fame in 1969.*

lined a ball to right field – but this time second baseman Bobby Richardson snared it. The Yankees were the World Champions for the second year in a row.

The 1962 season saw a number of records set. Maury Wills overtook and tied Ty Cobb's 47-year-old record of 96 stolen bases (in 156 games, as Detroit had played two extra games due to ties) and then went on to steal 104, a major-league record. Stan Musial got his 3431st hit, thus taking over first place in the National League from Honus Wagner. Sandy Koufax tied his own (1959) and Bob Feller's (1938) record of 18 strikeouts in nine innings. One record that did not get set in 1962, however, was Early Wynn's 300th victory: he ended up the season only one short of that pitcher's pantheon. The White Sox allowed him to report for spring training in 1963, but didn't sign him on; however, his old team, the Cleveland Indians did, and in July, on his fifth try that season, Early Wynn became the 14th major-league pitcher to post 300 wins.

And in 1963 the Yankees repeated as American League champions, despite the heavy-hitting Minnesota Twins – in one doubleheader, they hit eight home runs in the first game and four in the second – and despite injuries that kept Mantle and Maris from playing more than 65 and 90 games, respectively. In fact, the Yankees led the league by 10 and a half games, their largest margin since 1947.

Meanwhile, over in the National League, the Dodgers were avenging their humiliating loss to the Giants in the playoffs of 1962. The Giants had fine pitching from Juan Marichal (25-8), but it didn't do them any more good than did the fine pitching by 42-year-old Warren Spahn for the Milwaukee Braves: Spahn's 23-7 record was his 13th (although last) 20-game season. In the end, it was the Cardinals that gave the Dodgers their closest call, but with solid hitting from Frank Howard and Tommy Davis, great base-running from Maury Wills, Willie Davis and Jim Gilliam, and superb pitching from Don Drysdale, Johnny Podres and Sandy Koufax, the Dodgers came out with the pennant. Koufax had an especially strong season, turning in a 25-5 record with an ERA of only 1.88, 306 strikeouts and 11 shutouts. Another National League player who had a season to remember was Stan Musial, who got the final hit – number 3630 – of his career on 29 September. Among those who witnessed this National League record that day was the Cincinnati Reds' rookie second baseman, 21-year-old Pete Rose.

The 1963 World Series was one that the Yankees would like to forget. They lost the first game to the Dodgers when Koufax struck out 15 of them (breaking a World Series record of 14, set by Carl Erskine in 1953); they lost the second game, 4-1, to the pitching of Podres and Perranoski; they lost the third game, 1-0, to Drysdale, who gave up only three. hits; and they lost the fourth game, 2-1, to Koufax again. The Yankees no longer seemed invincible.

ABOVE: *Lefthander John Joseph Podres pitched for the Dodgers, first in Brooklyn and then in Los Angeles, for 12 years of his 15-year career. Podres won game two of the 1963 Series for the Dodgers to help his team take the World championship.*

RIGHT: *Hall of Famer Sandy Koufax pitched in four World Series for the Dodgers during his 12-year career. In 1963 his league-leading 25 wins, 1.88 ERA, 306 strikeouts and 11 shutouts helped his team to the Series, and the two wins he hurled in that contest, including one in which he set a new Series record of 15 strikeouts, helped the Dodgers take it all. Koufax threw four no-hitters from 1962 to 1965, one of them a perfect game. He led the league in ERA for the last five years of his career, which ended in 1966.*

The National League Rides High

Invincible they may not have been, but the Yankees rebounded from their '63 Series shutout to once again take the American League pennant in 1964, their 29th. It wasn't as if the other teams in the league lacked for good players. There was a new generation of strong players, in fact, who were beginning to challenge the old standbys. The Orioles, for instance, had John 'Boog' Powell, who hit 39 home runs in 1964. The Angels boasted of the talents of Dean Chance on the mound and Jim Fregosi at shortstop. The Indians had a fine young pitcher in Luis Tiant, while the Kansas City Athletics had Bert Campaneris in the infield. And the Boston Red Sox had Tony Conigliaro who, even though he had his arm broken by a wild pitch in July, ended up hitting .290 with 24 home runs; the Red Sox also had Dick 'The Monster' Radatz who pitched in 79 games in relief, only two short of the American League record set by John Wyatt (and in fact Radatz appeared in 29 more innings).

Under their new manager, and former catcher, Yogi Berra, the Yankees played lackluster ball during the greater part of the season and were only in third place in August. Perhaps the catalyst of the turnaround was Mel Stottlemyre, a pitcher brought up from the Richmond farm team in August, who from his win in his debut seemed to spark the team. Whitey Ford and Jim Bouton were there to pitch, and Mantle, Maris, Elston Howard and Joe Pepitone were there to hit, and the Yankees ended up in first place.

In the National League, the Phillies appeared to have it all wrapped up when they came into the final two weeks with a six and a half game lead; then, starting on 20 September, the Phillies lost 10 straight, and

LEFT: *Tony Conigliaro became the youngest player ever to hit 100 home runs. In his rookie season (1964) he slugged 24 homers, then led the league the following year with 32. In August 1967 a fastball hit him in the face, sidelining him for the rest of the season and curtailing his rise to greatness.*

ABOVE: *John Wesley 'Boog' Powell hit 39 homers and 17 doubles for a league-leading .606 slugging average in 1964. The big power-hitter played first base and outfield for the Baltimore Orioles from 1961 to 1974, ending his 17-year career with the Indians and then the Dodgers in 1977. During the five seasons Powell went to the league championships with Baltimore, he averaged 23 home runs and 85 RBI's each year.*

while they were going cold, the Cardinals got hot, won eight in a row, and ended up winning with a one-game lead over the Phillies.

Going into the Series, the Yankees were once more the favorite, although Mantle had a bad leg and Tony Kubek was out because of a sprained wrist. But the Cardinals had some solid hitters in the likes of Dick Groat, Ken Boyer, Bill White, Tim McCarver and Curt Flood; they also had a new outfielder who could steal bases – Lou Brock – and a pitcher who had a wicked fastball, Bob Gibson. The Series went back and forth through the first six games, and then in the seventh it was Stottlemyre against Gibson. By the fifth inning, the Cardinals were leading 6-0. Mantle hit a three-run homer in the sixth, and Clete Boyer

OPPOSITE: *Jim Fregosi played shortstop for the Angels, first in Los Angeles and then in California, from 1961 to 1971, when he was traded to the Mets in exchange for Nolan Ryan. A fine defensive player, Fregosi ended his 18-year career with Pittsburgh in 1978, after three seasons with Texas.*

RIGHT: *In the four years big Jim Bunning pitched for the Phillies (1964-67) after nine years with Detroit, he averaged six shutouts a season. In 1968 he moved to Pittsburgh, then LA, and ended his 17-year career in 1971 with the Phillies again. In 1964 Bunning hurled the first of three consecutive 19-win seasons for the Phillies.*

BELOW RIGHT: *The great lefthander Sandy Koufax became the first pitcher to strike out 300 batters in three seasons. Twice he struck out 18 batters in a game. When an arthritic elbow forced his early retirement in 1966, he became an NBC broadcaster, a position he held for six years.*

and Phil Linz hit solo homers in the ninth, but the Cardinals held on and won the game, 7-5, to take the Series.

But in 1965, the Cardinals couldn't take even the pennant, for both the Giants and Dodgers got hot in September – the Giants winning 14 in a row, the Dodgers 13 in a row. Willie Mays hit 52 home runs for the Giants, but in the end it was the Dodgers' pitchers who made the difference. Drysdale had a 23-12 record, Koufax had 26-8, and together they struck out almost 600 opponents, with Koufax alone taking out 382 (a new major-league record that would hold until Nolan Ryan struck out 383 in 1973). Koufax also joined perhaps the most exclusive of all sports circles when he pitched a perfect game against the Cubs (although as it happened, Jim Bunning of the Phillies had pitched a perfect game for the Phillies only the year before).

The Yankees also failed to repeat in 1965, slipping into sixth place (their lowest finish since 1925). First place in the American League was then taken over by none other than the Minnesota Twins (formerly the Washington Senators until they moved to Minnesota in 1961). The Twins relied on power hitting by such as Harmon Killebrew, Bob Allison, Don Mincher, Jimmie Hall and Tony Oliva, and so the 1965 World Series promised a showdown between a pitchers' team and a hitters' team.

In the opener, the Twins' hitters swamped Drysdale and the Dodgers lost, 8-2; then in the second game, the Twins proceeded to knock Koufax out, 5-1. But back in Los Angeles, the Dodgers took three straight with a combination of pitching, hitting and base-running. The Twins took the sixth game, forcing the Series into the seventh, where Sandy Koufax faced Jim Kaat; Kaat pitched a fine game, but Koufax pitched just that much finer, giving up only three hits, and the Dodgers won 2-0.

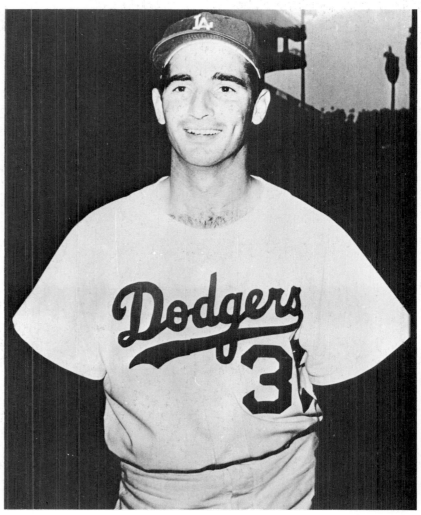

ABOVE: *Twins' first baseman Harmon 'Killer' Killebrew led the league in home runs six times in his 22-year career. He was elected to the Hall of Fame in 1984.*

RIGHT: *Outfielder Tony Oliva was selected as Rookie of the Year in 1964. He won the batting title three times during his 15 years with the Twins.*

LEFT: *Lou Brock leaps over the tag at home. This speedster played outfield for the Cardinals from 1964 to 1978, and led the league in stolen bases eight times.*

OPPOSITE: *Hall of Famer Lou Brock at bat. Brock retired in 1979 with 938 stolen bases.*

Changing of the Guard

If the Yankees thought their sixth-place finish in 1965 was a disaster, then the phrase 'Wait till next year!' took on a bitter twist in 1966, when the Yankees finished last in the league. Johnny Keane, who had been hired to manage the team in 1965, was dropped as manager, and Ralph Houk took over, but it did no good. (In mid-September, CBS would gain control of the club, with Mike Burke named as president and Lee MacPhail as general manager.) The American League in 1966 was dominated by the Baltimore Orioles, the team that had been the St Louis Browns until 1954. The Orioles had built up a 13-game lead by the end of July and were never in much danger after that. With such strong players such as Boog Powell, Luis Aparicio and Paul Blair, the Orioles were even further inspired to reach the heights by the two Robinsons, Frank and Brooks. Frank, an outfielder obtained the previous winter from the Cincinnati Reds, had earned the Most Valuable Player of the Year Award in 1961. In 1966 he would win the American League Triple Crown *and* the MVP Award (thereby becoming the only player to win that title in both leagues). Brooks Robinson had been with the Orioles for some years but only now was beginning to gain the recognition he deserved as one of the finest third basemen of all times.

The National League race in 1966 was no such runaway. The Pirates were strong contenders, with such hitters as Matty Alou, Willie Stargell, Donn Clendenon and Roberto Clemente (who was the league's Most Valuable Player). But the Pirates lacked strong pitching, and the Giants took second place with their hot pitchers, Juan Marichal (25-6) and Gaylord Perry (21-8). It was the Dodgers, again, that put it all together: they had strong batting, fielding and base-

running from Maury Wills, Willie Davis, Lou Johnson, Jim Lefebvre and Tommy Davis; and they had brilliant pitching from Sandy Koufax (27-9), decent pitching from Drysdale (13-6), and back-up pitching from Claude Osteen, Ron Perranoski and Don Sutton. (Both Koufax and Drysdale had held out for what was regarded as big money in those days, $100,000, and they proved to be worth every penny to the Dodgers.)

Little wonder that the Dodgers went into the 1966 Series as the favorites over the Orioles. But the Orioles' pitchers – Dave McNally, Jim Palmer, Wally Bunker and Moe Drabowsky – just about blanked the Dodgers (who went scoreless for the final 33 innings). The Dodgers went down to the Orioles, four straight. It turned out to be the end of an era for the Dodgers, as Maury Wills and Tommy Davis would be traded away over the winter, while Sandy Koufax, long bothered by painful arthritis in his left elbow, retired. With his 111-34 record for the previous five peak seasons, many would agree that Koufax was one of the all-time great pitchers of modern baseball.

With Koufax retired and the Dodgers collapsing to eighth place in 1967, the National League was up for grabs. Indeed, the league's overall batting average rose from .249 in 1966 to .256 in 1967. The Chicago Cubs looked promising, with their new young pitcher, Ferguson Jenkins, acquired in 1966 from the Phillies; Jenkins won the first of his seven 20-game seasons in 1967. The Mets had their own young pitcher, George Thomas Seaver; originally signed to a $50,000 bonus contract by the Braves, he had been declared a free agent because he had signed before his college class had graduated, and the

OPPOSITE: *Brooks Robinson takes a cut. This Hall of Fame third baseman played for the Baltimore Orioles for his entire 23-year career, retiring in 1977 with all-time records at his positon for fielding average, games played, putouts, assists and double plays. In 1964, when he was selected as the league's MVP, Robinson led the league in RBI's (118) and batted for a .317 average. In his first two playoffs he batted .500 and .538. Brooks Robinson was elected to the Hall of Fame in 1983.*

RIGHT: *Paul Blair after a close play at home plate. This Baltimore outfielder (1964-76) hit 26 homers and scored 102 runs in 1969.*

Mets had won him in a draw from a hat. In this first year with the Mets, Seaver won his first 16 games in the majors. But in the end, it was the Cardinals that took the pennant, with the aid of Orlando Cepeda (acquired from the Giants) and Roger Maris (acquired from the Yankees, where he had never been happy with the constant publicity), Bob Gibson and Nelson Briles.

The big surprise of the 1967 season, however, was to find the Boston Red Sox taking the pennant on the last day of the season, just beating out the Twins, the Tigers, and the White Sox in the final weeks. Boston's manager, Dick Williams, deserved much of the credit for getting the team to outdo itself, but the inspiration on the field was undeniably Carl Yastrzemski, with his .326 batting average, 121 RBIs and 44 homers. But could Boston go all the way? Few believed they had much of a chance against the experienced Cardinals, but the Sox took the Cardinals to seven games, where Bob Gibson – with two wins already in the Series – faced Jim Lonborg. The Cardinals got to Lonborg, Gibson gave up only three hits, and the Cardinals won the game 7-2 to become the world champions.

OPPOSITE: *Frank Robinson rounds first base. In the first of six years outfielder Robinson played for Baltimore (1966-71), he won the batting title with a .316 average and led the league in home runs (49), runs (122) and RBI's (122). Robinson, who played for the Reds, Dodgers, Angels and Indians as well, is the only player to win MVP Awards in both major leagues.*

OPPOSITE INSET: *Hall of Famer Frank Robinson when he managed San Francisco. He became the first black manager in the majors when he was hired by Cleveland in 1975.*

LEFT: *Ferguson Arthur 'Fergie' Jenkins threw six 20-game seasons in his nine and a half years with the Cubs (1966-73, 1982-83). Jenkins won the Cy Young Award in 1971.*

BELOW: *Orlando 'Cha-Cha' Cepeda hits a liner up the middle. 'The Baby Bull' played first base for six teams in his 17-year career, retiring from Kansas City in 1974.*

ABOVE: 'Tom Terrific' Seaver pitched for the Mets from 1967 to 1976 and in 1983, when he was lost to the White Sox through a front office error. Seaver won the first of three Cy Young Awards in 1969, when he won 25 games and lost only seven.

LEFT: Juan Marichal pitched for the San Francisco Giants from 1960 to 1973, ending his career with the Dodgers in 1975 with a 2.89 ERA.

OPPOSITE: Dodger Maury Wills poses at bat. Shortstop Wills, the National League MVP in 1962, played for LA for 12 years (1959-66, 1969-72). Wills ended his career with 2134 hits and 586 stolen bases.

LEFT: The big righthander Jim Lonborg pitched for Boston from 1965 to 1971, striking out a league-leading 246 batters in 1967 to win 22 games and the Cy Young Award. Lonborg won two of the three games he pitched in the '67 Series, including a one-hit shutout.

Pitchers, Changes and Miracles

The 1968 season was dubbed 'The Year of the Pitcher' because of some spectacular records run up by several pitchers. Bob Gibson of the Cardinals finished up the season with an ERA of only 1.12, the lowest in major-league history (breaking the major-league mark of 1.14 set by Walter Johnson in 1913 and the National League mark of 1.22 set by Grover Cleveland Alexander in 1915); Gibson also won 15 games in a row and pitched 13 shutouts. Equally as spectacular, Denny McLain of the Tigers ended up with a 31-6 record – the first major leaguer to win 30 games since Dizzy Dean had done so in 1934. Meanwhile, Don Drysdale pitched six consecutive shutouts (breaking Doc White's record set in 1904) that included 58 and two-thirds scoreless innings in a row (which broke Walter Johnson's record of 56, set in 1913). Altogether there were 185 shutouts in the National League alone – a major-league record – while the combined batting average for both leagues came to only .236, also a record. Carl Yastrzemski captured the American League batting title with an average of .3005, a record-low for the majors. Yet not all hitters were shut down. Pete Rose hit .335 and added 210 hits to his steady accumulation; Willie Mays raised his home run total to 587, putting him in second place behind Babe Ruth, while Mickey Mantle picked up 18 more homers to take over third place with his 536 total.

In the 1968 pennant races, the Cardinals led the National League for the second consecutive year; in second place (for the fourth year in a row) were the San Francisco Giants. In the American League, the Tigers ended up with a 12-game lead, thanks to McLain and another pitcher, Mickey Lolich, and strong support from Al Kaline, Norm Cash, Dick McAuliffe and others. With Gibson and McLain both due to become their league's Most Valuable Players as well as the winners of the Cy Young Awards, the World Series was inevitably regarded as a duel between these two aces. Gibson posted 17 strikeouts in the first game, a Series record, and the Cardinals won, 4-0; the Tigers came back with Mickey Lolich in game two and won, 8-1. The Cards then won the next two games – with Gibson getting his seventh straight Series win, another major-league record – but Lolich pitched the Tigers to a victory in the fifth game and McLain held on to win the

OPPOSITE: *The Orioles' pitching phenomenon, Jim Palmer, threw eight 20-game seasons with them in his 19-year career. Palmer won the first of three Cy Young Awards in 1973.*

ABOVE: *Voted the National League's MVP in 1968, Bob Gibson pitched for the Cardinals from 1959 to 1975. A* two-time *Cy Young Award winner, Gibson won 251 games with a 2.91 ERA, striking out 3117 in his career.*

LEFT: *Righthander Denny McLain hurled his way to 31 wins in 1968, winning the Cy Young Award and helping the Tigers win it all.*

171

Pete Rose performing one of his famous head-first slides while teammate Tony Perez looks on. Rose is defying one of his own rules: 'I don't recommend the headfirst slide for sliding into home plate. One time I tried it and cut up my face on the catcher's shin guards.' Selected as the National League's Rookie of the Year in 1963, 'Charlie Hustle' played for the Reds until 1978. He played for the Phillies in 1979-83 and the Expos in 1984 before returning to the Reds as player-manager in 1984.

sixth. In the seventh game, Lolich faced Gibson and the score was still 0-0 in the seventh, when Gibson gave up two singles; Jim Northrup hit one that the usually flawless Curt Flood misjudged; two runs scored, and the Tigers went on to win, 4-1, and take the Series.

After this season, the men who were running organized baseball became worried that such pitching would stymie the hitters and thus lose fans, so the rules committee adopted two major changes that went into effect in 1969. The pitching mound was lowered to 10 inches from 15 inches, thus reducing somewhat the advantage the pitcher gained from the height; and the strike zone was reduced from the longstanding shoulders-to-knee range down to the armpit to top of knee. Whatever impact these changes had on baseball was soon lost in the general unpredictability of the game. A far more obvious and enduring change, however, came about in 1969, when each league expanded to 12 teams and then divided itself into Western and Eastern divisions, with the league championship to be determined by the division winners going into playoffs for the first to take three out of five games. The National League's new teams were the San Diego Padres and the Montreal Expos; the American League added the Seattle Pilots and the Kansas City Royals.

Not unreasonably, there was some concern over whether these new expansion teams would be able to hold their own against the long-established teams. Students of the game would point to the New York Mets, which in their seven years had never finished above ninth place. But in 1969 something happened to the Luckless Mets to turn them into the Miraculous Mets. They were a young team and not especially strong as hitters. Although Tom Seaver was to have a great year, 25-7, their pitching staff wasn't all that exceptional. And in fact, as late as 13 August, the Mets were trailing the seemingly unstoppable

OPPOSITE TOP: *Detroit Tiger Mickey Lolich lets go a fastball. This superb lefthander won all three games he pitched in the 1968 Series, and hit a home run as well. After 13 years with Detroit, Lolich moved to the Mets and then the Padres, ending his career in 1979 with a 217-191 career record.*

OPPOSITE BOTTOM: *An ecstatic Jerry Koosman after winning game five of the 1969 World Series for the Amazing Mets, giving them the World championship. Koosman pitched for the Mets for 12 of his 18 years in the majors.*

RIGHT: *In the nine years shortstop Bert Campaneris played for the Oakland A's (1968-76), he averaged 44 stolen bases per season. Campaneris ended his 19-year career in 1983 after one season with the Yankees.*

Cubs by nine and a half games. But then the Cubs lost momentum and the Mets raced ahead, winning 38 of their last 49 games and taking first place in the Eastern Division. Then the Mets had to go up against the Atlanta Braves, winners of the Western Division; with Hank Aaron's 44 home runs and Phil Niekro's 23 victories, the Braves were regarded as the superior team. Again, the Mets astounded everyone by taking three straight.

Their opponents in the 1969 World Series were the Baltimore Orioles, who looked unbeatable; they had great pitching from Mike Cuellar, Dave McNally and Jim Palmer, they had six hitters who batted over .280, and they had superb defensive play from Brooks Robinson, Mark Belanger and others. Baltimore had beat the American League Western Division champion, the Minnesota Twins, in three straight, and everyone conceded that the Mets' joyride was about to end. Baltimore did take the first game, but the Mets went on to take the next three – with special credit to Tommy Agee for two spectacular catches. In the deciding fifth game the Orioles had a 3-0 lead, but the Mets tied it up by the seventh inning on a home run hit by Al Weis and then went on to win, 5-3 after Cleon Jones and Ron Swobodo both doubled in the eighth. The Mets had done the impossible!

Youth Baseball

If, as has been claimed, the Battle of Waterloo was won on the playing fields of Eton, then it is equally true that the World Series is won on the sandlot diamonds of America. For if anything makes baseball America's true national pastime, if anything explains how year in and year out, team after team can field new and skillful young players, it is because baseball is a game that is played by young Americans from a relatively early age. Toss a ball to a young European boy, it has been observed, and he will kick it. Toss a ball to a young American, and he will throw it. He will, that is, if he wants to make Little League.

The Little League is not the oldest program for boys' amateur baseball, but it has certainly become the best-known and most far-flung. It was begun in 1939 by Carl E Stolz of Williamsport, Pennsylvania, who decided that boys from about the ages 8 to 12 would benefit from more organized games of baseball. Only three teams played that first year in this city in northeast Pennsylvania, but the idea soon began to spread, until World War II put a brake on such activities. As soon as the war ended, though, Americans took up baseball with renewed enthusiasm, and Little League began to take off. There were only 60 teams to compete for positions in the first Little League World Series in 1947 – hardly national, let alone 'world' – and not surprisingly it was won by a team from Williamsport, where the Little League World Series is still played each year.

The publicity from that first Series in 1947 greatly stimulated the growth of the Little League. By 1948 there were 416 teams, in 1949, this number almost doubled, and it continued to double for several successive years. Eventually Little League became so popular that it

ABOVE: Children's Amusements, *published in 1820, pictured boys playing ball.*

BELOW: *A Little Leaguer takes a big cut for a strike.*

OPPOSITE: *The 1985 Bronco League World Series entry from Vera Cruz, Mexico, takes a break to gather around the Gatorade jug in San Jose, California.*

expanded to sponsor teams for boys 13 to 15 years old and another division for boys 16 to 18, while it split off the youngest into a Farm League division, 8 to 9, leaving Little League to the 10 to 12 year-olds. By 1964 Little League baseball had become such an institution that Congress gave it a federal charter, although it receives no governmental funds, while as further testimony to baseball's closeness to all currents of American society, in 1974 Congress passed a law requiring Little League to give girls a chance to compete for the teams. And since everyone who goes out for Little League is assured of assignment to a team and at least a couple of innings of play each game, this means that girls get to play Little League ball.

Meantime, Little League had been spreading around the world, so that by the 1980s it could count over 14,000 leagues, with some 145,000 teams and about two and a half million youthful participants in over 30 countries. (Almost half those teams and participants are in the USA.) To accommodate the international dimensions, the World Series of the Little League is now played out by the finalists from eight regions: four from the USA (Eastern, Western, Northern, Southern), Canada, Europe, Latin America and the Far East.

Although Little League in recent decades has become almost synonymous with organized baseball for young Americans, it was not the first such program. That honor belongs to the American Legion Junior League, founded in 1925 to sponsor teams for teenagers up to the age of 17. The first national competition was held in 1926, and by 1929 there was at least one team representing each of the then-48 states. In 1950 18-year-olds were admitted, then the 'Junior' was dropped from the official name. Meanwhile, American Legion baseball has spread to the two newest states, Hawaii and Alaska, as well as to Puerto Rico and the Panama Canal Zone. (Because it depends on

LEFT: *A pitcher from Lynnhaven, Virginia, is ready to let one fly at the 1985 Pony League World Series in Washington, Pennsylvania.*

BELOW: *In a close play at the plate, a runner from Oak Park, Illinois, slides home as the catcher from Washington, Pennsylvania, applies the tag at the 1985 Pony League World Series.*

ABOVE: *The 1985 American Legion Baseball National Championship team poses for their victory photo.*

BELOW: *A young Little Leaguer at bat.*

RIGHT: *In the 1985 American Legion National Championship Series, a runner dives into the bag as the first baseman leaps for a throw.*

sponsorship by American Legion posts, the program is not in as many countries as Little League is.) By the 1970s there were some 3200 teams in the American Legion program, involving boys from 16 to 18 years of age.

And there are several other programs that sponsor baseball teams for boys and young amateurs. The largest organization in the USA that sponsors amateur baseball teams of all ages, in fact, is the American Amateur Baseball Congress (AABC), founded in 1935 (although 'Amateur' was not added until 1955), with its headquarters in Battle Creek, Michigan. Its program began with adult teams, but over the years it has expanded to include five divisions: Pee Wee Reese (12 and under); Sandy Koufax (14 and under); Mickey Mantle (16 and under); Connie Mack (18 and under); and Stan Musial (19 and older). The AABC program claims over 3000 teams and about 75,000 participants. Then there was the Pony (Protect Our Nation's Youth) League, founded in Washington, Pennsylvania, in 1950, for boys 13 and 14 years old. A similar program, the Colt League, was founded in 1953 in Martins Ferry, Ohio, for boys 15 and 16. The Colt League merged

A Little Leaguer smacks a grounder up the middle in the 1985 State Championship Playoff Series in Chisholm, Minnesota.

with some similar programs and then in 1959 joined with the Pony League to form Boys' Baseball, operating out of Washington, Pennsylvania, which has since started a Junior League for boys 8 to 12. Another well-known program is the Babe Ruth League (originally the Little Bigger League), founded in 1952 in Trenton, New Jersey, for boys 13 to 15.

Not to mention that some 15,000 American junior high and high schools sponsor at least one baseball team, with perhaps 500,000 participating youths. So youth baseball in America seems very much alive and well, and although its official goals do not specifically call for preparing youths for careers in the major leagues, the fact is that at least 50 percent of the active players in the major leagues in any given year have played in such programs as the American Legion and/or Little League.

The Challenge of the Seventies

The 1970s would prove to be one of the most revolutionary in the history of baseball, one that seemed to call into question some of the most hallowed traditions of the sport. Fittingly, this assault on tradition began in January 1970 when Curt Flood, former St Louis Cardinals' outfielder, chose to fight his post-season trade to the Phillies on the grounds that he was being treated as 'a property . . . a chattel . . . a slave for a team against his will.' In other words, Flood was challenging the so-called reserve clause that had been at the core of organized baseball since its inception. The owners had always insisted that unless they were allowed to own and trade players throughout their careers, baseball would come apart as all the best players gravitated to a few rich teams. In the end, Flood lost his case right up through the US Supreme Court, but when it ruled in 1972 the Court called organized baseball's exemption from antitrust laws an 'aberration' and invited Congress to do something about it.

Meanwhile, the 1970 season got underway (although Flood sat it out). In the National League's Eastern Division, the Mets couldn't repeat a miracle and they ended up in third place, one game behind the Cubs but six behind the Pirates. In the Western Division, the Reds ran away with it, thanks to four .300 hitters (Tony Perez, Pete Rose, Bobby Tolan and Bernie Carbo) and the stellar catching and hitting of Johnny Bench. The Reds then rolled over the Pirates in the playoffs in three straight games and prepared themselves to confront the winner of the American League pennant. That league's season had been a repeat of 1969, with the Orioles taking the Eastern Division and the Twins winning the Western. And also as in 1969, the Orioles beat the

LEFT: *The enthusiastic Ernie Banks, who played shortstop and first base with the Cubs for his entire 19-year career (1953-71), hit his 500th home run on 12 May 1970. The first Cub to have his uniform retired, Banks was elected to the Hall of Fame in 1977.*

ABOVE: *Outfielder Curt Flood, who began the fight against the reserve clause in 1970, played mainly with St* *Louis, and ended his career with Washington in 1971.*

OPPOSITE: *In the nine years lefthander Vida Blue pitched for Oakland, he won 124 games and lost 86. Blue, who pitched a no-hitter in 1970, went on in 1971 to win 24 games with a 1.82 ERA, walking away with both Cy Young and MVP Awards.*

LEFT: *Cesar Cedeno, who joined the Houston Astros in 1970, waits in the on-deck circle. This slugging outfielder led the league in doubles in 1971 and 1972. He moved to the Cincinnati Reds in 1982, and ended his 15-year career in 1984.*

BELOW: *Mike Cueller, the Orioles' lefthanded hurler from 1969 to 1976, tied Denny McLain for the Cy Young Award in 1969. His four 20-win seasons helped the Orioles take three pennants.*

OPPOSITE: *Johnny Bench drives a long ball. Johnny Lee Bench, the all-time great catcher who played his whole career with the Reds (1967-83), was selected as National League MVP in 1970 and 1972. Bench was an integral part of the Big Red Machine, a dynasty team that dominated the 1970s.*

Twins in the playoffs in three straight. After their loss the previous year to the Mets, the Orioles weren't given that much of a chance against 'The Big Red Machine,' but once again baseball proved to be a game that defied the odds. The Orioles swept the first three games and it was only Lee May's three-run homer in the eighth inning of the fourth game that kept the Reds alive. But the Orioles took the fifth game, with their Brooks Robinson named as the Series' MVP.

Several players would make 1970 a season they at least would remember. Tom Seaver struck out 19 batters on 22 April, tying Steve Carlton's major-league record and setting a new one of his own by striking out 10 of these in succession. Luis Aparicio, shortstop for the White Sox, set a league record of 2219 games at his position (on his way to an all-time career record of 2581 games at shortstop). Hank Aaron became the ninth player in major-league history to get 3000 hits, Willie Mays followed as the tenth, and Ernie Banks of the Cubs became the ninth man to hit 500 homers.

The 1971 season was relatively non-controversial. The Orioles repeated as winners of the Eastern Division for the third straight year. With Palmer (20-9), McNally (21-5), Cuellar (20-9) and Pat Dobson (20-8), the Orioles were only the second team in major-league history (the White Sox of 1920 had been the first) to boast of four 20-game winners. In the American League Western Division, a newcomer appeared in the spotlight, the Oakland A's. They were a new type of team, too, somewhat brash and unorthodox in their carryings on, but with Reggie Jackson hitting 32 homers and Catfish Hunter winning 21 games and Rollie Fingers working his magic constantly in relief, they won games. The Athletics' biggest star, however, was their 22-year-old lefthanded fastballer, Vida Blue, who ended up with a spectacular 24-8 record, 301 strikeouts and an ERA of 1.82, taking the league's Cy Young Award as well as the MVP Award. In the playoffs, however, the Orioles' experience paid off and the A's lost three straight.

Over in the National League in 1971, the Reds failed to repeat in the Western Division, which was taken by the San Francisco Giants. But only barely: the Giants had a 10 and a half game lead at one point, but only secured first place on the last day of the season by beating the Dodgers. The Pittsburgh Pirates did repeat in the Eastern Division, thanks to a team of solid players such as Willy Stargell, Roberto Clemente, Al Oliver, Dave Cash, Rob Robertson and Manny San-

guillen. In the playoffs, the Pirates beat the Giants, three games to one, and then went on to the Series as the underdogs. When the Orioles took the first two games, it seemed that they could not be stopped, but Pittsburgh took the next three. The Orioles won the sixth game, but in the seventh, Steve Blass held the Orioles to four hits and the Pirates won the game and the Series. Many fans would long remember that 1971 Series as the one in which Roberto Clemente finally got the national recognition that had long been his due as one of the finest all-around ballplayers of his generation.

Undesignated Strikes, Designated Hitters

Although it was in 1972 that the Supreme Court ruled that the reserve clause was still binding on Curt Flood and all baseball players, there were rumblings of a new world to come when the players of both leagues went out on strike during the spring training exhibition season to demand that the owners contribute more to the medical and pension funds. The strike soon ended, but not before 86 regular season games had been missed (and rather than try to make them up, different teams ended up playing different numbers of games in 1972).

Once on the field, though, the players gave their all. In the National League's Eastern Division, the Pirates won for the third straight year, thanks in part to the hard-playing Roberto Clemente; on the last day of the season, he got his 3000th hit, only the 11th player in major-league history to achieve this. (Unfortunately, it turned out to be his last hit, for he died in a plane crash on 31 December 1972, while taking relief supplies to victims of an earthquake in Nicaragua.) The Western Division was led by the Cincinnati Reds, managed by Sparky Anderson, who acquired a new nickname, 'Captain Hook,' in reference to his penchant for 'pulling' his pitchers at the slightest sign of trouble (with the result that Reds' pitchers only got to complete 25 games all season). The Reds beat the Pirates in the playoffs, but it took five games and a wild pitch by the Pirates' Bob Moose in the bottom of the ninth in the fifth game to do so.

In the American League for 1972, the Oakland A's repeated as Western Division champs, despite the increasingly abrasive behavior of the club's owner, Charles O Finley. The one real contest in the majors this year was in the American League's Eastern Division,

where as late as Labor Day, four teams – the Red Sox, Orioles, Tigers and Yankees – were separated by only one game. In the end, the Tigers snuck by Boston with a half-game lead. In the playoffs, though, the Tigers lost to the A's.

The 1972 World Series thus saw the exuberant, individualistic Oakland A's confronting the disciplined organization known as The Big Red Machine. It was a tight series, with six games decided by only one run and with both teams batting an average of .209. The lead seesawed back and forth, until the seventh game saw the A's come out with a 3-2 victory and their first World Championship since 1930.

The 1973 season had no strike but it had something even more controversial: the American League teams adopted the designated hitter – supposedly on a three-year trial basis, but the American League teams were so satisfied with it that they adopted it permanently at the end of the 1973 season. The National League refused to try the designated hitter but went along with allowing teams to use the DH in World Series played in odd-numbered years. The debate over the DH, however, would go on. It did produce the desired result of upping the American League teams' batting averages, but as it

BELOW: *Roberto Clemente smacks his 3000th hit on 30 September 1972. He was elected to the Hall of Fame in 1973.*

OPPOSITE: *The Oakland A's powerhitting outfielder and growing* *superstar Reggie Jackson. In his eight years with the A's (1968-75), Jackson led the league in home runs twice, in runs scored twice and in RBI's once, helping his team take two pennants and earning the American League's MVP designation in 1973.*

OPPOSITE: *Johnny Bench argues a call with the home plate umpire. In 1973 Bench's league-leading 40 home runs and 125 RBI's helped his team to the league championship playoffs. Bench's ninth-inning homer won the first game of the playoffs, but the Reds went down to the Mets in five games.*

RIGHT: *Reds' manager Sparky Anderson in a dispute. George Lee Anderson played one season at second base for the Phillies in 1959 and batted .218. But he came into his own as a manager, first at Cincinnati, where he won five pennants and two World Series, and then at Detroit, where he won one pennant and one World Series. Between these two stints he tried his hand at broadcasting.*

turned out 1973 also saw 12 of the league's pitchers win 20 or more games, including five no-hitters. The most remarkable feats were those of Nolan Ryan, who had been traded to the California Angels by the New York Mets; Ryan not only pitched two no-hitters and two one-hitters, he ended up the season with 383 strikeouts, thus setting a new major-league record (that beat Sandy Koufax's previous record by one).

In the American League's Western Division for 1973, the Oakland A's took first place again, while the Baltimore Orioles took over first place in the Eastern Division. In the playoffs, the A's beat the Orioles, three games to two.

In the National League's Western Division, the Cincinnati Reds came from 11 games behind the Dodgers and ended up in first place.

But this was nothing compared to the 'charge' of the Mets. On 30 August, they were in last place in the Eastern Division. Inspired by their relief pitcher Tug McGraw's cry of 'Ya gotta believe!,' the Mets then won 20 of their last 28 games and on the last day of the season just managed to clinch first place in the Eastern Division. The Mets did this with a winning percentage of only .509, the lowest of any pennant winner in major-league history, while their team batting average of .246 left them in ninth place in the National League for 1973. But behind the pitching of Seaver, Jerry Koosman and Jon Matlack, the Mets went on to beat the Reds in the playoffs. But the growing balloon of fantasy – that the Mets were about to repeat their miracle of 1969 – burst when the Mets met the A's in the Series and lost the last two games after leading three games to two.

LEFT: *Lefthander Tug McGraw throws a curve. In 1973 the Mets lost the World Series to Oakland in seven games, despite McGraw's one win and one save. Frank Edwin McGraw pitched for the Mets until 1975, when he was traded to the Phillies. He ended his 19-year career in 1984.*

BELOW: *Willie Mays pleads with home plate umpire Augie Donatelli in the 1973 World Series. Willie Howard 'Say Hey' Mays played for the Giants (1951-52, 1954-72) and the Mets (1972-73). This superb and popular outfielder retired with a .302 batting average, 338 stolen bases, 3283 hits and 660 home runs. He was elected to the Hall of Fame in 1979.*

OPPOSITE: *Nolan Ryan after his record-setting 383rd strikeout on 27 September 1973.*

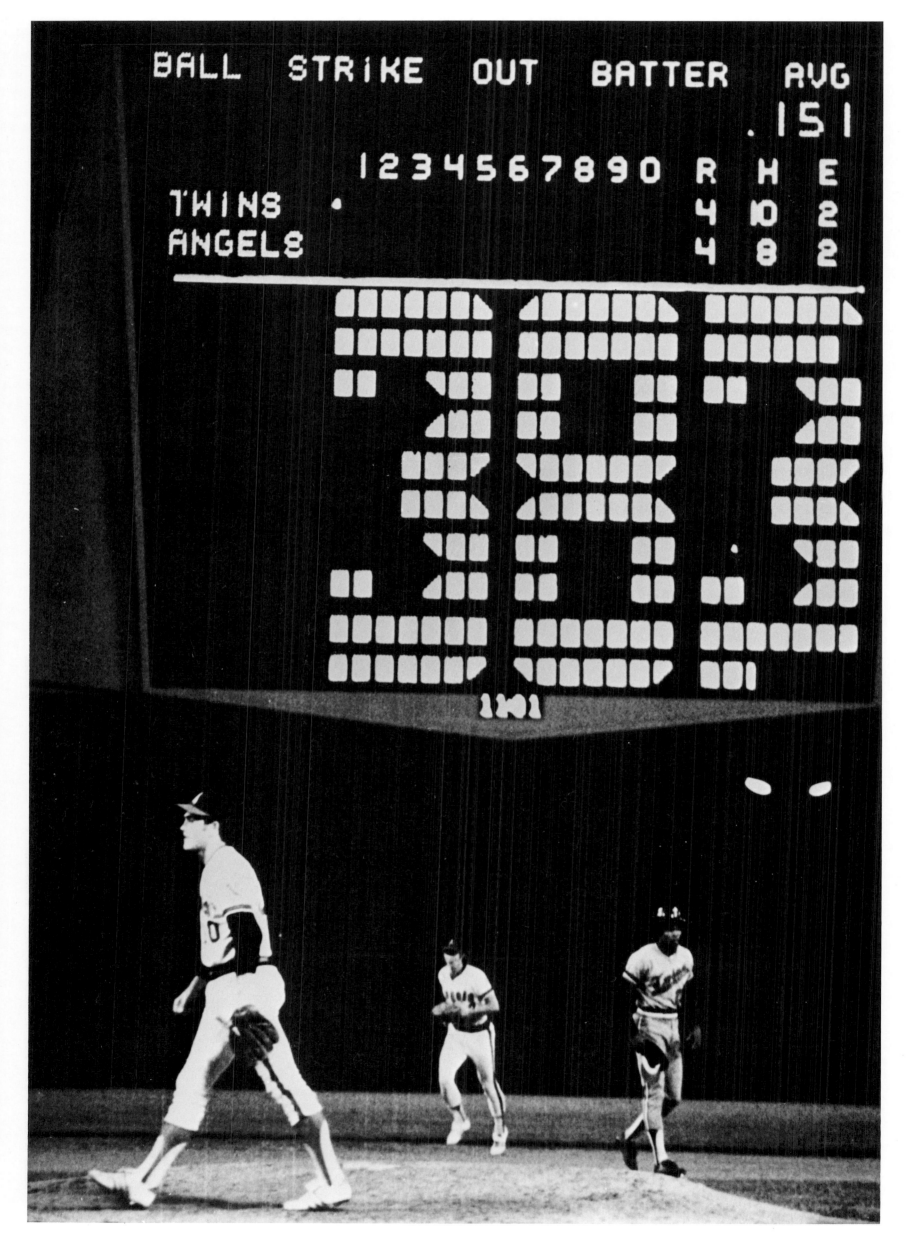

The End of a Record
– And a Clause

When the 1973 season ended, Hank Aaron of the Atlanta Braves had hit a total of 713 home runs – one short of Babe Ruth's career total of 714. It was obvious that Aaron was going to take over one of the all-time super-records of American sports, and the owners of the Braves, not unnaturally, wanting Aaron to set his record in his home stadium, said they would bench him for the opening games scheduled for Cincinnati. But Commissioner Kuhn ordered the Braves to put Aaron on the field, and he obliged by hitting his record-tying 714th homer on the opening game of the season. Then, on 8 April, in the first game back in Atlanta, Aaron hit his record-breaking 715th (with a television audience estimated at 35 million looking on). Although many old fans found it hard to concede this record by their beloved Babe (and some even wrote abusive and threatening letters to Aaron), most accepted that like all records, it had been made to be broken.

The 1974 season, in fact, saw two other new records. Lou Brock of the Cardinals stole 118 bases and thus broke Maury Wills' record of 104, set in 1962. Brock's record would not stand that long, but another set in 1974 still stands: Mike Marshall of the Los Angeles Dodgers appeared in 106 games as a relief pitcher.

The 1974 season turned out to be a rather predictable one, with both the A's and the Orioles repeating in their divisions of the American League. In fact, it was no walkway for the Orioles, who had to win 27 of their last 33 games. Meanwhile, the A's had to contend with their interfering owner, Finley, and various intrasquad squabbles. But with the superb pitching of Hunter, Blue, Holtzmann and Fingers, the A's then went on to defeat the Orioles in the playoffs, holding them

OPPOSITE TOP: *As a lawyer familiar with baseball affairs, Bowie Kuhn had been elected to the role of Baseball Commissioner in February of 1969. Kuhn served in the position for 15 years.*

OPPOSITE BOTTOM: *Henry Aaron after hitting his 723rd home run on 4 June 1974. Aaron, who had surpassed Babe Ruth's all-time home run record two months earlier, retired two years later with the all-time record of 755. Aaron also holds the all-time RBI record of 2297. Hammerin' Hank played for the Braves in Milwaukee and Atlanta (1954-74), and ended his 23-year career with the Milwaukee Brewers in 1976. He was elected to the Hall of Fame in 1982.*

ABOVE: *Ken Holtzman's shutout in game two of the 1974 American League Championship Series helped the A's take the pennant. In the World Series that year Holtzman scored the winning run in game one, then smashed a home run in game four to help the A's take it all.*

LEFT: *Rollie Fingers pitched for the A's his first nine years in the majors (1968-76). An ace reliever, Fingers holds the all-time record for saves. In the '74 Series Fingers was credited with one win and two saves.*

to only one run in the final 27 innings of the four-game series.

In the National League for 1974, the Pirates took the Eastern Division, but only by one and a half games over the Cardinals. In the Western Division, the Dodgers went out in front during the first week of the season and never trailed, ending up four games ahead of the Reds. The Dodgers had a superbly coordinated infield of Steve Garvey, Davey Lopez, Bill Russell and Ron Cey, and they had the pitching that the Pirates lacked, so it was no surprise when the Dodgers beat the Pirates in the playoffs. In the World Series, though,

the A's defeated the Dodgers, four games to one, proving that uniforms, moustaches and off-field antics had little effect on the game.

After his record-breaking 1974 season, Hank Aaron expected he might be asked to manage the Braves, and when he wasn't he got himself traded to the Milwaukee Brewers. So it was that the honor of becoming the first black manager in the major leagues fell to Frank Robinson. He was signed on by the Cleveland Indians and took the Indians onto the field in 1975; although the Indians came in fourth place in the Eastern Division, they had won almost half their games and

OPPOSITE: *Jim Rice came up from Boston's minor league Pawtucket club in 1974. Although an injury kept him out of post-season play in 1975, Rice sparked the Red Sox to a league championship that year, batting .309 with 22 home runs and 102 RBI's. Three years later Rice took over left field from Carl Yastrzemski.*

ABOVE: *Right fielder Dwight Evans hits a liner through the gap. 'Dewey,' who joined the Red Sox in 1972, became a perennial Golden Glover. The Red Sox lost the 1975 World Series to Cincinnati despite Evans' five RBI's.*

Robinson was given a second year's contract, and the last major barrier to blacks in organized baseball had fallen.

The big surprise of the 1975 season was the performance of the Boston Red Sox. With Carl Yastrzemski playing at his peak, and with some standout play by Dwight Evans, Carlton Fisk, Jim Rice and Fred Lynn, Boston won the Eastern Division of the American League and then beat the A's in the playoffs. In the National League, the Pirates repeated in the Eastern Division while the Cincinnati Reds won 108 games – the third highest total in major-league history – and left the

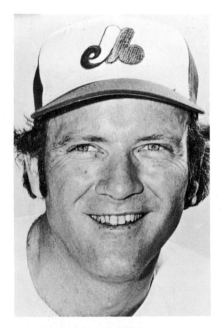

LEFT: *Pitcher Dave McNally in a Montreal Expos cap. As one of the first two free agents, McNally helped usher in a new age in baseball. McNally threw four 20-win seasons during his 13 years with the Orioles (1962-74) and ended his career with the Expos in 1975.*

RIGHT: *Red Sox first baseman Cecil Cooper poses in his stretch. Power-hitting Cooper played for Boston from 1971 to 1976, then moved to the Milwaukee Brewers. Although he went 4 for 10 in the 1975 pennant playoffs, in the World Series that year he got only one hit. Cooper has led the league in doubles and in RBI's twice.*

LEFT: *Pitcher Andy Messersmith was one of the first two free agents, with Dave McNally. John Alexander Messersmith pitched in both the National and the American League, beginning with the Angels in 1968. In 1975 Messersmith threw seven shutouts.*

OPPOSITE: *Dave Parker takes a big cut. 'The Cobra' played outfield for the Pittsburgh Pirates from 1973 to 1983, then moved to Cincinnati. In 1975 Parker's league-leading .541 slugging percentage helped his team win their division.*

Dodgers 20 games behind in second place. The Reds then beat the Pirates in three straight in the playoffs, and went into the World Series against Boston as the heavy favorites. The Red Sox, however, stretched the Reds to seven games, and the Reds only won the seventh when Joe Morgan hit a single in the ninth inning.

The most enduring showdown of 1975, however, came not in a stadium but when on 23 December an arbitrator ruled that two players, Andy Messersmith and Dave McNally, who had chosen to play without signing contracts, were now free agents – in effect, ruling that the reserve clause was no longer inviolable. (The difference between this and Curt Flood's challenge was that these players did not treat it as a fundamental legal issue but simply as a contractual dispute.) The owners immediately argued that this ruling was limited to these two players and said they would go to court, after all, to uphold the reserve clause. Things did not look good for the 1976 season.

Free Agents and Costly Hitters

When spring training time arrived on 1 March 1976, the owners and players had still failed to reach an agreement on how to handle this new development with free agents, so the owners simply refused to open the camps. By 17 March, the players said they would be willing to negotiate over details so the camps opened and negotiations proceeded. It was on 12 July, the eve of the All-Star Game, that a new four-year contract was agreed to. The terms represented a compromise between total 'free-agency' and the old reserve clause: after five years in the majors, a player could ask to be traded (and could veto up to six clubs); if he was not traded, he became a free agent; after six years in the majors, a player automatically became a free agent, although he could only negotiate with 13 clubs (including his latest) that participated in a draft. Many people, not only the club owners, predicted that this would lead to the end of organized baseball for it seemed that a few rich clubs would soon buy up all the best players. In practice, it would not work out quite that simplistically. Some superstars did gravitate to a few clubs, but the unpredictable elements of baseball still held sway: the unknowns and rookies who led teams to outdo themselves; the 'over-the-hill' veterans who came up with incredible final years; players traded by one team because they failed to produce and then who produced fantastically; and the inexplicable team spirit that continued to defy the odds.

In any case, the 1976 season remained unaffected by the new era of free agents. In the National League, the Reds swept the Western Division, again leaving the Dodgers well behind. In the Eastern Division, the Pirates lost out to the Phillies. But the Big Red Machine – with its team batting average of .280 and five players who hit over .300 – was too powerful for the Phillies in the playoffs. In the American League, the Kansas City Royals beat out the A's in the Western Division, but the Royals came up against the winner of the Eastern Division, the Yankees, and lost the playoffs, three games to two. The Yankees seemed to be a reconstituted team, for their primary owner, George Steinbrenner, had assembled such star players as Thurman

ABOVE: *Pete Rose (middle) and a teammate congratulate Johnny Bench after a run scored. In 1976 Rose and Bench helped the Reds become World Champions. Rose led the league in hits (215), doubles (42) and runs scored (130), while Bench came up with a nearly-perfect .997 fielding average.*

ABOVE: *Yankee third baseman Graig Nettles readies himself for a play. The agile Nettles played a strong offense for the Yankees as well, leading the league in home runs in 1976 with 32. Two years later he would help his team* take the pennant, smashing 27 homers and batting .333 in the playoffs. Nettles played with the Yankees from 1973 to 1983, when he joined the Padres.

LEFT: *Catcher Thurman Munson's solid playing helped the Yankees to three pennants and two World Championships beginning in 1976. In 1976 Munson batted in 105 runs with a .302 average. His career was cut tragically short by an airplane crash that claimed his life.*

OPPOSITE: *Big Dave Winfield waits to bat. Winfield played outfield for the San Diego Padres from 1973 to 1980, when he moved to the Yankees. In 1979 Winfield would bat .308 with a league-leading 118 RBI's.*

Munson, Mickey Rivers, Chris Chambliss, Catfish Hunter and Ken Holtzman, and brought in Billy Martin as manager (midway in 1975). But the Yankees proved no match for the well-coordinated Reds, who took the 1976 Series in four straight.

The 1977 season saw yet another expansion of the American League, with two new teams, the Seattle Mariners and the Toronto Blue Jays, though the National League remained with 12 teams. But much of the sports columns this season was filled with the bickerings of the Yankees' Terrible Trio – George Steinbrenner, Billy Martin and the newly acquired superstar, Reggie Jackson. The carryings-on didn't prevent the Yankees from winning 38 of their last 51 games, though, and taking first place in the Eastern Division. In the Western Division, the Kansas City Royals repeated, but they also repeated their 1976 loss to the Yankees in the playoffs.

In the Western Division of the National League, the Dodgers were under a new manager, Tom Lasorda (Walt Alston having retired after 23 years at the helm), and they ended up beating out the Reds for first place. In the Eastern Division, the Phillies repeated, but they fell to

the Dodgers in the playoffs. The Dodgers then went on to face the Yankees in the World Series, and it was assumed that the Dodgers, with four players who had hit at least 30 home runs, would outgun the Bombers. Instead, it was one Yankee player's hits that did in the Dodgers: Reggie Jackson had a record-making Series, hitting five homers, including three in a row on only three pitches, and scoring 10 runs, including four in a single game. The Yankees won four games to two and ended up once again as World Champions.

But perhaps the most significant record set in 1977 was that by Lou Brock, when he stole his 893rd base (thus breaking Ty Cobb's lifetime record of 892). Brock would steal 938 before he retired. Another extraordinary season was posted by Rod Carew, who won his sixth American League batting title with his .388 average (the highest since Ted Williams' .388 in 1957), and a total of 239 hits, the most since Bill Terry's 254 in 1930.

Lou Brock of the St Louis Cardinals breaks for second base in an attempted steal against the Pittsburgh Pirates. This Hall of Fame outfielder played for the Cubs (1961-64) and the Cardinals (1964-78). He led the league in stolen bases eight times. In 1977 Brock broke Ty Cobb's long-standing stolen base record of 892, on his way to achieving the all-time record of 938.

ABOVE LEFT: *Steve Carlton in his powerful windup. Stephen Norman 'Lefty' Carlton pitched for the Cardinals for seven years before joining the Phillies in 1972. In 1977, with a 23-10 record, Carlton won the second of three Cy Young Awards he would garner.*

ABOVE: *One of the first players to enter the open market as a free agent, Catfish Hunter signed with the Yankees on a $3-plus million contract after seven successful years with the Oakland A's. His first year with New York Hunter won a league-leading 23 games.*

LEFT: *Reggie Jackson waits for the call. In the five years Jackson played for the Yankees (1977-81), New York won four division titles, three pennants and two Series victories. Mr October holds the all-time World Series record for slugging average, with .755.*

OPPOSITE: *Tom Lasorda talks with first baseman Steve Garvey in the Los Angeles dugout. Lasorda, who took over as manager in 1976, has brought his team in first place five times to date.*

Baseball
as an International Game

Quite understandably, most Americans tend to regard baseball as 'native' to their country, in the sense of its having been both 'invented' and played mainly in the US. There has been considerable publicity given to the popularity of baseball in Japan, but that is usually treated as an exotic exception. And after all, everyone knows that the world's most popular spectator sport is soccer. All of this is true as far as it goes, but it is also true that baseball has a much wider following around the world than is generally realized. For one thing, Americans themselves have carried the game with them wherever they have gone, both in peace and war. American servicemen, for instance, have been playing the game among themselves for many decades now and in so doing have introduced the game to many foreigners. Meanwhile, the American-based Little League has also spread the game among young people in many countries. And with a moment's thought, almost everyone would realize that baseball must be widely played and enjoyed in Canada and Mexico, America's immediate neighbors, whose minor leagues have long been feeding players to the major leagues. (There was an attempt in 1946 by wealthy Mexicans to start a third major league, based in Mexico, but it was quickly squelched by organized baseball in the USA.)

Baseball has long been extremely popular throughout Latin America, and not only in places where the USA has had direct contacts, such as Puerto Rico, Panama and the Virgin Islands. Baseball is popular in Venezuela, Nicaragua and the Dominican Republic, and there is a lengthening list of players from Latin America who have moved up to become prominent players in the major leagues. Indeed,

ABOVE RIGHT: *Curious spectators watch the first American baseball game at Eton College, Buckingham County, England on 14 July 1944. World War II was instrumental in spreading the sport, as American servicemen brought the game with them wherever they went.*

RIGHT: *A baseball game being conducted under adverse conditons in Luxembourg during World War II.*

TOP: *The Venezuelan Vargas Baseball club poses for a team picture.*

ABOVE: *Cuban President Batista and his staff enjoy a Giants exhibition game in Havana.*

ABOVE AND RIGHT: *French soldiers play baseball, then pose for a photograph, at La Valbonne during World War I.*

LEFT: *French children play baseball during World War I.*

RIGHT: *American soldiers pose for a group picture after playing an exhibition game in France during World War I.*

one town in the Dominican Republic, San Pedro de Macoris, with a population of only 79,000, had 14 of its youths playing for the majors in 1985. During the winter in North America, it has long been the custom for many players from the major leagues to go to play with various Latin American teams, which since 1947 have had their own Latin American championship series.

Cuba is a special case. Baseball was first played there as early as 1878, and Cuba eventually supported a team that belonged to the Triple A International League. After Fidel Castro took over, the USA severed diplomatic relations with Cuba in 1961 and thus cut off movement between the two countries. Now there are two independent leagues in Cuba, and baseball remains as popular as ever: Castro himself likes to appear in games to show his people he's still a regular guy!

And then there is baseball in Japan. It was introduced there by Horace Wilson, an American teacher in Tokyo, back in 1873. The sport caught on quickly and was supported by schools and universities, spurred on by occasional tours by American collegiate teams. Up until the 1930s baseball in Japan remained an amateur sport, with the strongest teams coming out of the Japanese universities (which to this day serve as the 'farm' teams for the professional leagues). The big impetus to baseball in Japan came after the first visit of an American 'all-star' team of professionals in 1931 and then with Babe Ruth's visit in 1934. Since then, the Japanese have embraced baseball with the intensity that they seem to bring to so many activities, especially those adopted from the West. In fact, one of their star players, Sadaharu Oh, ended his 22-year career with an amazing record of 868 home runs. They now support two professional leagues, the Pacific and the Central, each with six clubs that play 130-game seasons and play their own Japan Series. Game draw huge crowds and the atmosphere at the games is much like that at American games. One major difference, however, is that the teams in Japan are owned by big industrial companies. The level of play is high, and although no Japanese player has ever had much success in coming over to the American majors, the best of their players could probably hold their own were there not cultural and language differences.

Elsewhere around the world, baseball has yet to catch on as it has in Japan and Latin America, but it is played by semi-professional teams in such countries as Italy and enjoys some popularity in countries such as France, the Netherlands, Belgium, Spain, England, South Africa, Australia, Taiwan – and Tunisia! Perhaps one of the most significant indications of the growing internationalization of baseball was its introduction as a demonstration sport in the 1984 Olympics at Los Angeles – where the winner turned out to be Japan. And since non-American teams have taken to winning the Little League World Series with some regularity, perhaps it is time to recognize that baseball has truly gone international.

ABOVE: *The Japanese slugger, Sadaharu Oh, begins his swing balanced on one leg. Sadaharu Oh retired with an astounding 868 home runs.*

LEFT: *Olympic baseball teams receive their medals in 1984, the first year baseball was played as an Olympic demonstration sport.*

The Japanese left fielder for the
Hankyu Braves, Masafumi
Yamamori, scales a fence to make the
spectacular catch that was voted by
major leaguers as the best catch in
baseball when it was aired on 'This
Week in Baseball.'

Dynasties and Upsets

The 1978 season was in some respects a rerun of 1977 – the same four teams won in their divisions in the two leagues – but there were enough aberrations on and off the field to keep baseball fans occupied. The most notorious episodes once again involved the feuding trio of Steinbrenner, Martin and Jackson of the Yankees. The infighting began when Jackson refused to follow Martin's signals to hit but simply went ahead and tried to bunt, and climaxed when Martin quipped to a reporter about Jackson and Steinbrenner, 'One's a born liar, the other's convicted' (this last a reference to Steinbrenner's having pleaded 'no contest' to federal charges of illegal campaign contributions). On the next day, Martin found himself resigning and Bob Lemon took over as manager, all of which was further confused when the Yankees announced that Martin would return as manager in 1980.

When Lemon took over in late July, the Yankees were 10 and a half games behind the division-leading Red Sox. The Yankees proceeded to play solid ball, the Red Sox came apart in September, and on the last day of the regular season, the Yankees had pulled into a dead heat for first place in the Eastern Division. In a one-game playoff, the Yankees beat the Red Sox – thanks in great part to the pitching of Ron Guidry (whose season winning percentage of .893 was the best for a 20-plus game winner in major-league history). Over in the Western Division, the Kansas City Royals took the title for the third consecutive year, paced by the batting of George Brett and the solid pitching of Dennis Leonard, Paul Splittorff, Larry Gura and Rich Gale. The Royals then lost to the Yankees in the playoffs.

In the Western Division of the National League, the Dodgers beat

ABOVE: *Ron Guidry winds up for a pitch. In his first full season with the Yankees (1977), 'Louisiana Lightning' won 16 games. In 1978 he won the Cy Young Award with 25 wins and a 1.74 ERA.*

LEFT: *Lefthander Tommy John joined the Yankees in 1979, winning 21*

games that year and 22 the following year.

OPPOSITE: *George Brett at bat. Third baseman Brett joined Kansas City in 1974 and collected 539 hits in his first three seasons. Brett won batting titles in 1976 and 1980 (an MVP year).*

out the Reds again, mainly because the Reds collapsed in August and the Dodgers won 22 of their last 37 games. In the league's Eastern Division, the Phillies beat the Pirates again and took their third consecutive division title. Then in the playoffs, the Dodgers downed the Phillies three games to one and advanced to the Series to meet their opponents of the previous year, the Yankees. The Yankees lost the first two, but when the bats of Jackson, Lou Piniella, Bucky Dent and Munson got going, they came back, won four in a row, and ended up World Champions.

Just when it seemed that the four divisions were being locked up by permanent dynasties, 1979 turned everything upside down and all four divisions had new winners. In the National League West, the Reds displaced the Dodgers, while in the National League East the Pirates displaced the Phillies. (Ironically, the Phillies had just acquired Pete Rose of the Reds.) The Pirates had no superstars but they drew inspiration from the 39-year-old 'Pops' Stargell who hit 32 homers. In the playoffs, the Pirates swept the Reds three games to none.

OPPOSITE: *Carlton 'Pudge' Fisk at bat for the Red Sox. Catcher Fisk joined Boston in 1972 and was selected Rookie of the Year. Perhaps the most memorable hit of his years with the Red Sox (1972-80) was the twelfth-inning, game-winning home run that sent the 1975 World Series into a seventh game.*

RIGHT: *San Diego's big righthander Gaylord Perry kicks high in his wind-up. Perry, who had won the Cy Young Award in 1972, threw a 21-6 season for a league-leading .778 winning percentage in his first year with the Padres.*

BELOW: *Mike Torrez pitched for the Red Sox for five years (1978-82). Torrez came from the Yankees as a free agent in 1978. That same year he started and lost the memorable one-game playoff that sent the Yankees to an eventual World Championship.*

In the American League, the Western Division had a surprise winner in the California Angels, who had been finishing an average of 23 and a half games down for the previous 18 seasons. In the Eastern Division, the Yankees on- and off-field turmoil finally caught up with them, but aside from that the Baltimore Orioles won fair and square, winning 102 games in the regular season and then going on to defeat the Angels for the American League pennant.

The Orioles went on to meet the Pirates in what was billed as a 'railroad series' – because Baltimore and Pittsburgh were conveniently linked by train – but it might better have been billed 'the storm-gear series': it was so rainy and cold that several key plays were affected. But both teams played under the same conditions, and when the Orioles took three of the first four games, it appeared that the Pirates were about to be blown away. Instead, the Pirates won the next three games to become the World Champions. (As extraordinary as this sounds, three other teams had previously done this in the World Series.) And so the 1970s ended with a reminder that major-league baseball was as full of surprises – and excitement – as ever.

213

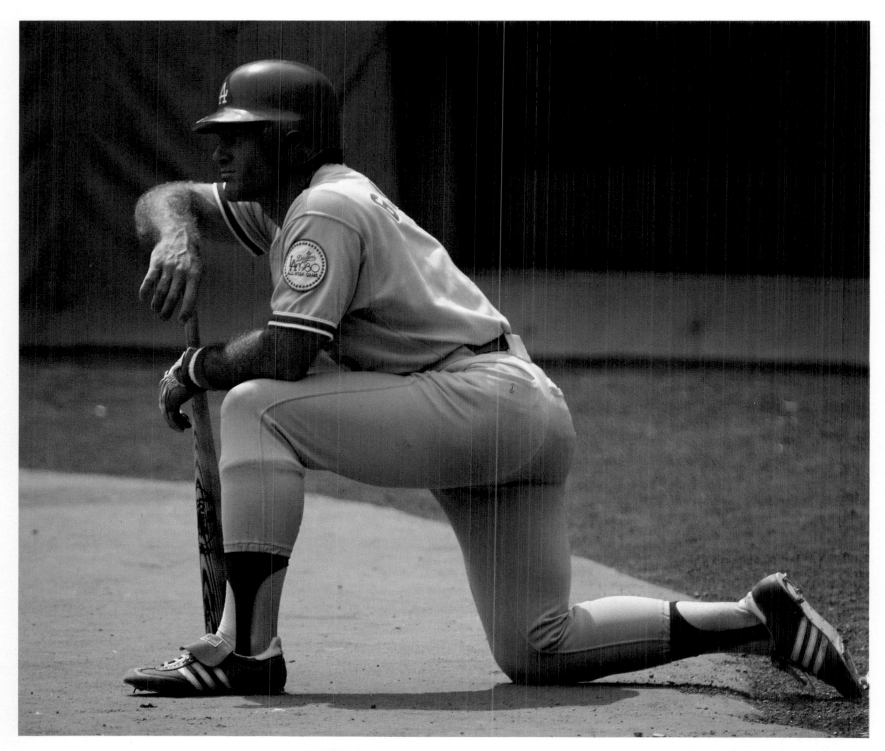

OPPOSITE: *Frank White turns a double play for the Kansas City Royals. This Golden Glove second baseman has been an important part of a winning team since 1973, when he joined the Royals.*

ABOVE: *Dodger first baseman Steve Garvey on deck at the All-Star game at Los Angeles on 8 July 1980. Garvey led the league in hits twice in three years, with 202 in 1978 and with 200 in 1980.*

RIGHT: *Willie Stargell hits a double in the 1979 World Series. Stargell's four doubles and three home runs helped the Pirates defeat Baltimore in seven games, and earned him a World Series MVP title to add to his National League MVP designation that same year.*

The Big Strike

Major-league baseball had gone through a number of changes since the nineteenth century, but two of the most significant ones finally collided by the 1980s. One was the striking down of the reserve clause, with the result that all players were sooner or later free to negotiate as free agents; the second was the large sums of money paid by television. Naturally the players wanted to get their share of this money and many of them began to get it: between 1978 and 1981, 43 players negotiated contracts worth over $1 million – the highest at that time being Dave Winfield's, worth at least $13 million, with a cost-of-living clause that made it possibly $20 million. And all the players began to ride the wave generated by the star free agents: the average salary of major-league players went from $50,000 in 1976, when the reserve clause was still in effect, to $200,000 by 1981.

So it was that when the agreement between the owners and the players expired on 31 December 1979, the owners decided to regain what they felt was lost territory by laying down a new condition: a club that lost a free agent must be allowed to choose a player from the club that signed the free agent. The players rejected this, claiming that this would put a brake on the bidding for free agents. During the final week of spring training in 1980, the players staged a walkout and threatened to go on strike on 23 May if there was no agreement. Just before that deadline, both sides agreed to set up a committee to study the whole issue of free agents and the new deadline was set at 31 January 1981.

And so the the 1980 season got underway as usual. In the American League's Eastern Division, the 1978 winner, the Yankees, fought it out with the 1979 winner, the Orioles, and the Yankees prevailed. In

OPPOSITE TOP: *Outfielder Ken Singleton, who joined the Orioles in 1975, batted .375 in the 1979 American League Championship Series and .357 in the World Series that year. Singleton began his career in 1970 with the Mets, then moved to the Expos before joining Baltimore.*
OPPOSITE: *Rickey Henderson breaks Ty Cobb's American League single-season stolen base record of 96.*

Henderson led the league in stolen bases five consecutive seasons, achieving the all-time single-season record of 130 in 1982.
ABOVE: *Willie Wilson slides into base. Wilson led the league in stolen bases his first full season with the Royals (1979) and won the batting title in 1982 with a .332 average. In 1980 his league-leading 230 hits and 133 runs helped his team take the pennant.*

the Western Division, the Kansas City Royals left the Oakland A's 14 games behind, despite Rickey Henderson's 100 stolen bases. Paced by George Brett (whose .390 average was the best in the majors since Ted Williams' .406 in 1941) and Willie Wilson's 230 hits, the Royals beat the Yankees three straight to take the pennant.

In the National League's Eastern Division, the Phillies won, but only clinched it in the next-to-last game of the season. The Western Division was even closer, with the Houston Astros in a tie with the Dodgers at the end of the regular season; in the one-game playoff, the Astros won on Joe Niekro's pitching. The Astros took the Phillies into

five games in the playoffs, but the Phillies won. In the 1980 World Series, the Phillies beat the Royals, four games to two, with Mike Schmidt leading the way as he had all season.

The 1981 season then began under a cloud, for the players and owners had still not resolved their differences. Still, the season brought new attendance records and lots of excitement over such new talents as Fernando Valenzuela, the Dodgers' rookie, who by 14 May had an 8-0 record, including five shutouts. But on 12 June, just as they had warned, the players went on strike – and stayed out for fifty days, the longest strike in professional sports in American history. Ameri-

cans fussed and fumed at the loss of their national pastime – although the minor leagues enjoyed a brief moment in the limelight – but a settlement was finally reached on 31 July: briefly, teams that lost 'premium' free agents would receive compensation from a pool of players made up from all clubs and the teams that lost players from this pool would be compensated from a fund maintained by all the clubs. The idea was that by dispersing the impact and cost, owners would be more inclined to compete for free agents.

By the time the teams got back on schedule, 741 games had been missed; the solution was to require the teams leading their respective

*A runner dives back to first base in an
attempted pick-off play with Pete Rose
awaiting the ball.*

divisions when the strike began to play the respective division leaders from the second half, thus producing a division winner. It also produced the possibility that a team might have the best total record for the year but not have led in either segment (the two segments not having the same number of games). That is exactly what happened. In the National League's Western Division, the Reds had the best total record, but they came in second – by only half a game – to the Dodgers in the first part, and to the Astros in the second part. And in the National's Eastern Division, the Cardinals had the best overall record, but the Phillies beat them in the first part and the Expos took the second part (again, with the Cardinals only half a game out). In the American League, the Yankees led in the Eastern Division in the first part, while Oakland led the Western Division; in the second part, the Milwaukee led the Eastern Division, while the Royals won in the Western Division.

Then began what seemed like an endless series of playoffs. In the

OPPOSITE TOP LEFT: *Mike Schmidt hits a fly ball. Michael Jack Schmidt has played third base for the Phillies since beginning his major-league career in 1972. Schmidt won consecutive MVP Awards in 1980 and 1981, and in 1980 he helped his team defeat Kansas City in the World Series by batting .381 in that contest.*

OPPOSITE TOP RIGHT: *Lefthander Fernando Valenzuela made his debut in 1981, winning both the Cy Young Award and the Rookie of the Year Award, and helping his Dodgers become World Champions.*

OPPOSITE BOTTOM: *Catcher Mike Heath goes into the stands for a foul ball. Heath joined the Oakland A's in 1979.*

National League's Western Division, the Dodgers beat the Astros, and in the Eastern Division, the Expos defeated the Phillies. In the play-offs for the National League pennant, the Dodgers beat the Expos. Over in the American League's Eastern Division, the Yankees beat the Brewers, and in the Western Division, the A's beat the Royals. In the pennant playoffs, the Yankees defeated the A's. And in the 1981 World Series, with the Dodgers meeting the Yankees for the 11th time, the Dodgers dropped the first two but then came back to take the next four. It had been a most confusing season, but one that again confirmed Americans' lasting affair with baseball.

ABOVE: *Andre Dawson runs on an infield hit. This Expos speedster came up at the end of the 1976 season and was selected as Rookie of the Year in 1978.*

221

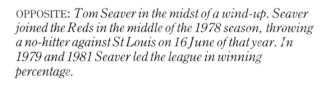

OPPOSITE: *Tom Seaver in the midst of a wind-up. Seaver joined the Reds in the middle of the 1978 season, throwing a no-hitter against St Louis on 16 June of that year. In 1979 and 1981 Seaver led the league in winning percentage.*

TOP: *The Expos' speedster Tim Raines attempts a stolen base.*

ABOVE: *Outfielder Tim Raines, who joined the Expos in 1979, has been a league-leading base-stealer since 1981.*

RIGHT: *Gary Carter began his major-league career with the Montreal Expos in 1974. A fine catcher, Carter wields a heavy bat as well. In the 1981 National League Eastern Division playoff, Carter's two home runs helped his team defeat the Phillies.*

Some Cliff-hangers,
Pine-tar and Cocaine

1982 turned out to be one of those rollercoaster years for the Commissioner of Baseball and the Atlanta Braves, but where the former was dumped from on high, the latter just managed to hang on. Bowie Kuhn had served as commissioner for 14 years and inevitably had been unable to satisfy all the owners; some of them got together and, after rumors and plots had swept the news media all year, they finally managed in November 1982 to end his contract – although he was asked to stay on till a successor was found. The Atlanta Braves, meanwhile, had opened the season with 13 straight wins – a National League record; by the end of July, they had a nine-game lead over the Padres, 10 over the Dodgers, and seemed unbeatable. But in August the Braves began to come apart and by the end of the month the Dodgers were in first place in the Western Division. It was not until the final day of the season that the Braves backed into first place – thanks to the Giants' defeating the Dodgers. In the National League's Eastern Division, despite strong opposition from the Reds, Pirates, Phillies and Expos, the St Louis Cardinals took first place, and then went on to defeat the Braves for the pennant.

In the American League's Eastern Division, it was a race between the Brewers and the Orioles. As chance had it, they ended their seasons with a four-game series with each other, but since the Brewers went into it with a three-game lead, they seemed safe. Then the Brewers lost three straight, and it was not until the final and tie-breaking game of the season that the Brewers finally secured first place. In the Western Division, the California Angels took first place, just beating out the Royals. In the playoffs the Angels beat the

ABOVE: *Detroit second baseman Lou Whitaker turns a double play. Named Rookie of the Year in 1978, 'Sweet Lou' has aided the Tigers' rise to the top.*

LEFT: *Toronto pitcher Dave Stieb winds up for a throw. Stieb joined the Blue Jays in 1979, turning in seven solid years before helping pitch his team to the division title in 1985.*

OPPOSITE: *Ace relief pitcher Bruce Sutter when he played for the St Louis Cardinals. Sutter has established himself as one of the greatest firemen of all time, from his beginning with the Cubs in 1976. Sutter won the Cy Young Award with the Cubs in 1979, and has led the league in saves five times.*

LEFT: *Power hitter Gorman Thomas accelerates out of the batters box after clubbing a long ball. With his league-leading 39 home runs in 1982, Gorman Thomas was a force in Milwaukee's drive to the pennant. After nine years with the Brewers, Thomas was traded to the Indians midseason the following year.*

BELOW: *Robin Yount pumps between bases. In 1982 Yount had a season that legends are made of, batting .331 while leading the league in hits (210) and doubles (46) on his way to an MVP year. Yount's performance helped his team take the pennant, but the Brewers lost the Series despite his batting .414 in that contest.*

OPPOSITE: *Ben Oglivie at bat. Benjamin Ambrosio Oglivie joined the Brewers in 1978 after three years with the Red Sox and four years with the Tigers. Free-swinging Oglivie clouted 34 homers in 1982, as yet another member of the Brewers' 'murderers' row' of 1982.*

Brewers two straight in Anaheim, but in Milwaukee the Brewers took all three. Then, in a hard-fought Series, which went to seven games and required a total of 72 runs, the Cardinals defeated the Brewers to emerge as the 1982 World Champions. 1982 was also the year in which Ricky Henderson, with the Oakland A's, set a new all-time season record for stolen bases, 130.

1983 might be remembered as the year that the drug problem finally couldn't be ignored by organized baseball and its supporters. Some individual players had previously been caught and even sentenced for drug use – particularly cocaine – but in 1983 four players for the Kansas City Royals were found guilty of using cocaine. Many explanations were produced – the high salaries, the nature of life on the road, the general acceptability of drug use in American society – but everyone agreed that professional athletes were going to have to beat this problem.

On the field, 1983 might better be recalled as the year of the pine-tar bat. In the American League Eastern Division, there was a fairly close race among the Yankees, Tigers and Orioles when on 24 July the Yankees met the Royals. In the top of the ninth, George Brett hit a two-run homer to give the Royals the game, 5-4, but Yankee manager Billy Martin protested that Brett's bat had more than the allowed 18 inches of pine-tar. The umpire upheld Martin's protest, but Lee

MacPhail, president of the American League, overruled the umpire and the final one and a third innings of the game were replayed later (and the Royals kept their lead). But the Yankees never regained their momentum and the Orioles took the Eastern Division. In the Western Division, the Chicago White Sox astounded even their most loyal rooters by holding onto first place and for the first time since 1959 got into post-season play – where they promptly lost three straight to the Orioles.

In the National League Eastern Division, the Phillies took first place, while in the Western Division, to no one's surprise, the Dodgers won. The Phillies then took the National League pennant and went on to confront the Orioles in what was billed as another 'railroad series.' The Phillies' stars such as Mike Schmidt went cold, however, and the Orioles won the World Series, four games to one.

ABOVE: *Eddie Murray takes a big cut. A Golden Glove first baseman who hits for power and consistency, Murray has been the backbone of the Orioles' offense since he entered the league in 1977. Murray's two home runs in the fifth game of the 1983 World Series helped Baltimore clinch the championship.*

LEFT: *Rickey Henderson attempts a steal. The chief base-thief in the American League, Henderson is an explosive offensive talent. To the chagrin of pitchers Henderson always seems to get on base: in 1983 he led the league in walks with 103, while batting .292. Henderson was traded for an army of Yankees in 1985.*

OPPOSITE: *Righthander Dennis Eckersly lets go one of his patent sliders. Traded from the Red Sox to the Cubs for Bill Buckner in 1984, Eckersly helped the Cubs win their division, and was pitching brilliantly in 1985 before joining the Cubs' disabled ward.*

LEFT: *Keith Hernandez, a clutch hitter whose consistent bat played a key role in the Cardinals' World Championship of 1982, was traded midseason the following year to the Mets.*

BELOW: *First baseman Cecil Cooper readies himself for a play. After being traded from the Red Sox to the Brewers in 1977, Cooper put together a string of five superlative seasons.*

And the Game Goes On

Major-league baseball, like all great institutions, is compounded of continuity and change, of tradition and turnover. The 1984 season saw several significant personnel shifts. For one, after the long search for a new Commissioner of Baseball, the club owners finally selected Peter Ueberroth, president of the Los Angeles Olympic Organizing Committee, who was to receive the highest accolades for his managing of the 1984 summer Olympics; it was 1 October 1984 before he took over. Meanwhile, the Yankees surprised many people by signing on the oldest active player in the majors, 44-year-old knuckleballer Phil Niekro. In the National League, Tom Seaver woke up one day to find himself claimed by the Chicago White Sox became the Mets had forgotten to list him as a 'protected' player.

But a few such surprises help to keep the game lively and the fans on edge – not to mention providing copy for sportswriters. Certainly there were few surprises in the American League Eastern Division's race for 1984: the Detroit Tigers won their season opener, went on to win game after game – at one point, 17 straight – and never did leave first place. In the Western Division, it was the Royals, but they had no chance to catch the non-stop express of the Tigers. In the National League's Eastern Division, there was a surprise of a different sort as the Chicago Cubs got up to first place in May, then managed to hang in there and come out with their first win since 1945. The San Diego Padres won the Western Division, but when they lost the first game of the playoffs to the Cubs, 13-0, everyone in Chicago went back to arguing whether the Cubs' home field, Wrigley, should or should not remain the last major-league stadium not to have lighting for night

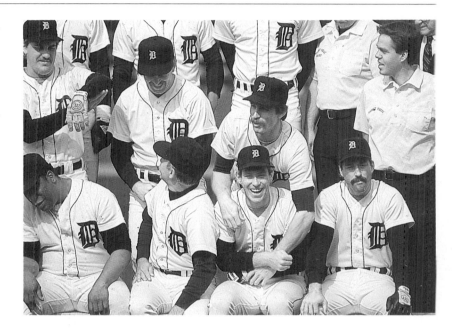

ABOVE: *The World Champions in 1984 – the Detroit Tigers. The crew that started off 35-5 went on to sweep the American League West Champions, the Royals, in three straight, and win it all by dumping the Padres in five.*

BELOW: *Ozzie Smith swings for a strike. The Wizard of Oz forgot about hitting, along with the rest of the Cardinals, in the 1985 World Series against the Royals.*

OPPOSITE: *Cubs fans bask in the sun at Wrigley Field.*

games. The traditionalists won – but the Cubs went on to lose to the Padres. In the end, though, it all proved to be immaterial, for the unstoppable Tigers continued their rampage and won the 1984 World Series, four games to one.

When the 1985 season opened, the talk of not just the baseball community but the country at large was Pete Rose's imminent take-over of one of the most sacrosanct records of major-league baseball: Ty Cobb's all-time record of 4191 hits. Rose undoubtedly helped to fan the flames of media interest, but he had earned the right to be proud, and when he broke Cobb's record, on 11 September, it was one of those sweet moments in American life that perhaps only baseball can generate. Certainly it helped to compensate for a couple of somewhat bitter moments in the 1985 season: the strike that cancelled two days of games (eventually made up) and the trials of drug-dealers in Pittsburgh that led to an unseemly contest among major-league players to see who could name the most of their fellow players as drug-users.

But as usual the real game was on the playing fields. In the National League's Western Division, the Dodgers won, while in the Eastern Division the Cardinals just managed to beat out the Mets by one game. (The Mets' try for the division title was aided by their pitching ace, Dwight Gooden, who became the youngest 20-game winner in modern baseball, ending up with a record of 24-4.) In the American League, the Toronto Blue Jays came out the division leaders after a close race with the Yankees, while the Kansas City Royals won the Western Division – this time the pundits got it right. The playoffs were extended to the best of seven games. When the Cardinals beat the Dodgers to take the National League pennant and the Royals beat the Blue Jays to win the American League, the country found itself with an

LEFT: *Leon 'Bull' Durham rounds the bases. The power-hitting first baseman joined the Cubs from St Louis in 1981, and helped his team to the division title in 1984 with 23 home runs. In 1985 the Cubs' decline affected Durham as well.*

BELOW: *George Brett, who may well be the best hitter of the era, clouts a home run over the left field wall. On a team that scored the second-fewest runs in the league, Brett hit .335 with 38 doubles, 30 homers and 112 RBI's in 1985. Needless to say, he was the primary offensive force in the Royals' championship year.*

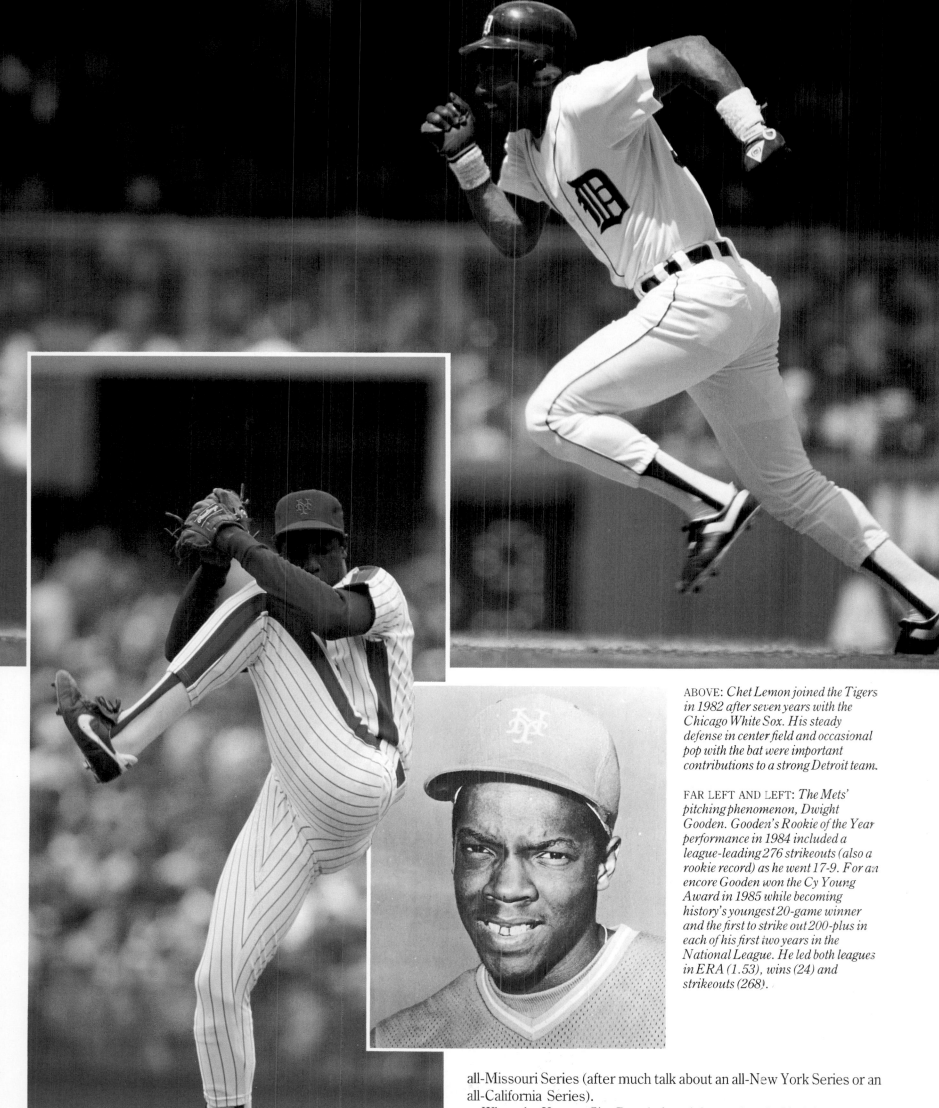

ABOVE: *Chet Lemon joined the Tigers in 1982 after seven years with the Chicago White Sox. His steady defense in center field and occasional pop with the bat were important contributions to a strong Detroit team.*

FAR LEFT AND LEFT: *The Mets' pitching phenomenon, Dwight Gooden. Gooden's Rookie of the Year performance in 1984 included a league-leading 276 strikeouts (also a rookie record) as he went 17-9. For an encore Gooden won the Cy Young Award in 1985 while becoming history's youngest 20-game winner and the first to strike out 200-plus in each of his first two years in the National League. He led both leagues in ERA (1.53), wins (24) and strikeouts (268).*

all-Missouri Series (after much talk about an all-New York Series or an all-California Series).

When the Kansas City Royals found themselves behind three games to one, everyone began to dismiss the 1985 Series as a foregone conclusion. But what many people forgot was that the Royals had also been behind 3-1 in the playoffs with the Blue Jays. And in what turned out to be an exciting Series – albeit with an anticlimactic 11-0 victory in the seventh game – the Royals won the World Series. All of which seemed to suggest that so long as baseball was played, it would continue to provide those continuities and surprises, those traditions and thrills, that have made it a nation's pastime.

TOP: *Carlton Fisk tags out the runner at home in a close play. Pudge muscled up in 1985, hitting 37 home runs and driving in 107 runs, both career highs.*

RIGHT: *In his sophomore season, the 21-year-old Bret Saberhagen had a dream year. He went 20-6 in the regular 1985 season, winning the Cy Young Award in the American League, and in one weekend became the father of a baby boy, winner of the final game of the World Series and was named World Series MVP.*

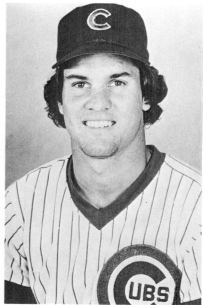

ABOVE: *Ryne Sandberg joined the Cubs in 1982 and in 1984 he put it all together with an MVP year in which he led the league in runs (114) and triples (19) while batting .314 and helping his team win their division. Sandberg followed up by batting .305 in 1985 with 54 stolen bases.*

LEFT: *Chicago White Sox catcher Carlton Fisk prepares to make a play.*

LEFT: *The Red Sox hitting machine, Wade Boggs. Boggs batted .349 in his rookie year of 1982, won the batting title the following year with a .361 average, and followed up in 1985 by leading both leagues in average (.368), hits (240) and on-base percentage (.450). His 240 hits were the most of any player since Bill Terry had 254 in 1930.*

RIGHT: *Don Mattingly's MVP year in 1985 yielded impressive stats as he led the league in RBI's with 145, doubles with 48, and first baseman fielding percentage with .995. The Yankee phenomenon pulled this off after winning the batting title the previous season with a .343 average.*

ABOVE: *Pete Rose acknowledges the applause after breaking Ty Cobb's long-standing all-time record of career hits by belting number 4192 on 11 September 1985. Rose's success as manager of the Cincinnati Reds has been overshadowed by his playing performances.*

RIGHT: *Teammates gather around Pete Rose on first base and fireworks brighten the sky following his landmark hit.*

Win Some, Lose Some

ABOVE: *A Bartlett Giamatti, former president of Yale University, became the president of the National League in 1986.*

RIGHT: *In 1986, Boston Red Sox pitcher Roger Clemens' outstanding 24-6 record helped take his team to the World Series. He won the Cy Young Award in 1986 and again in 1987, and the American League MVP award in 1986.*

BELOW: *The Mets put the tag on the Astros in the 1986 National League playoffs.*

OPPOSITE TOP: *Darryl Strawberry of the Mets steals second in the 1986 World Series. New York beat Boston, four games to three.*

OPPOSITE BOTTOM: *News of Met Dwight Gooden's cocaine problem shook the baseball world in 1987.*

The 1986 season was one of those increasingly rare ones where play on the field actually made all the games played out in the media seem irrelevant. The media made much of the emerging conflict over the issue of free agents: As more and more free-agent stars realized that clubs weren't bidding for them, they began to accuse the owners of collusion in trying to keep salaries down. Then there was the usual quota of personnel changes – the most surprising perhaps being the appointment of A Bartlett Giamatti as the new president of the National League, the very Giamatti who had just served as president of Yale University (leaving scholars to debate whether this was a step up or down in the American hierarchy). But none of this really distracted true fans from the game.

The first sign that something was stirring came on 29 April, when Roger Clemens, a not especially well-known Red Sox pitcher, struck out 20 Seattle Mariners, a modern record for a nine-inning game. Clemens then continued his winning ways, racking up 14 consecutive victories and helping the Red Sox take over first place in the American League's Eastern Division by 15 May. They would not give it up all season. In the American League's Western Division there was another surprise as the California Angels and Texas Rangers left the 1985 World Championship Royals behind and fought it out for first place, with the veteran Angels eventually taking it. The playoffs that ensued were among the most exciting in recent memory. The Angels went into the fifth game with a 3-1 game lead and by the ninth inning were winning 5-2 – they actually had the champagne ready in their locker room – but the Red Sox's Dave Henderson hit a two-run homer, the Sox won the game and then took the final two and the pennant.

In the National League the only surprise in 1986 was that the Houston Astros beat out the favored Dodgers, Giants and Reds. In the Eastern Division the Mets were heavily favored and came through in high style, taking over first place on 23 April and ending up with 108 wins. The playoffs thus featured two expansion teams celebrating their 25th anniversaries, and although the Mets continued to be the favorites, they were taken to six games by the Astros before winning the pennant.

The Mets were inevitably regarded as the heavy favorites in the 1986 World Series, so it seemed incredible when the Red Sox won the first two games – in Shea Stadium, no less. The Mets then took the next two at Fenway Park, but the Red Sox took the fifth. In the sixth game the Sox took a lead into the ninth inning – and then lost the game. The Mets took the seventh game and came out as World Champions, but all agreed that baseball and its fans had been the true winners in the 1986 season.

The 1987 season began with a series of episodes that seemed to strike at the very heart of the game. For one, there were a number of truly outstanding free agents who could not find any bidders, so the charge of collusion by the owners seemed self-evident. Some of these free agents ended up returning to their teams, but two – Ray Knight and Andre Dawson – deliberately signed with other teams for lower salaries just to express their resentment (and Bob Horner went off to play in Japan to show where *he* stood). Then on 21 September an arbitrator ruled that there had indeed been collusion among the owners, at least in 1985, but the question of what was now to be done about it remained open. No less unsettling was the matter of Dwight Gooden's

be hitting an embarrassing number of home runs during 1987. The most spectacular example was rookie Mark McGwire of the Oakland As, who not only broke the all-time rookie best for homers but went on to win the American League's home-run title with 49. Any number of players beat their personal best for homers, and the major league total was some 17 percent over the 1986 total. There was no final agreement as to what caused this, although many concluded it was a combination of better-conditioned batters and inexperienced pitchers.

In any case, it made for an exciting season, with all kinds of records broken. Paul Molitor of the Brewers hit safely in 39 consecutive games – hardly a threat to DiMaggio's record, but respectable. Don Mattingly of the Yankees hit homers in eight consecutive games (to tie Dale Long's 1956 record) and also hit six grand slam homers, a season record for the majors. Another record went all but unnoticed: catcher Bob Boone of the California Angels broke Al Lopez's career record (1918) with the most games caught. In the category of questionable records was Don Baylor's, with a career total of 255 awards of first base for being hit, the major league high.

On the playing field what characterized 1987 was the upsetting of all the expert prophets. In the American League's Western Division the Twins were hardly taken seriously before the season began, but by 6 July they took over first place and stayed there. The fact that they won their division with only 85 victories only shows how tough their competition was. In the Eastern Division the Tigers took over first place on 19 August, then lost it to the Toronto Blue Jays in the next-to-last weekend of the season, only to take it back in the three final games against those same Blue Jays. In the playoffs, the young Twins continued their surprising ways by shutting down the veteran Tigers, taking four games to one and the pennant.

In the National League, Cincinnati appeared to have the Western Division under control, leading much of the season. Then, beginning on 7 August, they lost 18 of the next 25 games, while the Giants exactly reversed that record and ended up by taking first place. In the Eastern Division the highly-touted Mets never really got going; instead, the Cardinals swept ahead of the division and held a 9½ game lead by 23 July. They slipped after that, but they held on to first place and then, in an exciting playoff, staved off defeat in the sixth game, taking it 1-0, and went on to rout the Giants in the seventh to take the pennant.

In the 1987 World Series, it was the relatively inexperienced Twins up against the seasoned Cardinals. When the Twins took the first two

coming up positive on a test for cocaine. He had to spend a month in a drug clinic and then lost more weeks in the minors getting back into shape. Even though he did fairly well in the rest of the season, no one pretended that this resolved the problem of drug-use by athletes.

But the most disturbing problem exploded on the scene in the midst of the observance of the 40th anniversary of Jackie Robinson's breaking the color barrier. An unconsidered and inconsiderate remark by a Los Angeles Dodgers' executive had the effect of giving the public a look into the select chambers reserved for management and administration in the major leagues, revealing that there were virtually no blacks or Hispanics there. There was much scurrying around and promises of actions to be taken, but given the special role that baseball plays in American life it was a sobering reminder of how far the country still has to go to become a truly integrated 'team.'

More in the department of light relief was the issue of whether the regulation baseballs were being 'juiced up' and/or whether some bats were being 'corked.' In fact, several tests showed the balls were no different, and only a couple of doctored bats ever were reported. The reason for such concern was that everyone and his cousin seemed to

ABOVE: *Don Baylor's career total of 255 awards of first base for being hit became a new major league record in 1987.*

LEFT: *Ozzie Smith of the St Louis Cardinals leaps over Don Mattingly of the New York Yankees as he tries to complete a double play in the first inning of the 1987 All-Star Game.*

BELOW: *World Series action: the Minnesota Twins versus the St Louis Cardinals. The Twins surprised baseball fans by taking the Series from the Cardinals, four games to three.*

OPPOSITE TOP: *Another home run for Oakland As rookie Mark McGwire. His 49 homers broke the record for homers by a rookie and won the American League title in 1987.*

OPPOSITE BOTTOM LEFT: *Yankee Don Mattingly hammered a record six grand slams in 1987 and tied the record for homers hit in consecutive games (eight).*

OPPOSITE BOTTOM RIGHT: *Paul Molitor of the Milwaukee Brewers hit safely in 39 consecutive games in 1987.*

games everyone concluded this was due to the homefield advantage of the Metrodome, with its unusual lighting and acoustics. When the Cardinals swept the next three in St Louis it appeared that experience was finally paying off. Back in the Metrodome, though, the Twins swamped the Cardinals 11-5 in game six, and then managed to win the seventh, 4-2. Homefield advantage or not, the Twins emerged as true World Champions. It was their first ever World Series victory, and ecstatic Minnesotans hope they will be back for more.

There were some other upsets in 1987. In the Pan American Games the US could only take the silver medal, as Cuba's team won the gold in baseball, while in the Little League World Series the United States, represented by a team from Irvine, California, also came in second to a team from Taiwan. But such losses were a tribute to the international appeal of baseball and did not signify any slackening of its hold on Americans. Evidence of this came with the publicity that attended the Salt Lake Trappers, a Class A team that won 29 consecutive games, an all-time record in the 117-year history of organized professional baseball. So long as Americans could exult in such achievements, there would be little danger of baseball's losing its place as the national pastime.

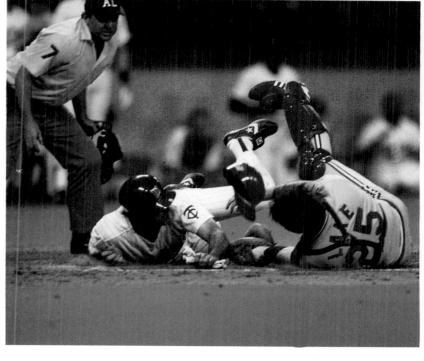

The 1988 season was one of the rare ones that began with unanimity about what was going to happen on the field and no great controversy off the field. Practically all close observers of the baseball scene agreed that this was the year for a Subway Series – the Mets and Yankees were shoe-ins for the pennants. The San Francisco Giants and the Oakland A's were picked to be the also-rans in their respective leagues. The only mildly controversial issue was the threatened strict enforcement of the balk rule, and, indeed, the standing season record for called balks (356 for both leagues) was quickly wiped out. Although balks eventually ceased to gain much publicity, many fans were worried that so many called balks could influence the outcome of games.

The season got underway with an American League record that the Baltimore Orioles would prefer to forget: their 21 straight losses. By the end of April the Cleveland Indians and Oakland A's were in the lead in their divisions, while the Pirates and Dodgers led their divisions. Still, the experts didn't lose faith: on 8 May a *New York Times* sports writer was seriously declaring 'that it's evident the Mets and Yankees will win the Eastern Division championships.' By All-Star break the Mets had indeed taken over first place in the NL East, but the Tigers were now leading the Yankees – with Lou Piniella having replaced Billy Martin, fired for the fifth time by Steinbrenner. The A's seemed securely in first, as expected, but so, too, were the Dodgers.

Then something most unexpected happened. The Red Sox fired manager John McNamara and replaced him with their third-base coach, Joe Morgan, who proceeded to lead the Sox on a miraculous turnaround that included a record-setting 24 successive wins at Fenway Park. On Labor Day the Red Sox took over first place from the Yankees, and after holding off the Tigers and a last-minute charge by the Milwaukee Brewers, the Red Sox took the AL East. The Oakland A's and the Los Angeles Dodgers had never faltered, and the Mets had stayed on to vindicate the experts.

TOP LEFT: *Twins hurler Frank Viola had 24 wins in 1988.*

TOP RIGHT: *Formidable Mets hitter Darryl Strawberry.*

ABOVE: *One of the shocks of 1988 occurred when the great Pete Rose, manager of the Reds, was suspended after arguing with an umpire.*

ABOVE: *Tom Browning of the Cincinnati Reds pitching his perfect game, the fourteenth in big league history.*

LEFT: *At long last Chicago's venerable Wrigley Field bowed to the times and installed lights for nighttime play.*

243

In the playoffs, however, the Mets found themselves stymied by a Dodgers team that, on paper, didn't have a chance, and the Dodgers won the pennant 4 games to 3. In the American League playoffs, Boston's dream year came up against harsh reality as the A's overpowered them in four straight games. Never daunted, the experts continued to pronounce Oakland a sure winner over the Dodgers, who went into the Series with the lowest team batting average ever. But the Dodgers ignored the experts and defeated the A's 4-1, to become the World Champions.

It was a strange year in several respects. Not only were called balks up 160 percent, home runs were down 29 percent from 1987's record-setting pace, and team batting averages and earned run averages were also down. Inevitably there was talk again of a new ball, but the consensus attributed it to better pitching. The Dodgers' Orel Hershiser, for instance, besides going 23-8 and picking up the Cy Young Award, pitched a record-breaking 59 consecutive scoreless innings. Tom Browning, of the Cincinnati Reds, pitched a perfect game, only the 14th in the history of major league baseball. Jose Canseco of the A's became the first player in organized baseball to hit 40 home runs *and* steal 40 bases, while Don Baylor upped his own record to a total of 267 'hits' by pitches.

Elsewhere, Jim Abbott, the one-handed pitcher who has been signed by the California Angels, led the US team to a gold medal in the Olympics. Chicago's Wrigley Field, the last holdout, finally installed lights and hosted its first night game. A Bartlett Giamatti, who had resigned the presidency of Yale to become the president of the National League, was voted in to succeed Peter Ueberroth as Commissioner of Baseball. The Year also saw umpires in the news, starting with the rejection of Pam Postema as the first woman in the majors and climaxing with the argument that led to Pete Rose's suspension.

Back in the ballparks, major league teams for the fourth consecutive year set a new single-season attendance record during 1988. Thus, for all the shenanigans and despite the experts, baseball had once again shown that it had lost nothing of its enduring ability to surprise and attract the fans.

ABOVE: *Dodgers pitcher Jay Howell was ejected from one of the NL playoff games for having pine tar on his glove.*

LEFT: *Ed Vargo, supervisor of NL umpires, showing the offending Howell glove to NL president, and soon-to-be Baseball Commissioner, Bart Giamatti.*

LEFT: *Cy Young Award winner and World Series MVP, Dodgers pitcher Orel Hershiser was 23-8 in the 1988 season.*

BELOW LEFT: *José Canseco of the A's was the American League MVP in 1988, with 42 home runs, 124 RBIs and 40 stolen bases.*

BELOW: *Tommy Lasorda (left), the ebullient Dodgers manager, deserved much credit for LA's surprising triumphs in the 1988 season and Series.*

Picture Credits

All photographs courtesy of The National Baseball Hall of Fame and Museum Inc, with the following exceptions:

American Legion: 179 (top, bottom right)
Fabian Bachrach and The National Baseball Hall of Fame and Museum Inc: 192 (top)
Robert C Bartosz: 192 (bottom), 213 (right)
Baseball Nostalgia, Cooperstown, NY: 157 (top)
Beacon Journal Photo, Akron, Ohio: 153 (bottom)
Marcello Bertinetti: 230
Bison Picture Library: 206 (all 4)
Bernard Stephen Croker: 15 (center)
Daily Democrat Photo: 174 (bottom)
Denver Zephyrs: 41 (bottom left)
Detroit Free Press photo by Dick Tripp: 171 (left)
Globe Democrat Photo: 174 (top)
The Greer Studios, Inc: 135 (top)
Nancy Hogue: 160, 163, 170, 184 (top), 185, 188, 189, 194, 195, 197, 198 (all 3), 199, 202 (top left, bottom), 203, 212, 213 (bottom), 215 (both), 216 (top); 218-19, 221, 222, 223 (bottom), 226 (top), 227, 228 (top), 229 (top 2)
Hollywood Citizen-News: 158 (top)
Le Presse, Montreal: 142 (bottom)
Little League Baseball, Inc: 176 (bottom), 179 (bottom left)
Ron Modra: 210 (both), 211, 214, 220 (top right, bottom), 223 (top), 224 (left), 225, 226 (bottom), 228 (below), 229 (bottom), 231 (both), 232 (both), 233 (top right, bottom left), 234, 236-37 (both), 238 (all 3), 239 (both), 240 (all 3), 241 (top right, bottom), 242 (all 3), 243 (both), 245 (all 3)
NEA Service: 138
Observer Reporter Publishing Comp, Washington, PA: 178 (both)
Lou Pavlovich: 146
Plain Dealer Photo: 139
PONY Baseball Inc, Washington, PA: 177
Russ Reed, Photo Dept, Oakland Tribune: 190 (bottom)
John W Ripley: 12 (bottom), 14 (all 6)
Rochester Times-Union: 145 (bottom right), 168 (bottom right)
© 1916 Estate of Norman Rockwell, Courtesy of the Estate of Norman Rockwell: 13
John Savage: 180-81
Signal Corps Photo: 204-05 (bottom)
T Spalding: 144 (top left)
© Topps Chewing Gum, Inc: 12 (top left)
UPI/Bettmann Newsphotos: 244 (both)
US Air Force Photo: 204 (top)
US Marine Corps Photo: 108
US Navy Photo: 109 (bottom), 111 (top)
Angela White: 15 (bottom)
Don Wingfield: 159 (top)
Larry A Woolis: 145 (top)

Acknowledgements

The authors and publisher would like to thank the following people who have helped in the preparation of this book: Alan Gooch of Design 23, who designed it; Barbara Paulding Thrasher, who edited it; Donna Cornell and Mary Raho, who did the picture research; Cynthia Klein, who prepared the index. Special thanks go also to the following personnel at The National Baseball Hall of Fame and Museum, Inc: Thomas R Heitz, librarian; Pat Kelly, manager, photo collection; Stacy Fundis, associate, photo collection.